Beginning SharePoint with Excel

Gini Courter and
Annette Marquis

Apress®

Beginning SharePoint with Excel

Copyright © 2006 by Gini Courter and Annette Marquis

ISBN-13 (pbk): 978-1-59059-690-6

ISBN-10 (pbk): 1-59059-690-0

Printed and bound in the United States of America 9 8 7 6 5 4 3 2 1

Trademarked names may appear in this book. Rather than use a trademark symbol with every occurrence of a trademarked name, we use the names only in an editorial fashion and to the benefit of the trademark owner, with no intention of infringement of the trademark.

Lead Editor: Jim Sumser
Technical Reviewer: Alexzander Nepomnjashiy
Editorial Board: Steve Anglin, Ewan Buckingham, Gary Cornell, Jason Gilmore, Jonathan Gennick, Jonathan Hassell, James Huddleston, Chris Mills, Matthew Moodie, Dominic Shakeshaft, Jim Sumser, Keir Thomas, Matt Wade
Project Manager: Kylie Johnston
Copy Edit Manager: Nicole LeClerc
Copy Editor: Susannah Pfalzer
Assistant Production Director: Kari Brooks-Copony
Production Editor: Kelly Winquist
Compositor and Artist: Kinetic Publishing Services, LLC
Proofreader: Nancy Riddiough
Indexer: Broccoli Information Management
Cover Designer: Kurt Krames
Manufacturing Director: Tom Debolski

Distributed to the book trade worldwide by Springer-Verlag New York, Inc., 233 Spring Street, 6th Floor, New York, NY 10013. Phone 1-800-SPRINGER, fax 201-348-4505, e-mail orders-ny@springer-sbm.com, or visit http://www.springeronline.com.

For information on translations, please contact Apress directly at 2560 Ninth Street, Suite 219, Berkeley, CA 94710. Phone 510-549-5930, fax 510-549-5939, e-mail info@apress.com, or visit http://www.apress.com.

The source code for this book is available to readers at http://www.apress.com in the Source Code section.

This is a book about collaboration. Never was collaboration more important than it is in New Orleans and the Louisiana, Mississippi, and Alabama Gulf Coasts as they rebuild from Hurricane Katrina. This book is dedicated to all of the organizations collaborating to ensure that every hurricane victim is treated equitably and humanely as they recover from this unprecedented crisis.

Contents at a Glance

Contents

About the Authors

GINI COURTER is a partner in TRIAD Consulting, a technology consultation and training company. Gini's expertise in technology planning, information architecture, and database design, and her ability to synthesize and communicate this expertise, is invaluable to the varied clients she serves. From Fortune 1,000 companies to small businesses and not-for-profit organizations, Gini has proven over and over again that technology can effectively solve business problems as long as the humans designing it understand the needs of the business.

ANNETTE MARQUIS is also a partner in TRIAD Consulting. Annette has more than 15 years of executive management experience in health care and nonprofit organizations, and 10 years of experience providing software consultation, training, and technical writing to a wide variety of businesses. She offers expertise in the practical uses of computers in business settings and in designing and providing effective, customized staff training and documentation of software applications and solutions.

Gini and Annette are coauthors of more than 25 books on Microsoft Office and related software topics, including *Mastering Microsoft Office 2003 for Business Professionals* (Sybex, 2004) and *Mastering Microsoft Office XP* (Sybex, 2001). This is their first book with Apress.

About the Technical Reviewer

ALEXZANDER NEPOMNJASHIY works as a Microsoft SQL Server DBA with NeoSystems North-West Inc., an ISO 9001:2000–certified software company. As a DBA, he's responsible for drafting design specifications for solutions and building database-related projects based on these specs. As an IT professional, Alexzander has more than 11 years of experience in DBMS planning, designing, securing, troubleshooting, and performance optimizing.

Acknowledgments

For making this book happen, our hats go off to Jim Sumser. Jim was the very first acquisitions editor we ever had—Gini worked with him on her first book, *The Learning Guide to Windows 95* (Sybex 1995)—but soon after that, he went on to find fame and fortune in other circles. We are thrilled to be working with him again after all these years. Thanks, Jim, for agreeing to put up with us again!

We would also like to thank all the great people who worked on this book. Our special thanks to senior project manager Kylie Johnston, who stayed with us in the dark days between submissions. We appreciate your support and patience. Susannah Pfalzer, our copy editor, is responsible for making our meaning clearer and our sentences smoother. Thanks for all your attention to detail. Speaking of detail, we want to thank Alexzander Nepomnjashiy for his attention to technical detail. He helped keep us on target and made sure we didn't miss a critical step along the way. Thanks, Alexzander.

We know that we have just scratched the surface here in terms of the number of people who have been involved with this book. We extend our heartfelt thanks to them all.

We would be remiss if we didn't thank Leonardo Brito, senior IT analyst for Valassis, Inc., for all his help as we learned the ins and outs of SharePoint. He was invaluable as we worked with him on implementing a corporate-wide SharePoint portal and innumerable Windows SharePoint Services sites to departments and teams throughout the company. Muchas gracias, Leo!

Introduction

Whether you work in a large multinational corporation or in a tiny family-owned company, you have at least one thing in common: it's a challenge to secure IT resources to solve common everyday business problems. In a large corporation, resources are typically spent on the big projects that have a significant cost benefit to the company. When you make a request for assistance, you're probably called upon to justify the business value of your request. If you aren't planning to save the company millions of dollars, you're out of luck. At the other end of the spectrum, all a small company might know about IT is that it was a member of the cast of the Addams Family TV show.

Although initial installation of Microsoft SharePoint Portal Server requires administrative expertise, even a company with no technical staff can buy hosting from a SharePoint hosting company (see Appendix C), and in minutes have a Windows SharePoint Services site for its team. As we've delved deeper and deeper into the possibilities that SharePoint offers, one thing has become crystal clear: a high-end user within a department can develop highly sophisticated SharePoint sites, business dashboard, and data sharing systems without a lick of programming. This puts tremendous power in the hands of end users and IT business analysts who want quick, easy-to-implement solutions for their users.

Who This Book Is For

This book is intended for IT professionals and for business users who see the benefits of electronic collaboration and want to maximize the tools they already have available. Most books of this type are written for programmers and require a high level of technical knowledge. Because there's so much you can do with SharePoint and Excel without programming, we intentionally excluded techniques and solutions that require programming. Our intention was to make this book accessible to those high-end users who aren't programmers but who, with the right level of knowledge, can still make a big difference in solving business problems in their organizations. In other words, even if you don't know the difference between XML, SQL, and .NET, you can create powerful team collaboration solutions with SharePoint and Excel.

How This Book Is Structured

To work with SharePoint and Excel effectively, you'll sometimes be working primarily in Excel and other times primarily in SharePoint. Deciding what make sense given what you want to do, the team you're working with, and what works best for your situation is a critical part of developing the best solution.

In this book, we take you back and forth between SharePoint and Excel with relative fluidity. However, each chapter has a focal point—that is, in which program you work with the data. For example, Chapter 2 focuses on working with lists in SharePoint. The data might originate in SharePoint or might have come from Excel, but SharePoint is where you want your team to access the data. Chapter 3, on the other hand, takes data that originates in SharePoint and shows you how to work with it in Excel. If you know which direction you're heading with the data, in this book you'll find everything you need to know about getting it there and working with it after you do.

The first six chapters focus on the how-tos of creating, using, and exchanging data between SharePoint and Excel. Beginning with Chapter 7, the focus changes to taking the skills you've learned in the preceding chapters and putting them to use solving specific business problems. In addition, you'll learn higher-level skills, such as creating your own web parts to manage and display data your way. If you're eager to get to solutions, you might want to jump to Chapter 7. You can then use the earlier chapters as a reference when you get stuck, or to develop a deeper knowledge of what you're doing.

Following is a chapter-by-chapter overview of what you'll find in this book.

Chapter 1: SharePoint and Excel: The Perfect Partnership

This chapter is designed to give you an overview of Windows SharePoint Technologies, specifically SharePoint Portal Server and Windows SharePoint Services. It also outlines the relevant features of Microsoft Excel. However, because this is a book about how they interact, the real focus of this chapter is how SharePoint and Excel work together.

Chapter 2: Working with Lists in SharePoint

To truly understand how to work with data in SharePoint, you have to understand how to work with SharePoint lists. Lists share some functionality with Excel but also have their own unique characteristics. This chapter focuses on creating lists, working with list data, publishing Excel data to SharePoint, and synchronizing lists between Excel and SharePoint.

Chapter 3: Working with SharePoint Lists in Excel

In Chapter 3, we look at lists in the other direction: taking SharePoint lists into Excel. Here, you learn how to export SharePoint lists into Excel and maximize integration. This chapter includes a discussion of how to add calculations in Excel and synchronize the offline data with SharePoint.

Chapter 4: Creating SharePoint Views

One of the distinct advantages of working with lists in SharePoint is the ability to create and switch between custom views of the data. This chapter covers how to create views that display the data you want to see in the way you want to see it.

Chapter 5: Creating Custom Calculations in SharePoint

SharePoint lists aren't as flexible as Excel worksheets, especially in the arena of calculations. However, you can create calculated fields and add them to a SharePoint list. In fact, almost all of Excel's rich set of functions is available in SharePoint. The challenge comes in creating the formulas, and what you can include in a formula (only row data can be calculated). In this chapter, you'll learn how to create a calculated field and how to use many of the most commonly used functions.

Chapter 6: Publishing Excel Web Pages for SharePoint

Sometimes you want to make data available for ad hoc reporting and analysis, but displaying it on a Web page is a better option than expecting users to work directly with a list. In this chapter, you'll see how to create interactive web pages where users can add formulas, sort and filter data, analyze data, and edit charts.

Chapter 7: Building Out-of-the-Box Business Solutions

Chapter 7 takes what you learned in the first six chapters and puts it to use. In this chapter, we demonstrate two commonly needed business solutions: tracking issues related to a project and displaying sales performance data. Even if you don't have a specific need for these scenarios, these chapters will show you how to take a business problem and combine the functionality of SharePoint and Excel to develop a comprehensive solution.

Chapter 8: Using Excel to Query SharePoint

Excel's Web Query is a powerful query tool that allows you to query any accessible table on an intranet or the Internet, including tables and lists in SharePoint. This chapter shows you how to develop useful web queries of SharePoint data. If you're managing a number of internal or external Windows SharePoint Services sites, you'll find this chapter especially useful. In this chapter, you'll see how you can use Web Query to track users on up to 255 sites in one workbook. If you're responsible for removing contractors or employees who have left the company, this is an invaluable tool.

Chapter 9: Using SharePoint's Office Web Parts

Reporting on and analyzing data is just as important as maintaining good data. In this chapter, you'll learn how to use the SharePoint Office web parts to create highly interactive pivot tables and pivot charts. To make this functionality available to site users, you can use the PivotView web part to let users choose how they want to see the data: as a datasheet, as a pivot table, or as a pivot chart.

Chapter 10: Building Excel Spreadsheet Web Parts

By this time, you've seen all that SharePoint and its integration with Excel has to offer—out of the box, that is. But why stop there? You can create your own web parts that include the functionality you need to have. This chapter shows you how to create a simple custom web part and then include that web part on a page of your SharePoint site. For a more advanced example, we've included information about how to create a web part that returns a data set, such as all the documents in a SharePoint document library that have been created or modified on or after January 1, 2006. With this functionality, you have the ability to create data from other data and develop valuable reports on the data you have. We need to warn you that this chapter includes some references to XML mapping (see Appendix C to get you started).

Appendixes

For those of you who want just a little bit more, we've included three appendixes:

- **Appendix A: Creating and Using Excel Lists** is an introduction to the functionality of Microsoft Excel 2003's new List feature. This is helpful when you're publishing Excel data to SharePoint and when you're bringing it back again. If you haven't used lists in Excel, you'll want to review this appendix before moving into Chapters 2 and 3.

- **Appendix B: Mapping Excel Spreadsheets for XML** is a basic introduction to Extensible Markup Language (XML) for those who want to explore the limits of SharePoint and Excel integration. It's a good idea to review this appendix before hitting Chapter 10.

- **Appendix C: Resources** is a list of web-based resources about SharePoint that we think are especially useful. We have no investment or relationship with these resources, so they're truly objective from our point of view. They're the places we go when we're stuck, or the services we use when we're outside of a corporate environment.

Prerequisites

To make the most of this book, readers should already have a working knowledge of Windows SharePoint Services and a comfortable level of knowledge of Microsoft Excel.

Downloading the Code

This book contains no code, but to access SharePoint resources on the web, you can download a web version of Appendix C so you can click rather than type those ugly URLs. You can find the web version in the Source Code area of the Apress web site (http://www.apress.com).

Contacting the Authors

If you'd like to make comments, give feedback, send accolades, or ask questions, you can contact the authors at info@triadconsulting.com.

CHAPTER 1

■■■

SharePoint and Excel: The Perfect Partnership

This is a book about collaboration; specifically, how you can collaborate with others you work with to get the job done with style and grace. It's a book about how you can take a tool you're probably intimately familiar with—Microsoft Excel—and extend the data you collect there to members of your team. But most importantly, it's a book about how you can solve common business problems with another sort of collaboration: the collaboration of two pieces of software, Microsoft Excel and Microsoft SharePoint.

In this chapter, we'll look at the richness of Microsoft Excel and the enhancements in Excel 2003 that make true collaboration possible. We'll also look at this thing called SharePoint. We'll differentiate between Microsoft SharePoint Portal Server and Microsoft Windows SharePoint Services. We'll explore how these technologies can change the way we work together. And we'll look at why tools such as SharePoint matter in today's business environment.

Finally, we'll examine the interaction between Excel and SharePoint, because when you understand how these products work together, you'll see a whole new world open before you. You'll begin to see solutions to business problems that in the past would have taken a cadre of database administrators and months of programming to solve. You'll begin to see how in a couple simple steps you can not only provide access to information, but also get incredible potential for data sharing.

Before we look at Excel 2003, we'd like to make a disclaimer. Although Microsoft Excel has been around for many years and is probably one of the most developed products on the market, SharePoint Technologies are the new kids on the block. As a result, some of their features are awkward to use, some things you'd like to be able to do are missing, and some things just don't work as well as they should. We'd like to emphasize, though, that this shouldn't discourage you from using SharePoint. In this book, we've tried to point out the awkward places, and whenever possible, we include workarounds for those missing features. SharePoint takes what previously was a convoluted and hard-to-manage process— that is, effectively sharing documents and data with coworkers—and makes it not only possible, but easy and accessible to all levels of users. Combined with Excel, SharePoint has tremendous potential and abundant possibilities. It's worth whatever challenges it presents.

Excel Has Something for Everyone

Microsoft Excel has played a critical role in most businesses from the early days of PCs. Excel is not only a workhorse, it's a treasure trove of invaluable features that can make both novices and techies smile. Whether you need to create a simple budget for your home-based business or make long-range financial projections that pave the way for a small company to become a multinational corporation, Excel has something for everyone. With Excel, you can create complex formulas that calculate the distance to newly discovered planets, analyze the cost per part of a supersonic jet aircraft, or gauge the time it takes to print, bind, and ship a print-on-demand book.

Using Excel As a Database Tool

Excel isn't limited to number crunching. Excel has become the de facto database of choice for millions of users. Excel is a flat-file database tool, so its uses are limited to nonrelational data, but that doesn't stop those who need to keep lists. A single Excel spreadsheet can hold 65,536 records with 256 columns of data. That's a lot of data even for a large company to track. Some of this data might be better housed in Microsoft Access, Microsoft Outlook, or a SQL Server database. However, Excel is, in fact, the home of transaction data, contact information, inventories, customer lists, store locations, newspaper listings, and a host of other types of data. Using Excel's data tools, users can sort, filter, subtotal, conditionally format, and analyze and report with pivot tables.

XML Makes Data Truly Portable

Excel 2003 offers even greater adaptability with the integration of Extensible Markup Language (XML). XML converts data in a worksheet to a text file that a variety of applications can read and understand through the use of standardized tags. XML offers new freedom from the limitations of data importing and exporting. With XML, you can create custom schemas that allow you to extract business data, such as customer information, from your worksheets for use in other databases or reports.

Excel Lists Simplify Data Management

Also new to Excel 2003 is a feature, for lack of a better name, called an *Excel list*. You might have thought that whenever you entered data into a worksheet you were creating an Excel list. Although technically you were, Excel 2003 has taken list creation to a new level. Using Excel list features, you can segregate data in a worksheet and work with it independently from other data in the worksheet. By designating a range of cells as a list, you can sort and filter the data defined by the list parameters, ignoring everything else in the worksheet. You can toggle a total row on and off that allows you to apply a number of aggregate functions quickly—such as SUM, AVERAGE, MIN, and MAX—to your list. Because the totals row automatically creates a SUBTOTAL formula, you can be assured that your totals are correct even when you filter the list data. Figure 1-1 shows the features of an Excel list.

AutoFilter Buttons

List Toolbar

New Record Row

Totals Row

	A	B	C	D	E	F	G	H
1	ID	First Name	Last Nam	Street Address	City	Sta	Zip	Telephone
2	1	Heather and Donny	Adams	15221 Parkwood Drive, N	Gulfport	MS	39503	338-555-5832
3	2	Mary	Alde					38-555-2281
4	3	Terrie	Aldri					
5	4	Bridget	All					38-555-3152
6	5	Carol	Becker	309 Bayly Drive	Biloxi	MS	39530	338-555-5359
7	6	Scott and Angela	Benson	3523 Old Bay Road	Biloxi	MS	39531	388-555-2053
8	7	Oscar	Carpenter	3301 Atkinson Road, # 1C	Biloxi	MS	39531	338-555-5719
9	8	Larry & Laural	Goldberg	310 Belvedere Drive	Biloxi	MS	39531	
10	9	Melinda	Gray	13925 Crepe Myrtle Lane	Gulfport	MS	39503	338-555-8805
11	10	Mike & Chris	Grinsell	510 Evergreen Drive	Long Beach	MS	39550	338-555-3501
12	11	Aaron	Hahn	1013 Debra Drive	Gulfport	MS	39503	338-555-5507
13	12	Wilma	Lopez	133 Edgewater Drive	Biloxi	MS	39531	338-555-5535
14	13	Jane	Lopez	559 Cutler Ave	Maple Shade	NJ	08053	855-555-0535
15	14	Carol	Lodge	13085 Glennwood Place	Gulfport	MS	39503	338-555-8723
16	15	Bill	Meyer	25 35th Street	Gulfport	MS	39507	338-555-8119
17	16	David & Elizabeth	Morrow	3511 Parkview Drive	Biloxi	MS	39531	338-555-5591
18	17	Alice Lewis & Kim	Murray	13530 Crystal Court	Gulfport	MS	39503	338-555-5823
19	18	Bob & Keitha	Rogers	15221 Parkwood Drive N	Gulfport	MS	39503	338-555-2353
20	*							
21	Total		18					

List — Toggle Total Row

Figure 1-1. *An Excel list is a designated range of cells within a workbook with added functionality.*

Excel lists are also great for ensuring that formatting and formulas are carried down to subsequent rows. Even conditional formatting is automatically applied to new rows of data in a list. You can analyze list data with Excel's PivotTables feature and chart it using the Chart Wizard.

SharePoint Makes Collaboration Possible

Microsoft SharePoint Technologies, comprised of Microsoft SharePoint Portal Server (SPS) and Microsoft Windows SharePoint Services (WSS), provide a framework for collaboration and teamwork in both large multinational enterprises and small entrepreneurial organizations. Microsoft SharePoint uses Microsoft Internet Explorer so that users can browse collections of web pages containing content specifically relevant to their team or user group. However, SharePoint sites aren't merely passive information sources. With appropriate permissions, users can add content directly to lists on the site, modify page layouts, upload and download documents, run photographic slide shows, participate in discussions, and create personalized views of pages in the site. SharePoint sites can become critical resources for teams that need to work together efficiently and effectively.

Before we discuss the common characteristics of SPS and WSS, let's first differentiate between the two SharePoint technologies.

Microsoft SharePoint Portal Server

SPS provides an enterprise-wide intranet that's powerful, flexible, scalable, and completely customizable. A SharePoint Portal provides a single point of entry to corporate information stores. Because SPS is so easy to use and so powerful, it can easily replace the multitude of shared network drives most enterprises use to manage where corporate documents are stored.

SPS portal administrators can target information to specific groups based on the Microsoft Windows Server Active Directory group to which a user belongs (see the section "Permissions" later in this chapter). For example, when opening the home page of the portal, a user in the sales division in Seattle might see the most recent sales figures, sales projections for the remainder of the year, a calendar of sales meetings and trade shows, and the Seattle weather. At the same time, a user in the human resources department at the home office in Traverse City, Michigan might see a listing of open positions, a report on the number of positions filled this year by department, a calendar of upcoming professional development trainings and job fairs, and the weather in Traverse City.

Unlike for other web sites, content providers don't need to learn web design and publishing to contribute to the site. They can post documents and other content by saving them to existing libraries (see the section "Web Parts, Lists, and Libraries" later in this chapter). When implemented appropriately, an SPS portal improves the organization of corporate information and reduces the amount of time users spend searching for documents. Let's look at a typical scenario before SPS, and then one after SPS has been deployed.

Before SPS

Mary Jones is a dedicated executive assistant who reports to the CEO, Nancy Suregood, of MNL Corp. Nancy is preparing for a meeting of the board of directors, and has asked Mary to pull together a package of last quarter's sales reports and PowerPoint presentations that highlight goals for the upcoming quarter from each of the company's six major areas of business.

Mary contacts the executive assistants in each of the six divisions and tells them what she needs. Three of the executive assistants tell her they'll e-mail her the relevant documents. The other three direct Mary to the network shares where she can find the folders that contain the information she needs. In one case, she's told that she'll find it in three different folders: `\\salesdivision\newprods\sales\sales reports\2006\1st quarter\jan 06\`, `\\salesdivision\newprods\sales\sales reports\2006\1st quarter\feb 06\`, and `\\salesdivision\newprods\sales\sales reports\2006\1st quarter\mar 06\`. She can copy the documents from there, but this executive assistant informs her that the March 06 documents are still being finalized, and might change before the board packet goes out. Mary is encouraged to check back with the assistant next week to determine the status.

In the meantime, two of the three executive assistants e-mail her the documents as promised. The second PowerPoint presentation is quite large and it causes her mailbox to exceed its size limit. Mary has to spend some time cleaning up her mailbox to get back down below the limit before it disrupts other mail delivery.

The third set of documents she was promised by e-mail never arrive, so Mary sends out a reminder e-mail to the executive assistant in that area, Judith Smith. Mary promptly receives an out-of-office message telling her that Judith is on vacation for the next two weeks. Mary scrambles to find someone else who knows about the documents and where she can find them. When someone finally gets back to her, she's told that they must be in Judith's private folders and can't be accessed. She'll have to wait for Judith to return from vacation, three days after the board meeting.

After spending about ten hours on this task, Mary finally has everything pulled together—except, of course, for the division that can't produce its documents. She reports the status of the task to the CEO. Unhappy about the missing reports, the CEO asks Mary to contact the division director and have that person reproduce the documents if necessary. As this particular director isn't known for having a gracious manner, Mary gulps hard and says she'll see what she can do. After much haggling, the director finally sends the documents, one day before the packet is due to go out to the board. The director had to completely re-create the reports from scratch, because even the director didn't have copies of them or of the previous month's reports to use as a model. After a total of about 12 hours on this task, Mary gets the board packet out the door and breathes a huge sigh of relief.

After SPS

MNL Corp.'s IT department, in cooperation with each administrative department and the sales division, rolls out the MNL Portal on January 1, 2006. The Sales area of the portal contains a document library designed to contain sales reports. When documents are loaded to this document library, the executive assistants in each area categorize them (using metadata fields) by division, type of document, year, quarter, and month. The SPS portal area administrator has created a number of custom views in the document library that display the documents in these groupings, depending on what the user wants to see.

■**Note** *Metadata* is data about data. In SharePoint document libraries, you can create custom metadata fields to capture data that describes the documents. By entering metadata when you upload documents, you can maintain a large number of related but distinctly different documents in a single document library. To organize the documents, you can then create views to sort, filter, and group the data in logical ways.

When the CEO gives Mary the assignment to pull together a package of last quarter's sales reports and PowerPoint presentations that highlight goals for the upcoming quarter from each of the company's six major areas of business, Mary immediately clicks the Sales area of the portal. She opens the Sales Reports document library and clicks the view that groups the documents by Quarter and by Division. She reviews the Last Modified dates to see that the documents are current. In the process, she notices that two divisions haven't uploaded their documents for the last month. She e-mails the executive assistants in those areas and asks them to upload the documents to the document library as soon as possible.

Mary sets an alert on the document library to notify her automatically when any of the documents in the document library have been changed or new documents have been added. Within minutes of sending the reminder e-mail to the delinquent departments, Mary receives an SPS alert notifying her that new documents have been added the library. She reviews the document names in the e-mail and is satisfied that one of the two departments has complied.

The other department is a bit harder to work with. The executive assistant, Judith, is on vacation, and no one has seen the report from the last month of the quarter. Mary sends the department director links to the previous month's reports in the document library on the Sales area of the portal, and asks him to make any necessary changes for the current month and save the new report to the document library. The director agrees, and Mary receives an SPS alert that new documents have been added to the library. Mary double-checks that she has everything she needs. The day before the board packet is due to go out, Mary prints the documents from the document library. Altogether, Mary has spent less than an hour on this task and is ready to move on to something else.

As is evident from these two scenarios, SPS can dramatically streamline access to documents across an enterprise. Of course, this isn't possible without buy-in from strategic leaders within the company and active participation of other key people. Successful implementation of SPS requires a culture change within an organization. However, culture change is much easier to accomplish when workflow is simplified and people find more efficient ways to get their jobs done. As SPS does this for the enterprise, WSS helps smaller teams and workgroups collaborate more efficiently.

Microsoft Windows SharePoint Services

WSS is a sister to SPS, and is designed to help teams share documents and information. When WSS runs as part of an overall SPS installation, WSS sites are integrated into the larger portal. For example, a user who is a member of a WSS site can enter search criteria and see results that meet the search criteria on both the portal and on the WSS site.

However, smaller organizations and large enterprises that aren't running SPS might still choose to run WSS to manage team collaboration. A typical WSS site has 2 to 100 members, although sites that are primarily information-sharing sites might run considerably larger. WSS sites can be created on the fly as the need arises, or can be the result of a carefully planned strategy to involve partners in a comprehensive workflow system.

A WSS site, such as the one shown in Figure 1-2, can effectively serve as a department's intranet site where department leaders can post announcements, calendars, contacts, department-specific documents, photos, discussions, and task lists. A WSS site can also house documents and other items related to a specific time-limited project. WSS sites are flexible, adaptable, scalable, and customizable to meet just about any need of a group of people who want to work together.

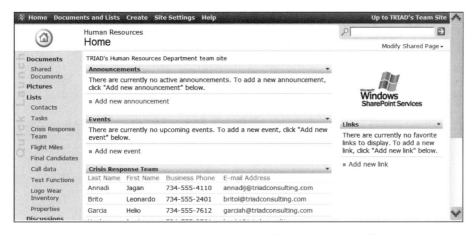

Figure 1-2. *A WSS site can serve as a department's intranet and collaboration site.*

Common Features of SPS and WSS

SPS and WSS share a number of common features. This simplifies training and provides
consistency for users between the portal and their work in smaller teams and workgroups.
In this section, we'll briefly describe the common features before talking about the integration of Excel and SharePoint.

Permissions

Organizations that use Microsoft Windows Server Active Directory (AD) to administer
user rights on a network can use the same system to manage SharePoint security. AD
effectively controls access to SharePoint sites without adding another layer to an already
complex system of security. Only individuals and groups that exist in AD can be granted
SharePoint permissions. Organizations that use externally hosted SharePoint sites or that
don't use AD can add users, based on their e-mail addresses, directly to a SharePoint site.

SharePoint site administrators can take permissions a step further within each
SharePoint site by designating permissions to document libraries, lists, and other site
content (see more about site content in the section "Web Parts, Lists, and Libraries" later
in the chapter). For example, all users within a company might be granted reader permissions to an SPS site. However, only specially designated and trained individuals can add
site content or modify the site. Other users might be granted contributor access to a WSS
site that was created for a team project they're working on. When a new user is added to
a WSS site, the site administrator can set permission levels for the user. Figure 1-3 shows
the Add Users page of a WSS site.

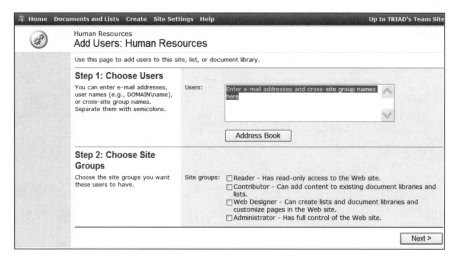

Figure 1-3. *When a site administrator adds a new user, the administrator can choose the level of permission to assign the user.*

By being able to customize permissions easily based on the need to know, organizations can manage security and document compliance effectively with regulatory authorities.

Web Parts, Lists, and Libraries

A SharePoint site is nothing more than a web site, but it's a web site with a distinct advantage. Rather than using web site design tools or HTML to lay content out on blank pages, a SharePoint site consists of web part pages, web parts, document libraries, and lists. A *web part* is a component designed to display specific information, such as an announcements list, a calendar, or a document library. A *web part page* is a web page that contains preestablished zones where web parts can be positioned. Figure 1-4 shows a newly created web part page and a list of available web parts to add to the page.

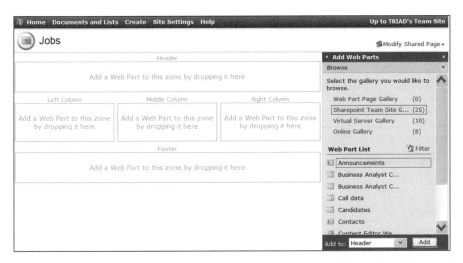

Figure 1-4. *You can add web parts to a web part page to display information such as announcements, events, and document libraries.*

A *document library*, shown in Figure 1-5, is a folder for holding documents, images, or forms. Each document library can have its own custom permissions separate from the general WSS site. For example, someone might have Contributor permissions that allow them to add and delete content to a WSS site, but still might have only Reader permissions in one of the document libraries. WSS document libraries can hold a variety of document formats, such as Microsoft Office documents, Adobe PDF files, image files, and Microsoft InfoPath forms.

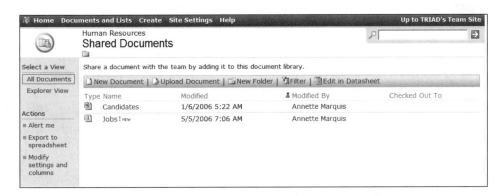

Figure 1-5. *A document library is a container for documents, images, or forms.*

A *list*, such as the one shown in Figure 1-6, is a folder that holds data organized into customizable columns and rows. A list can also have its own permissions, and can be displayed in a standard list view and in Datasheet view, resembling a spreadsheet.

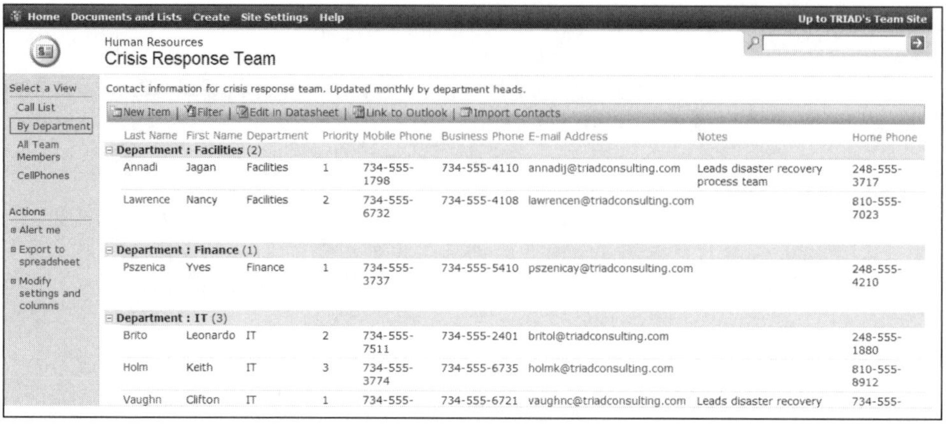

Figure 1-6. *You can group, sort, and filter a SharePoint list to show only the data you want to see in the order in which you want to see it.*

Note In addition to libraries and lists, discussions and surveys can be added to SharePoint sites. Although in their most basic forms these are simply other types of lists, each contains its own special characteristics. Discussions consist of threaded conversations with topics and replies. Surveys can contain a variety of questions, from multiple choice to open-ended text questions. Answers are automatically tabulated and displayed in graphic form on the site.

Document Collaboration

SharePoint is fundamentally about collaboration, so it's no surprise that SharePoint document collaboration features are especially well developed. SharePoint document libraries include the following collaboration features:

- *Document check in and check out*: By checking out a document, you can assure that someone else doesn't overwrite your changes. Users who have permission to access the document library can see if a document is checked out, and to whom. When you check in a document, you can record comments specific to the changes you made to the document, or other pertinent information.

- *Versions*: SharePoint can automatically track versions of a document for you. You can switch between versions and maintain an accurate record of document changes for auditing purposes. This is especially valuable in light of new corporate rules introduced due to Sarbanes-Oxley regulations.

- *Document workspaces*: A document workspace is a mini-version of a WSS site focused on a document or a set of related documents. Users can be invited to a document workspace through an automatically generated e-mail message. They can click the link to open the document; add comments; and through the use of a Document Workspace task pane, check off tasks related to the document, contact other members of the shared workspace, access other related documents, and set alerts to be notified of changes to the document (see the section "Uploading an Excel Workbook to SharePoint" later in this chapter).

- *Presence integration*: Members can easily detect if another member of the team is currently online, and depending on that person's status, make contact with the team member through instant messaging, send the team member an e-mail, add the team member to their contacts, and check the team member's free/busy status.

- *Alerts*: Members can set alerts to receive e-mail notifications if a document has been added to a document library, or if a document in a document library has been modified (see the section "Alerts for Content Changes" later in this chapter).

Powerful Search Tools

SharePoint has a powerful search engine that can help you quickly locate the information you need. Using Search, you can find documents, people, list items, web sites, and other useful information. If a user conducts a search from an SPS portal page, SharePoint searches the portal and any WSS sites to which the user has access. Users can access documents on any area of the portal or on any WSS site directly from the search results.

By default, the results are categorized by the site on which they were found, and in order of relevance. However, you can choose a different view of the search results and see them by author, by date, and by area.

Using advanced search tools, you can narrow a search by entering specific search criteria by type, by source, by properties, and by date. For example, these advanced tools give you the ability to find all Microsoft Excel documents (by type), on the Sales area of the portal (by source), authored by John Smith and containing the word "elephant" in the description (by properties), modified in the last week (by date).

Alerts for Content Changes

One of the biggest advantages of maintaining documents and lists on SharePoint is that users can decide what's important to them and what they want to track. In the world without SharePoint, people are bombarded with group e-mail messages that contain information that has no relevance or interest to them. E-mail serves as the primary method of communication, information dissemination, document sharing, and document storage.

E-mail was never intended for this purpose. Handling the sheer volume of e-mail that arrives each day becomes a monumental task. If you spend two hours a day handling e-mail, and half of the e-mail messages you receive are inconsequential, you've just wasted an hour a day, 5 hours a week, 260 hours a year. That comes to six and a half weeks of work each year! Wouldn't you rather spend that time on vacation in the Caribbean than slogging through junk e-mail?

Then there's the size of e-mail messages. Not only does a 5MB PowerPoint presentation attached to an e-mail message clog your mailbox, when you multiply that by the number of people copied on the message, it can seriously impact the bandwidth in an organization's network.

SharePoint can drastically reduce the amount and the size of e-mail messages you receive. By setting daily or weekly alerts on the content that interests you, you receive one e-mail message that summarizes all the pertinent content. It tells you what has been modified or added, and includes a link to the related document or list. No more sending large e-mail attachments to 50 people. You upload the document to the SharePoint site, and users who want it can go and get it there.

If you're interested in a particular list, you can set an alert that notifies you that a list item has been added or a list has been modified. SharePoint lets you choose how frequently you want to be notified: immediately, daily, or weekly. You can also choose what level of notification you want: items that are discovered (added) or items that are changed.

Alerts are pervasive in SharePoint. You can find Alert Me links on every page, in document workspace task panes, and in drop-down menus on list items. After you've set a number of alerts, you can manage your alerts through Rules and Alerts on the Actions menu in Microsoft Outlook. This is part of SharePoint's excellent integration with Microsoft Office, and provides a convenient place to review the alerts you've set and make changes when necessary. Figure 1-7 shows an e-mail notifying you that an item has been added to a SharePoint list.

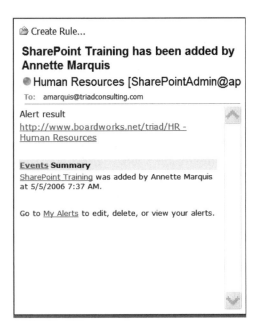

Figure 1-7. *Alerts are integrated into Outlook so you receive your alert notices in your Inbox.*

Working Together: Excel and SharePoint

In this chapter, we've talked about useful features of Microsoft Excel, and we've identified key benefits of SPS and WSS. But this is not a book solely about Excel or a book solely about SharePoint. It's a book about how these two tools work together to extend each other, to make each other more powerful, and to make it possible to develop low-cost business solutions that would otherwise be out of reach for many organizations. Because of the integration of Excel and SharePoint, data that was once hidden in an Excel spreadsheet can be easily shared with members of a team. SharePoint offers two ways to do this:

- Uploading a workbook to a SharePoint document library, and then sharing it with a team through a shared document workspace

- Publishing an Excel list to SharePoint so users have ready access to the data on the SharePoint site

Let's look at the benefits of each of these options, starting with uploading an Excel workbook to a SharePoint document library.

Uploading an Excel Workbook to SharePoint

Although at first glance uploading an Excel workbook to SharePoint might seem like it's no different than saving the workbook to a network folder and giving everyone access to it, you'll soon discover it's quite different. When you save an Excel workbook to a shared network folder, you first have to share the workbook if you want more than one person to access it at a time. Excel's version of sharing makes it possible for more than one person to make editing changes at the same time and to resolve conflicts if they arise. However, SharePoint takes sharing to a much higher level of true collaboration. SharePoint creates a Shared Document Workspace for the workbook, such as the one shown in Figure 1-8, that puts a lot of collaboration features close at hand through the Shared Workspace task pane.

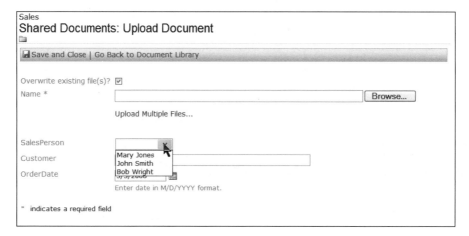

Figure 1-8. *From the Shared Workspace task pane, you can access a number of SharePoint collaboration features.*

Accessing SharePoint Options in Excel

When you open a workbook from a SharePoint site, you can do the following:

- Restrict which users have access to the workbook and what level of access they have

- Assign and manage tasks specifically related to the workbook, right in the workbook

- Check a workbook out to prevent other users from making changes

- Set up alerts to notify you that the workbook has been modified

- Add related documents to the document workspace

- Open other shared workbooks from the team site

- View the workbook history and versions

The following list describes each of the options in the Shared Workspace task pane:

- *Status*: Information about the status of a document

- *Members*: The members of the shared workspace and whether or not they're online

- *Tasks*: The tasks related to this shared workspace

- *Documents*: A list of documents in the document library on the WSS site or in this workspace

- *Links*: Hyperlinks related to this workspace

- *Document Information*: Properties of the document, including any metadata

At the bottom of the Shared Workspace task pane, you'll find additional options. Some of these options, such as **Add new task** and **Alert me about tasks**, are specific to the task pane button you've selected. In addition, on the General tab, you'll find these options:

- *Restrict permission*: Use this option to restrict permissions for individuals who have access to the workbook but who aren't members of the WSS site. Use WSS permissions to manage permissions for site members.

- *Alert me about this document*: Create an alert to notify you of changes in the workbook.

- *Version history*: If versions are enabled for the document library, use this tab to view the saved versions and review comments about them.

- *Get updates*: Send a request to the WSS site to update the workbook to incorporate any changes made by other users since you've had the workbook open.

- *Options*: Set options related to how you want to manage updates for the workbook.

Working with Document Libraries

Another clear advantage to uploading Excel workbooks to a SharePoint document library is that you can organize workbooks within a document library using views (see Chapter 4). For example, let's say that you have a collection of workbooks that contain details about specific orders. Each order consists of a collection of worksheets, so there's one workbook for each order. Organizing these in a shared network folder can be an arduous task. Do you alphabetize them by customer, list them by order date, or categorize them by sales person? To do any of these, you must standardize your file-naming convention. Even then, you're limited to one of these options, unless you create a convoluted system of subfolders to keep the workbooks organized. Finding a workbook for a specific order can be frustrating. Mary Jones was the sales person at the beginning of the order but John Smith took over—is the workbook filed under Mary or John? Was it last quarter or this quarter? This type of discernment takes times and wastes energy.

SharePoint eliminates this headache. By uploading all the workbooks to a single document library, and tracking important data such as sales person, customer name, and order date in metadata fields, you can slice and dice the workbooks any way you want. Look back at Figure 1-8. It shows metadata fields on the Upload Document page of a WSS document library. If you want, you can require any or all of the fields. You can also create drop-down lists or, for easy list management, tie a drop-down list to another list on the WSS site.

If you still can't find what you're looking for in a document library, you can use SharePoint's Search feature to search document properties, including metadata fields, and all the content of the workbook. For example, say you need to find all the order workbooks that include a specific product. You can enter all or part of the product name in the Search field, and SharePoint returns a list of all workbooks where that product was sold. Although theoretically you could use Windows Search to do the same thing, you'll find SharePoint's Search not only easier to use, but a whole lot faster.

Publishing an Excel List

The second option for sharing Excel workbook data in SharePoint is by publishing an Excel list. In Chapter 2, we explore publishing an Excel list to SharePoint in great detail, so here we'll just present a brief overview. In the previous section, we talked about uploading an Excel workbook to a document library. Although that has significant advantages over using shared network folders, it still has its limitations. For one thing, except through the use of metadata and searching, you cannot access data within the workbook without opening it up in Excel. However, by publishing an Excel list to SharePoint, you can display the contents of a worksheet directly on the site. In this way, you can control access to the workbook and limit users to seeing just the content you want them to see. Excel lists can be published as static data, or can be published to synchronize with the SharePoint server so changes made in either the Excel list or in the SharePoint list are reflected in the other. Figure 1-9 shows an Excel list published as a SharePoint list.

Human Resources
Job Candidates

New Row | Show in Standard View | Task Pane | Totals | Refresh Data

Street Address ▼	City ▼	State ▼	Zip ▼	Telephone ▼	
15221 Parkwood Drive, N	Gulfport	MS	39503	338-555-5832	
12359 Mosswood Drive	Gulfport	MS	39503	338-555-2281	
15538 Tourill Road, #13	Gulfport	MS	39503		
3335 Popps Ferry Road	Biloxi	MS	39533	338-555-3152	
309 Bayly Drive	Biloxi	MS	39530	338-555-5359	
3523 Old Bay Road	Biloxi	MS	39531	388-555-2053	
3301 Atkinson Road, # 1C	Biloxi	MS	39531	338-555-5719	
310 Belvedere Drive	Biloxi	MS	39531		
13925 Crepe Myrtle Lane	Gulfport	MS	39503	338-555-8805	
510 Evergreen Drive	Long Beach	MS	39550	338-555-3501	
1013 Debra Drive	Gulfport	MS	39503	338-555-5507	

For assistance with Datasheet view, see Help.

Figure 1-9. *Excel lists can be synchronized with SharePoint so that users are always viewing the most current data.*

From SharePoint to Excel and Back Again

In addition to uploading Excel workbooks and publishing Excel lists to SharePoint, you can also go in the reverse direction. You can publish SharePoint lists to Excel to make use of Excel's analysis, charting, and other advanced features (see Chapter 3). You can also publish Excel charts and tables as web pages to display in SharePoint so you can easily share them with others (see Chapter 6). If you need in-depth query capability, you can use Microsoft Query through Excel to query data in a SharePoint list (see Chapter 8).

As you can see, it doesn't matter where your data starts—with the integration of SharePoint and Excel, you can take it in whatever direction you need to go.

Summary

In this chapter, we reviewed features of Microsoft Excel that make Excel an excellent partner for a collaboration tool such as SharePoint. We took a high-level look at Microsoft SharePoint Technologies, including Microsoft SharePoint Portal Server and Windows SharePoint Services. We then ended with an introduction to the partnership between these two workhorses, Excel and SharePoint. In the remainder of this book, we'll explore this partnership in great depth so you can exploit this relationship to its maximum, including creating out-of-the-box solutions to move your business forward.

CHAPTER 2

■■■

Working with Lists in SharePoint

Every SharePoint site consists of three elements: web pages and web parts, document libraries, and lists. Lists can be used for everything from displaying contact information to real-time tracking of issues. Lists can contain static, read-only content or be populated by dynamic, collaborative content that changes every second.

Although lists can reside solely on the SharePoint site, through the integration of Microsoft Excel and SharePoint, you can combine the power of Excel lists with the collaboration features of SharePoint for a powerful new way to track and maintain data. You can publish Excel lists to SharePoint sites using powerful synchronization tools that allow for editing on the site or directly in the Excel workbook. By maintaining the list on a SharePoint site, team members can easily review the list's contents, modify the list when appropriate, and use database features such as sort and filter to analyze the list.

In this chapter, we examine SharePoint lists, including how to create a list, how to set list permissions, how to publish a list from Excel to SharePoint, and how to synchronize and manage lists.

Exploring SharePoint Lists

A SharePoint list is a collection of columns (fields) and rows (records) of data. You can create a list in SharePoint using one of the standard list templates, you can modify a standard list or create a custom list with your own columns, and you can import a preexisting list from Excel. What makes a list especially valuable in SharePoint is not in the creation of the list but in how you can display the data the list contains. By setting list permissions and creating custom views of SharePoint lists, you can control who sees the data and give authorized users the ability to view the data in the way that's most helpful to them.

SharePoint comes with the following standard list templates to help you get started:

- *Links*: Hyperlinks to documents or to internal and external web pages

- *Announcements*: News and other short bits of information

- *Contacts*: Name and address information, which can be linked to Microsoft Outlook

- *Events*: Meetings and other date-specific data, which can be displayed in a calendar format and linked to Microsoft Outlook

- *Tasks*: Items you want to track that need to be completed by the team

- *Issues*: Issues related to a project that you want to track

In addition to these standard lists, you can choose three additional methods to create lists:

- *Custom List*: A standard custom list where you create your own columns

- *Custom List in Datasheet View*: A custom list that's displayed in datasheet or spreadsheet view by default

- *Import Spreadsheet*: A custom list you create by importing a preexisting spreadsheet from Excel

Creating a SharePoint List

To create a list, choose the template or method that most closely resembles the list you want. Whichever you choose, you can customize the list after you create it by adding columns, choosing the order of the columns, defining sort order, filtering data, and adding totals. Depending on the type of list, you might also be able to group it and choose a display style.

To create a new list, follow these steps:

1. Click **Create** in the Windows SharePoint Services (WSS) top navigation bar or in SharePoint Portal Server (SPS), click **Manage Content** in the Actions menu, and then click **Create** to see a list of standard list templates.

2. Click the type of list you would like to create from the available templates.

3. On the New List page that opens, enter a name for the list. This is the name that site visitors see, so make it descriptive. However, because it becomes part of the URL (Uniform Resource Locator or address) to the list, it's better to make the list name as short as possible while still identifying the list.

4. Enter a description of the list. In addition to text that will help to distinguish the list, include any names in the Description text box that team members might use to search for the list.

5. Select **No** if you don't want a link to the list to appear on the Quick Launch bar on the left side of the site's home page. For example, select **No** if you're creating a list that will be used to supply data to a lookup field in another list or document library. If you want users to have easy access to the list, leave the default option set to **Yes**.

6. Click **Create**.

A new web page is created to display the list. The columns that display on the list page depend on the type of list you chose to create. The type of list also determines which views appear in the Select a View list on the left of the page.

If you already have a list in Excel, you don't have to re-create it in SharePoint. You can use SharePoint's **Import Spreadsheet** option to import the list directly from Excel to SharePoint. The steps for importing a spreadsheet are essentially the same as they are for creating a new list, with just a few exceptions.

To import a preexisting list from a spreadsheet, follow these steps:

1. Click **Create** in the WSS top navigation bar or in SPS, click **Manage Content** in the Actions menu, and then click **Create** to see a list of templates.

2. Select **Import Spreadsheet** from the list of available options.

3. On the New List page that opens, enter a name for the list.

4. Enter a description of the list.

5. Click **Browse** at the bottom of the New List page.

6. Choose the workbook that contains the list from the Choose File dialog box, and then click **Open**.

7. Click **Import** on the New List page.

8. In the "Import to Windows SharePoint Services list" dialog box, select the type of range that contains the list from the Range Type drop-down list, and then select the corresponding range:

   - **List Range** refers to a Microsoft Excel list (see Appendix A for information about creating and using Excel lists). If the workbook has only one list, SharePoint selects it automatically. If the workbook has multiple lists, select the list you want from the Select Range drop-down list.

   - **Range of Cells** is any selected range of cells in any worksheet in the workbook. To select a range, click the **Collapse** button on the right end of the Select Range field, select the range of cells you want to import, and click the **Expand** button (see Figure 2-1) to return to the "Import to Windows SharePoint Services list" dialog box (see Figure 2-2).

Figure 2-1. *Click the Expand button to return to the Import to Windows SharePoint Services list dialog box.*

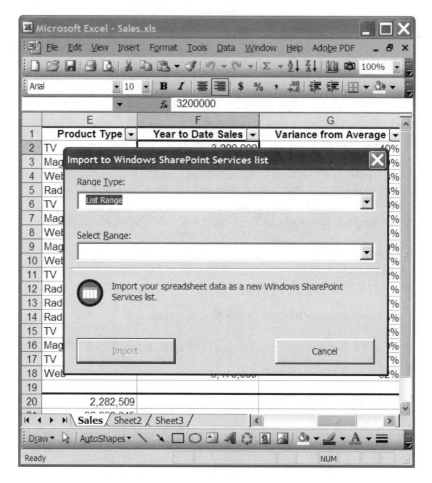

Figure 2-2. *Use the WSS "Import to Windows SharePoint Services list" dialog box to select the cells in a worksheet you want to import.*

- **Named Range** refers to a named range within the workbook. Select the named range from the Select Range drop-down list.

9. Click **Import**.

The contents of the Excel list are displayed in the new list on the SharePoint site.

■**Note** When you create a list using **Import Spreadsheet**, the option to display a link to the list in the Quick Launch bar is inexplicably missing from the New List page. When you import a spreadsheet, the link doesn't appear in the Quick Launch bar, by default. If you'd like to include a link after you create the list, see the upcoming section "Changing General Settings."

You're now ready to add records to the list, customize the columns in the list, or modify other list settings. To learn how to create custom views of any list you create, refer to Chapter 4.

Modifying a List's Settings

After you create a list, you can make changes to the list's general settings, such as its name and description; set list permissions; add or modify columns; and configure views of the list.

Changing General Settings

To change a list's general settings, click **Modify Settings and Column**s in the Actions menu on the left side of the list's page. This opens the Customize page. In the WSS General Settings section, shown in Figure 2-3, you can do the following:

- Change general settings

- Save list as template

- Change permissions for this list

- Delete this list

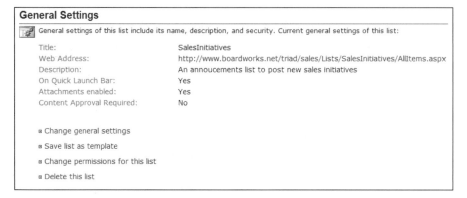

General Settings

General settings of this list include its name, description, and security. Current general settings of this list:

Title:	SalesInitiatives
Web Address:	http://www.boardworks.net/triad/sales/Lists/SalesInitiatives/AllItems.aspx
Description:	An annoucements list to post new sales initiatives
On Quick Launch Bar:	Yes
Attachments enabled:	Yes
Content Approval Required:	No

⊠ Change general settings

⊠ Save list as template

⊠ Change permissions for this list

⊠ Delete this list

Figure 2-3. *Use the General Settings options to modify a list's name, description, security, and other settings.*

Note In SPS, permissions are managed on the area level rather than the list level. Instead of **Change permissions for this list**, you'll find an option to **Select a portal area for this document library**. For more about changing permissions on a SPS portal, see "Managing SPS Security" later in this chapter.

Click **Change general settings** to modify the properties of the list, including its name and description. This opens the List Settings page.

Here's a description of the settings you can change:

- *Name and Description*: Change the list's name or modify the description.

- *Navigation*: Change whether you want a link to the list displayed on the Quick Launch bar.

- *Content Approval*: Select **Yes** if you'd like to require that before items are posted to a list, you'd like them approved by a site administrator or other team member with Manage List rights (see the section "Setting List Permissions" for more about WSS list permissions). The default option is **No**.

- *Attachments*: Specify whether file attachments to items in a list are enabled or disabled. Attachments are enabled by default.

- *Item-Level Permissions*: Specify which items in a list users can read—all items or only their own—and if they can edit all items, only their own, or no items.

Saving a List As a Template

You might decide that after you've customized a list to meet your needs, you might want to designate it as a template so that it can be reused for future lists. To do this, click **Save list as template** on the list's Customize page. Enter the following:

- *File name*: Enter a file name for the template. It's a good idea to keep this name short and avoid spaces to minimize the length of the template's URL.

- *Template title*: The title appears on the Create page in the list of available list types. Make it friendly and descriptive so users know what they're selecting.

- *Template description*: The description appears on the Create page in the list of available list types.

- *Include content*: Select this checkbox if you want to include the data from the current list in any lists based on this template. Don't select this checkbox if the data contained in the list should be kept confidential. List permissions don't carry over from the original list to the template.

The new template is available in the Lists list on the Create page when you click **Create** in the top navigation bar in WSS, or when you click **Manage Content** in the Actions menu in SPS, and then click **Create**.

To modify or delete a template you've created, follow these steps:

1. Click **Site Settings** on the top navigation bar.

2. Click **Go to Site Administration** in the Administration section of the Site Settings page.

3. Click **Manage list template gallery** in the Site Collection Galleries section of the Top-Level Site Administration page.

4. To delete:

   a. Click the **Edit** icon next to the template.

   b. Click **Delete**.

5. To edit:

   a. Click **Modify Settings and Columns** in the Actions list.

   b. Make changes as you would to any list.

   c. When you're finished making changes, click **Go back to List Template Gallery**.

Setting List Permissions

To control who has access to a list on a site, you can set varying levels of permissions. These permissions can be identical to, or different from, permissions on the site itself. Permissions to SharePoint lists are managed by adding site groups, user groups (Active Directory groups, for example), or individual users to the list. Groups provide the easiest and most useful method of managing list permissions and are considered the best practice. By assigning individuals to groups, rather than assigning them individual permissions, you have better control over access to each list.

■Note *Site groups* are custom security groups to which users can be assigned, in order to grant them permissions to a SharePoint site, library, or list. For information about restricting access to lists on an SPS portal using site groups, see "Managing SPS Security" later in this section.

By default, SharePoint sites have five predefined site groups. These predefined site groups have a variety of permissions in relation to the entire site. When applied to a list, these groups have the following list-related permissions:

- *Guest*: Limited reader access to a specific list without giving access to the entire site. Users cannot be added to the Guest site group. If you allow Guest access to a list, then any user who has access to the site is automatically given Guest permissions to the list. The Guest site group cannot be customized, but can be removed from specific lists.

- *Reader*: View items in the list.

- *Contributor*: View, insert, edit, and delete items in the list. Contributors cannot create new lists, but can add content to existing lists.

- *Web Designer*: View, insert, edit, and delete items; change list settings, including managing lists.

- *Administrator*: View, insert, edit, and delete items; change list settings; change list security, including the right to approve list items when content approval is required (see the section "Changing General Settings" earlier in this chapter).

You aren't limited to these site groups, however. You can mix and match permissions to assure that everyone has exactly the permissions they need and no one has more than they need. To add individual users to a WSS list and set custom permissions for them, while restricting others' access to the list, follow these steps:

1. Click **Modify Settings and Column**s from the Actions menu on the left side of the page.

2. Click **Change permissions for this list** in the General Settings section of the Customize page.

3. Select the default site groups that you want to restrict from accessing the list and then click **Remove Selected Users**. For example, if you want everyone who has access to the site to be able to read the list (Reader site group), but only a few people to be able to edit it, select Contributor and remove that site group.

4. Click **Add Users** to add the specific people to whom you want to grant unique permissions.

5. Click **Address Book** to select users you want to add to the list. Note that to access an address book, you must have an address book compatible with WSS, such as an Outlook Address Book, installed. You might have to click **Allow Access for 1 minute** and then click **Yes** in the Microsoft Office Outlook dialog box that opens. Click **OK** when you've finished adding users.

6. Select the level of permission you want to grant these users from the standard list, or click **Advanced permissions** to customize permissions.

7. Click **Next**.

8. Edit the user's display name, if desired, to make it a friendlier name.

9. If you want the users to be notified by e-mail that they've been added to the list, enter a personalized message to the users in the Body text box.

10. Click **Finish**.

Individual users are added to the list, and their names appear in the Users list on the Change Permissions page.

Managing WSS List Permissions Through Custom Site Groups

When you want to assign permissions to users of a list that are different from the default permissions on the SharePoint site, you can add individual users to the list and define permissions for each user, as described in the previous section. However, this process can become tedious if you have a large site with numerous users and multiple lists. A more efficient practice is to create one or more site groups that define the permissions you want to use on the list, and then assign users to the relevant site groups. As you add users to the site, it's then a simple step to assign them to the appropriate site groups for each list you want them to access. Doing this correctly involves some preplanning, but will save time in the long run. More importantly, assigning permissions using site groups provides tighter control over security for the lists on the site. Here are the steps to follow to create and assign custom site group permissions to a site.

Step 1: Identify what permissions you want users to have. You'll be creating a list-specific site group for each level of permission you want to assign, so it's important to be thorough in evaluating the needs for each list on the site. Table 2-1 shows the five default site groups, with the addition of two commonly used custom site groups: "Reader with insert" and "Contributor with no delete."

Table 2-1. *Site Groups and Permissions*

Site Group	View	Edit	Insert	Delete	Change Settings	Change Security
Guest	✓					
Reader	✓					
Reader with insert	✓		✓			
Contributor	✓	✓	✓	✓		
Contributor with no delete	✓	✓	✓	✓		
Web Designer	✓	✓	✓	✓	✓	
Administrator	✓	✓	✓	✓	✓	✓

■Note In most cases, you'll focus on creating list-specific site groups related to the permissions associated with the Guest, Reader, and Contributor site groups (view, edit, insert, and delete). Web Designers and Administrators typically have permissions that extend beyond specific lists.

Step 2: Create a site group that includes the name of the list and a description of the type of permission. For example, if your list is named Candidates and you want some users to have Reader permissions to the list, create a site group called "Candidates Reader." If you want some users to be able to read, insert, and edit items but not delete them, you might call the site group "Candidates Contributor with no delete". Follow these steps to create a site group:

1. In WSS, click **Site Settings** on the top navigation bar.

2. Click **Go to Site Administration** in the Administration section of the Site Settings page.

3. Click **Manage site groups** in the Users and Permissions section of the Site Administration page.

4. Click **Add a Site Group** in the Manage Site Groups toolbar.

5. Enter the site group name and description in the respective text boxes. Be sure to include the list name in the site group name—for example, Sales Initiatives Contributor—so it's easy to distinguish this site group from others in the site.

6. Select the list rights you want this site group to have (see Figure 2-4). Don't select rights from either the Site Rights or Personal Rights sections.

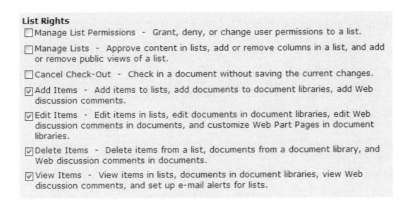

List Rights

☐ Manage List Permissions - Grant, deny, or change user permissions to a list.

☐ Manage Lists - Approve content in lists, add or remove columns in a list, and add or remove public views of a list.

☐ Cancel Check-Out - Check in a document without saving the current changes.

☑ Add Items - Add items to lists, add documents to document libraries, add Web discussion comments.

☑ Edit Items - Edit items in lists, edit documents in document libraries, edit Web discussion comments in documents, and customize Web Part Pages in document libraries.

☑ Delete Items - Delete items from a list, documents from a document library, and Web discussion comments in documents.

☑ View Items - View items in lists, documents in document libraries, view Web discussion comments, and set up e-mail alerts for lists.

Figure 2-4. *Select the list rights you want this group to have.*

7. Click **Create Site Group** at the bottom of the page.

The site group is created, and as shown in Figure 2-5, is displayed in the list of available site groups. Repeat steps 4–7 to create additional list-specific site groups.

Add a Site Group | ✕ Delete Selected Site Groups	
Site Group	Description
☐ Reader	Has read-only access to the Web site.
☐ Contributor	Can add content to existing document libraries and lists.
☐ Web Designer	Can create lists and document libraries and customize pages in the Web site.
☐ Administrator	Has full control of the Web site.
☐ Sales Initiatives Contributor	A contributor to the SalesInitiatives list on the Sales subsite.

Figure 2-5. *The newly created site group, Sales Initiatives Contributor, appears in the list of available site groups.*

■**Note** To create site groups at the subsite level, the site must be using unique permissions and not inheriting rights from the top-level site. If **Manage site groups** doesn't appear in the Users and Permissions section of the Site Administration page, click **Manage permission inheritance**, select **Use unique permissions**, and then click **OK**. **Manage site groups** should now appear in the list.

Step 3: Delete nonapplicable site permissions from the list. This step assures that only users with specific permissions to the list can access it. Follow these steps to remove nonapplicable site permissions:

1. Open the page that displays the list.

2. Click **Modify Settings and Columns** in the Actions menu.

3. Click **Change permissions for this list** in the General Settings section of the Customize page.

4. Select the general site permissions; for example, Reader, Contributor, and any other site groups that aren't relevant to the list.

5. Click **Remove Selected Users** and then click **OK** to confirm the deletion.

Now, only users assigned to the custom site groups you created can access the list.

Step 4: Assign users to the custom site groups. In this step, you'll assign site users to custom site groups to give them appropriate access to the relevant lists. To assign users to site groups, follow these steps:

1. Click **Site Settings** in the WSS top navigation bar.

2. Click **Manage Users** in the Administration section of the Site Settings page.

3. Select the users whose site group membership you want to modify.

4. Click **Edit Site Groups of Selected Users** in the toolbar.

5. Select the custom site groups to which you want the users to be assigned. Be sure to keep their general site group memberships—Reader, Contributor, and so on— so they can still access unrestricted areas on the site.

6. Click **OK**.

7. Repeat steps 3–6 to assign other users to unique site groups.

Users now have general permissions to the site and custom permissions to specific lists.

Managing SPS Security

SPS security is managed on the area level. To assign unique permissions to a list, you need to create the list in its own subarea. To create custom site groups on an SPS portal, you need portal administrator rights. You can add users and site groups to specific subareas and control access to lists in that way. Before taking any steps to restrict access to a list on the portal, talk with your portal administrator about your needs for unique permissions.

Deleting a List

To delete a list from a SharePoint site, follow these steps:

1. Click **Modify Settings and Column**s in the Actions menu on the left side of the list's page.

2. Click **Delete this list** in the General Settings section of the Customize page.

3. Click **OK** to confirm that you want the list deleted.

The list is completely removed from the site and the data is no longer available.

Working with SharePoint List Data

Regardless of how you create a list, SharePoint offers a number of tools for working with it after it's created. You can access these tools most easily by switching a list from Standard view to Datasheet view. To switch to Datasheet view, click the **Edit in Datasheet** button on the list toolbar.

Figure 2-6 shows a list in Datasheet view. Datasheet view resembles a spreadsheet, and has many of the characteristics of an Excel spreadsheet. In Datasheet view, you can sort and filter data, adjust column width and row height, rearrange the order of columns, use fill to copy data, add totals, and export data to Excel and Access.

Name	Years of Service	Region	Product Type	Year to Date Sales
Chelsea Alder	4.5	East	TV	3,200,000
David Geffen	8	East	Magazine	925,000
Rod Serling	0.5	East	Web	2,800,720
Bill Cooke	5.5	East	Radio	840,000
Veronica Smith	3	East	TV	2,920,500
Alicia Adams	3	North	Magazine	750,000
Don Wan	14	North	Web	4,200,350
Judy Abrams	13	North	Magazine	3,200,600
Mike Jones	6	North	Web	2,450,000
Sue Chaney	7	North	TV	1,770,000

Figure 2-6. *In Datasheet view, a SharePoint list has many of the characteristics of an Excel spreadsheet.*

The arrows at the top of each column include sort and filter options, including Custom Filter.

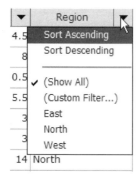

Adjust columns and rows, just as you might in Excel, by dragging or double-clicking the cell dividers in the header rows. To copy values up or down in a column, drag the fill handle in the bottom right of the cell.

To rearrange columns in the list, click a column header to select the column. Point to the column header, and when the pointer changes to a four-headed arrow, drag the column to a new position.

Inserting Column Totals

If you want to add totals to any of the columns, click the **Totals** button in the list toolbar. SharePoint automatically includes totals for any column with numeric values. You can choose from a number of functions, including **Average**, **Count**, **Maximum**, **Minimum**, **Sum**, **Standard Deviation**, and **Variance**. Select the function you want to display from the drop-down list in the Totals row. If you don't want a total in a particular column, select **None**.

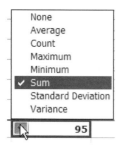

Using the SharePoint Datasheet Task Pane

To access addition tools, click the **Task Pane** button on the list toolbar, or click the **Show Task Pane** button on the right side of Datasheet view to open the Datasheet task pane. The task pane is divided into two sections. The top section includes **Cut**, **Copy**, **Paste**, **Undo**, **Sort**, **Remove Filter/Sort**, and **Help** buttons.

■**Caution** The **Undo** button works only with **Cut**, **Copy**, and **Paste**. If you change data in the list, you cannot use **Undo** to change it back.

The bottom section, Office Links, has options for working with SharePoint data in Excel and Access. Chapter 3 deals extensively with exporting and linking a SharePoint list to Excel, and using Excel to print, chart, and create an Excel PivotTable report. In addition to these options, you have three choices for exporting SharePoint data to Access:

- *Export to Access*: Exports the data into Access and creates an unlinked Access table

- *Create a linked table in Access*: Exports the data into Access and creates a linked Access table

- *Report with Access*: Exports the data into Access, creates a linked Access table, and generates an AutoReport

By taking the data into Access, you can use Access reporting tools to create sophisticated reports. In addition, you can use the data in the SharePoint list to link to other data in an Access database to create a full relational database.

In all three exporting options, the table that SharePoint generates in Access contains an Edit field, shown in Figure 2-7, that's linked directly back to the edit form for the list item in SharePoint.

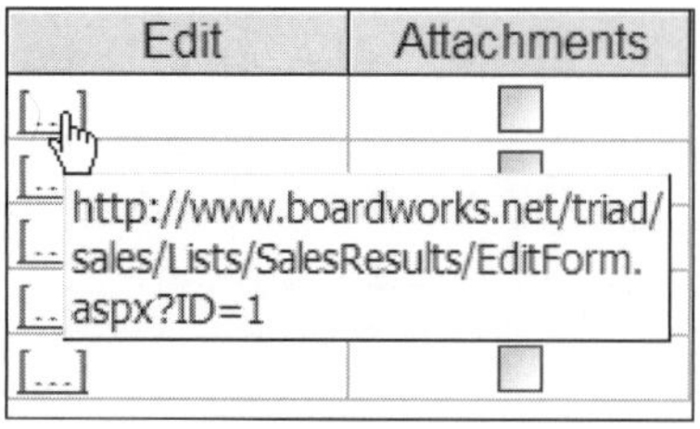

Figure 2-7. *When SharePoint generates an Access table, it includes an Edit field that's directly linked to the SharePoint record.*

■**Caution** If the data in either the SharePoint list or the Access table is edited, the Access table must be linked to SharePoint for the data to synchronize. If you choose the first option, **Export to Access**, the data isn't linked, so as soon as data is edited, differences will exist in the two data sources.

Publishing an Excel List to a SharePoint Site

The integration of Excel 2003's list function (see Appendix A for more about creating and using an Excel list) with SharePoint provides a new and valuable way to share Excel data. Publishing an Excel list to a SharePoint site offers several advantages:

- Users can access the list in a centralized repository rather than through a difficult-to-find network share.

- The list and its contents are easily searchable through SharePoint's extensive search tools.

- You can control access to the list with SharePoint's powerful security features.

- Users who don't have access to the corporate network can be given permissions to access the list.

In many ways, it's the best of both worlds. You can make data accessible while still retaining control of the Excel workbook and all of its functionality.

Publishing Lists with Formulas

Although you can publish any Excel list to SharePoint, formulas cannot be published. Cells that contain formulas are converted to values when the list is published to SharePoint. This is important to remember when deciding whether to publish a list from a workbook or to upload the entire Excel workbook to the list.

You can re-create formulas based on columns within one row in SharePoint (see Chapter 3 for more about creating formulas in a SharePoint list). However, formulas based on all the data in a column cannot be re-created, with the exception of totals (see "Inserting Column Totals" earlier in this chapter). For example, you can create a formula in Column C of a SharePoint list that multiplies Column A with Column B. However, you cannot create a formula that calculates a variance based on the average of the data in Column A. If it's important that users have access to the columns that contain this second type of calculation, it's probably better to provide them with access to the entire Excel workbook.

■**Tip** If you'd like some users to access the entire workbook and others to access only pertinent data from the workbook, one option is to upload the Excel workbook to a document library that has restricted access within the SharePoint site, and then publish a more publicly available list from the workbook as a SharePoint list within the same site.

Publishing Excel Lists Using the List Toolbar

To publish Excel data to SharePoint, it must first be a recognized Excel list (see Appendix A). To convert Excel data that exists in a worksheet to an Excel list, activate the List toolbar (View ➤ Toolbars ➤ List) in Excel if it isn't visible, and then follow these steps to publish the list:

1. Click **List** on the List toolbar and then click **Publish List**. The Publish List to SharePoint Site wizard, shown in Figure 2-8, opens.

2. Enter the address of the SharePoint site to which you want to publish. Open the SharePoint site and copy and paste the root address from the home page, excluding the page reference. For example, copy `http://www.boardworks.net/triad/HR/` from the complete address of `http://www.boardworks.net/triad/HR/default.aspx`.

3. Check the **Link to the new SharePoint list** checkbox if you'd like to maintain a dynamic link between the Excel list and the SharePoint list.

4. Enter a name and description of the list. Click **Next**.

5. In the second step of the wizard, verify that the data is being converted correctly. SharePoint supports a limited set of data types: Text (single line), Text (multiple lines), Date, and Numeric. All data in a column must conform to a single data type. SharePoint determines this based on the data in the first row. Any data in the column that doesn't conform to this data type is designated in the Key Cell column. If a value appears in the Key Cell column, you might want to close the wizard and verify that the data in that cell can be converted without creating problems. If it cannot, convert the data type of the column before attempting to publish again.

6. Click **Finish** to publish the list.

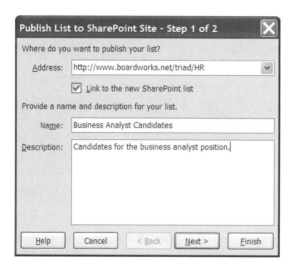

Figure 2-8. *The Publish List to SharePoint Site wizard walks you through the steps for publishing an Excel list to SharePoint.*

When the list is published, a Windows SharePoint Services dialog box opens that includes a link to the list on the SharePoint site. Click the link to see the published list.

Working with Lists on the SharePoint Site

The published list works the same way as any other SharePoint list. You can view the list in Datasheet or Standard view. Even if the list is linked to the Excel workbook, you can rearrange the columns and manipulate the data using all the Datasheet view features described in the section "Working with SharePoint List Data" earlier in this chapter.

Modifying a List

If you didn't choose to create a link between the Excel and SharePoint lists when you published the list, you can modify the data in either list without impacting the other list. If you created a link, you can modify the data in either list and then synchronize the lists to update the data in both lists.

Synchronizing a List

After you've made changes to the Excel or SharePoint lists, you can synchronize the changes between the two lists. From Excel, click the **Synchronize** button on the List toolbar. This writes any changes from either list to the other.

After you've synchronized a list in Excel, click **Refresh Data** on the SharePoint list toolbar to view the changes in SharePoint.

Resolving Conflicts

If the same cell is changed on both the Excel list and the SharePoint list, a conflict is identified that must be resolved. Figure 2-9 shows a typical conflict.

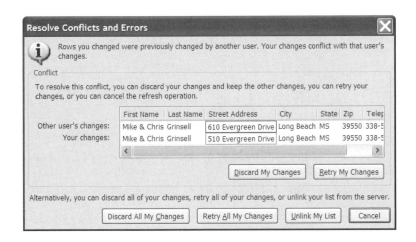

Figure 2-9. *When a conflict arises because the same cell is changed between lists, you can use the Resolve Conflicts and Errors dialog box to resolve the conflict.*

You can choose to discard your changes or retry your changes. If you realize that you shouldn't have been making any changes to the list, you can choose to **Discard All My Changes**, or if you want your changes to win over the other changes made, you can choose

Retry All My Changes. You can also choose to unlink the lists (**Unlink My List**) so both changes are preserved and the lists can function independently of each other.

Refreshing a List and Discarding Changes

If you've been working in the Excel list and want to discard changes you've made, click **Refresh List and Discard Changes** on the List toolbar. The list reverts to the last saved version of the workbook.

Setting External Date Range Properties

When you create a list in Excel and then publish it to SharePoint, SharePoint uses Microsoft Query functionality to synchronize and maintain the lists. You can change some of the Microsoft Query properties to control how the list refreshes. On the List toolbar in Excel, click the **List** button and choose **Data Range Properties** to open the dialog box shown in Figure 2-10.

Figure 2-10. *In the External Data Range Properties dialog box, you can control Refresh and other properties related to the link.*

To synchronize the data automatically at regular intervals, select **Enable background refresh**. To refresh data every time you open the file, click **Refresh data on file open**. You can also change options in the "Data formatting and layout" area to adjust column widths and preserve cell formatting.

Breaking the Link

If you decide that you want to unlink the Excel list from the SharePoint list, you can break the link between the two. On the List toolbar in Excel, click the **List** button and choose **Unlink List**. You're warned that this change cannot be undone. Click **OK** to verify that you want to continue. When the link is broken, the two lists function independently of each other, and changes in one list don't appear in the other one.

Summary

SharePoint offers a number of tools to manage lists, from easy-to-use sorting and filtering features to synchronizing with an Excel worksheet. Assigning permissions through the use of site groups gives you an organized way to grant the appropriate permissions to site users. By publishing an Excel list to a SharePoint site, you provide users with a helpful way to access data while preserving control over who can change the data, and how the data can be changed. In the next chapter, you'll learn how to modify list views in SharePoint to provide users with the data they need, in exactly the layout and format in which they need it.

CHAPTER 3

■ ■ ■

Working with SharePoint Lists in Excel

Corporate America is littered with Excel data that needs to be updated by multiple users: shared Excel workbooks stored on network drives, attachments e-mailed from one manager or administrative assistant to the next, and workbooks that are copied and then need to be consolidated or merged. Excel and SharePoint together provide superior support for multiuser lists, including offline editing and conflict resolution. This chapter will help you rethink your strategies for shared Excel lists.

Taking SharePoint Data Offline with Excel

One of the most useful yet least used SharePoint features is the ability to take list data offline in Excel. You can export any SharePoint list to Excel for offline use, including Contacts and Events lists that also integrate with Outlook.

Exporting to Excel from a Datasheet View

To export to Excel from a datasheet view, follow these steps:

1. In a datasheet view, use the task pane to export the list.

2. Click the **Task Pane** button to open the task pane (shown in Figure 3-1), and then click the **Export and Link to Excel** link to launch Excel.

Figure 3-1. *Open the Datasheet view task pane to export a list to Excel.*

3. When the Open Query dialog box appears, click the **Open** button to export the SharePoint data to Excel.

Exporting to Excel from a Standard View

To export to Excel from a standard view, follow these steps:

1. Choose a standard view that includes the columns of data you want to export. If a suitable view doesn't exist, create it (see Chapter 4 for detailed instructions on creating views). Don't worry about grouping or totals—they won't be included in the exported data.

2. With your view selected, click the **Export to Spreadsheet** link on the Actions list on the left side of the screen to open the File Download dialog box, shown in Figure 3-2.

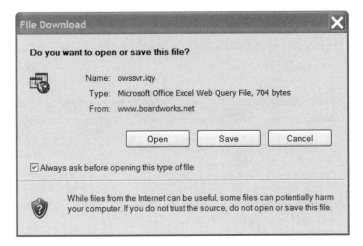

Figure 3-2. *Export the list to Excel or save the query separately in the File Download dialog box.*

3. To export the data to Excel, click the **Open** button.

4. After Excel launches, you'll be prompted to open or save the query. Click **Open** to export the SharePoint list data to Excel.

Saving and Using a Query

The **Export to Spreadsheet** link in the Datasheet view task pane creates a query and automatically opens the query in Excel to export the data. Exporting from a standard view provides an additional useful option. Instead of choosing **Open** in the File Download dialog box, you can save the query definition as a separate file. The query file can be used in Excel, Microsoft Query Editor, Access, or any other application that can process a query (IQY) file. If you have a SharePoint list that you want to use in more than one Excel worksheet, it's more efficient to save the query file separately.

Click the **Save** button in the File Download dialog box to save the query file. If you'll be the only person using the query, save it in the My Documents\My Data Sources folder on your computer, the default location for queries. (If other people will use the query, save it in a network shared folder. Choose a file name that accurately describes the data source rather than the name of the SharePoint site, which might have more than one list you'll want to query.)

After you've saved the query, follow these steps to use the query to create an offline copy of the SharePoint list data in Excel:

1. Open the Excel workbook where you want to display the SharePoint list data.

2. Choose Data ➤ Import External Data ➤ Import Data to open the Select Data Source dialog box, shown in Figure 3-3.

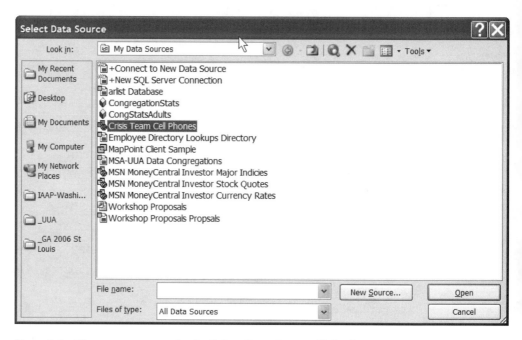

Figure 3-3. *Choose your query in the Select Data Source dialog box.*

3. Select the query and click **Open**.

4. In the Import Data dialog box, choose a location for the query results: a new work-sheet or a single cell in an existing worksheet (see Figure 3-4).

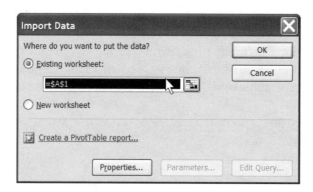

Figure 3-4. *Choose a location for the query results in the Import Data dialog box.*

5. Click the **Properties** button to open the External Data Range Properties dialog box, shown in Figure 3-5. If you want Excel to refresh the query automatically every time you open the workbook, select the **Refresh data on file open** checkbox. Click **OK** to close the dialog box.

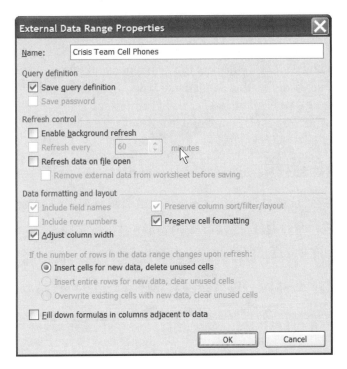

Figure 3-5. *Set options for the query in the External Data Range Properties dialog box.*

6. Click **OK** to close the Import Data dialog box and insert the query results into the Excel worksheet, as shown in Figure 3-6.

ID	Last Name	First Name	Department	Priority	Mobile Phone	Notes
1	Brito	Leonardo	IT	2	734-555-7511	
2	Hoeh	Jamie	Security	1	734-555-1212	Authorized to lock down physical facilities
3	Vaughn	Clifton	IT	1	734-555-3321	Leads disaster recovery process team
4	Garcia	Helio	PR	1	734-555-4071	Route all media contacts to Helio
5	Pszenica	Yves	Finance	1	734-555-3737	
6	Morse	Robb	Manufacturing	1	734-555-7512	
7	Annadi	Jagan	Facilities	1	734-555-1798	
8	Lawrence	Nancy	Facilities	2	734-555-6732	
9	Hurley	John	PR	2	734-555-8312	
10	Holm	Keith	IT	3	734-555-3774	
11	Holm	Aidan	Security	2	735-555-8798	

Figure 3-6. *The SharePoint data, imported as an Excel list*

Working with Offline Data in Excel

Working with the SharePoint data in Excel is similar to working with an Excel list that's been previously published in SharePoint. You don't have to be online to edit the SharePoint list data, even while online users are working with the SharePoint list. You can edit the list and add rows (records), then save the workbook locally until you're back on the network and ready to synchronize your offline data with the SharePoint list.

If you have a group of users who need to update the same data set, a SharePoint list allows each user to export and work with the data independently and simultaneously. As you'll see, SharePoint manages any conflicts that occur when two or more users make different changes to the same data element.

Many users prefer to work with their SharePoint lists offline in Excel:

- *Managers*: During budget "crunch time" when they're finalizing line items and many users need to update different rows in the same list

- *Sales people*: Logging sales leads and customer information on the road instead of waiting until they return to the office

- *Developers*: Recording actions taken to resolve items in an Issues log

- *Information workers*: Editing lists during peak hours on a slow network

- *Frequent flyers and other travelers*: Working with list data when they don't have access to their corporate SharePoint site

SharePoint Calculated Fields in Excel

If the SharePoint list you exported to Excel includes calculated fields, the calculations are reflected in the Excel list. For example, the Sales by Quarter SharePoint list shown in Figure 3-7 includes a calculated Year to Date column.

Product Type ▼	Q1 Sales ▼	Q2 Sales ▼	Q3 Sales ▼	Q4 Sales ▼	Year to Date ▼
TV	72,000	78,000	100,000		$250,000
Magazine	37,500	34,000	21,000		$92,500
Web	92,400	101,620	86,700		$280,720
Radio	0	39,000	45,000		$84,000
TV	98,500	100,000	94,000		$292,500
Magazine	25,000	21,000	29,000		$75,000
Web	130,000	150,000	140,350		$420,350
Magazine	100,200	130,200	90,200		$320,600
Web	81,000	70,000	94,000		$245,000
TV	59,000	61,000	57,000		$177,000

Figure 3-7. *Portion of a SharePoint list with a calculated field, Year to Date*

The following calculation is used for the Year to Date field:

```
=[Q1 Sales]+[Q2 Sales]+[Q3 Sales]+[Q4 Sales]
```

When the list is exported to Excel, Excel converts the SharePoint formula to an Excel formula, as shown in Figure 3-8.

	D	E	F	G	H	I	J
	Region	Product Type	Q1 Sales	Q2 Sales	Q3 Sales	Q4 Sales	Year to Date
2	East	TV	72000	78000	100000		=F2+G2+H2+I2
3	East	Magazine	37500	34000	21000		=F3+G3+H3+I3
4	East	Web	92400	101620	86700		=F4+G4+H4+I4
5	East	Radio	0	39000	45000		=F5+G5+H5+I5
6	East	TV	98500	100000	94000		=F6+G6+H6+I6
7	North	Magazine	25000	21000	29000		=F7+G7+H7+I7
8	North	Web	130000	150000	140350		=F8+G8+H8+I8
9	North	Magazine	100200	130200	90200		=F9+G9+H9+I9
10	North	Web	81000	70000	94000		=F10+G10+H10+I10
11	North	TV	59000	61000	57000		=F11+G11+H11+I11
12	North	Radio	71500	80500	78000		=F12+G12+H12+I12
13	West	Radio	97500	0	0		=F13+G13+H13+I13
14	West	Radio	115500	107500	107000		=F14+G14+H14+I14
15	West	TV	67000	87000	46475		=F15+G15+H15+I15
16	West	Magazine	70000	70000	110000		=F16+G16+H16+I16
17	West	TV	36000	44000	40000		=F17+G17+H17+I17
18	West	Web	110000	112000	125000		=F18+G18+H18+I18
19							

Figure 3-8. *Calculated fields in SharePoint are converted to formulas in Excel.*

The formulas are automatically protected in Excel. Users aren't allowed to overwrite or edit the calculated fields from SharePoint (for more about calculations in SharePoint, see Chapter 5).

Adding Calculations in Excel

You can add more columns of data in Excel and use the SharePoint list data in your calculations. Add fields starting with the first column to the right of the query results. To have Excel automatically fill the formulas down if the query data returns additional rows, modify the external data source properties:

1. On the List toolbar, click the **List** button.

2. Choose **Data Range Properties** from the menu to open the External Data Range Properties dialog box (see Figure 3-9).

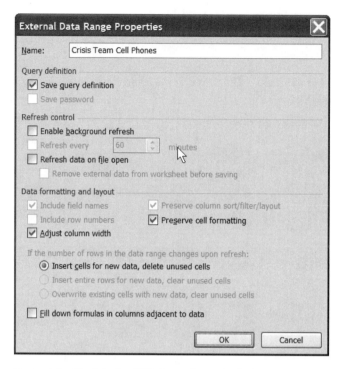

Figure 3-9. *Enable the "Fill down formulas" checkbox to copy formulas automatically.*

3. Select the **Fill down formulas in columns adjacent to data** checkbox. Click **OK**.

When you refresh the query data, Excel will automatically fill formulas in columns to the right of, and adjacent to, the query results if the query returns additional rows.

Synchronizing the Offline Data with SharePoint

When you're ready to synchronize your offline data, save the file locally and then click the **Synchronize** button on the List toolbar. If your synchronization causes a conflict because it includes changes to a data element that another user has already changed, the Resolve Conflicts and Errors dialog box opens, shown in Figure 3-10 (see Chapter 2 for more information about synchronization).

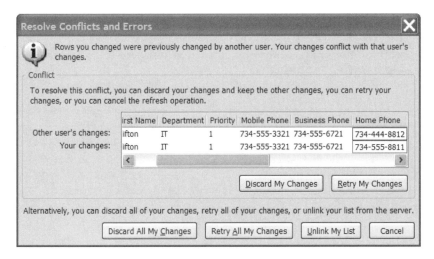

Figure 3-10. *Resolve conflicts that occur when more than one user changes the same data.*

Finally, you can choose to unlink your offline Excel list from the SharePoint list. You can't undo this choice, and if you unlink the list, you won't be able to synchronize the list with SharePoint in the future. If you want to retain the changes you made in Excel without handling any conflicts—perhaps so you can examine the list in SharePoint—click **Cancel** rather than unlinking the list.

Note that the first user is never asked to deal with a data conflict. It's the second user's changes that create the conflict. If a number of people are working with offline copies of the same SharePoint list and editing the same rows, it's a good strategy to synchronize frequently. The longer you wait to synchronize, the greater the possibility that another user has already synchronized a change to a list element you also edited.

If you're at the end of a project or process and won't be using the offline Excel data for a while, you can delete the worksheet or workbook. It's easy enough to create another, fresh offline Excel data set when you need to work with it in the future. If you've added other calculations in Excel, though, you might not want to discard the worksheet or workbook casually. The next time you open the workbook, begin by synchronizing so you start with the current data from SharePoint. If you begin with old data, you increase the potential for conflicts when you synchronize.

Scenario: The Crisis Response Team System

Most organizations have a crisis or disaster response team: a group of people from various departments who are immediately contacted in case of an emergency. When the power goes out in Michigan and New York, the levees break in New Orleans, or the wind and rain come ashore in Florida, someone pulls out the crisis response plan and starts making phone calls. This is an application that you can create easily using a SharePoint list and offline Excel lists.

We started with a SharePoint Contacts list customized by adding columns for Priority (a choice list indicating who is called first, second, and third) and Department, shown in Figure 3-11. The specifications for the columns from the Crisis Response Team SharePoint list are shown in Figure 3-12.

New Item | Filter | Edit in Datasheet | Link to Outlook | Import Contacts					
Last Name↓	**First Name**	**Department**	**Priority**	**Mobile Phone**	**Notes**
Annadi	Jagan	Facilities	1	734-555-1798	
Brito	Leonardo	IT	2	734-555-7511	
Garcia	Helio	PR	1	734-555-4071	Route all media contacts to Helio
Hoeh	Jamie	Security	1	734-555-1212	Authorized to lock down physical facilities
Holm	Keith	IT	3	734-555-3774	
Holm	Aidan	Security	2	735-555-8798	
Hurley	John	PR	2	734-555-8312	
Lawrence	Nancy	Facilities	2	734-555-6732	
Morse	Robb	Manufacturing	1	734-555-7512	
Pszenica	Yves	Finance	1	734-555-3737	
Vaughn	Clifton	IT	1	734-555-3321	Leads disaster recovery process team

Figure 3-11. *The Crisis Response Team list includes contact information for all members of the team.*

Columns

A column stores information about each item in the list. Columns currently in this list:

Column (click to edit)	Type
Last Name	Single line of text
First Name	Single line of text
Department	Single line of text
Priority	Choice
Job Title	Single line of text
Business Phone	Single line of text
Home Phone	Single line of text
Mobile Phone	Single line of text
E-mail Address	Single line of text
Notes	Multiple lines of text

Figure 3-12. *SharePoint column list for the Crisis Response Team list*

Team members and employees in the organization's security department must have fast and direct access to this list. It's a SharePoint contacts list, so this is easy to accomplish. Anyone who wants access to the list can click the **Link to Outlook** button to add the Crisis Response Team list to Outlook, as shown in Figure 3-13.

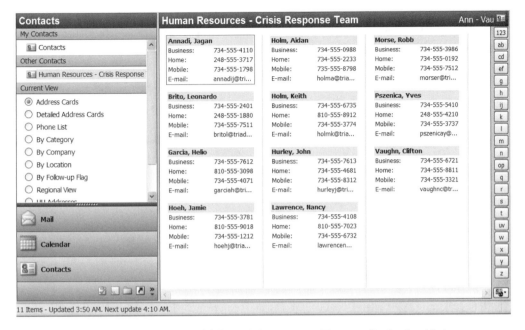

Figure 3-13. *Team members can add the Crisis Response Team to Outlook with just one click.*

Outlook automatically keeps this list synchronized with the list on the SharePoint site, and Outlook provides a number of different page setups (card style, booklet, phone list) that the team members can use to print the team's contact information to keep at home or in their car. They need a hard copy of the list when the power goes out!

Every month, each department manager is required to update the information for his or her department. Department managers can export the list to Excel and make their changes offline, then synchronize their changes. A SharePoint list exported to Excel, changes in Excel synchronized to SharePoint, SharePoint synchronized to Outlook on team members' desktops: a powerful system created using the built-in functionality of Excel, SharePoint, and Outlook.

Charting SharePoint Data in Excel

Windows SharePoint Services and SharePoint Portal Server include specialized web parts to create charts and pivot tables for use on SharePoint sites. But you don't have to do all your charting on a web site. After you've exported SharePoint data to Excel, you can do anything with it that you can do with native Excel data, including creating charts to illustrate the data.

■**Note** Placement is important. If a query returns ten rows this time, it might return eight or fifteen next time, so you shouldn't place charts below the query results. Locate charts above or to the right of the query results, or on another worksheet.

In Excel, select the exported SharePoint data you wish to chart, then click the **Chart Wizard** button on the Standard toolbar to launch the Chart Wizard. Create the chart as you would with native Excel data.

You don't need to export the data first. You can launch Excel's Chart Wizard directly from SharePoint. Follow these steps to create a chart directly from SharePoint:

1. Open the list you want to chart in Datasheet view. If it's in Standard view, click the **Edit in Datasheet** button on the list toolbar to switch to Datasheet view.

2. Click the **Task Pane** button to open the task pane.

3. Click the **Chart with Excel** link to open Excel, return the query results, and launch the Chart Wizard with all the query results selected.

4. Complete the steps of the Chart Wizard to create the chart.

■**Note** If you have a SharePoint list that's often used for a chart, consider creating a view, Chart Data, that only includes the columns needed for the chart. For information on creating views, see Chapter 4.

Creating PivotTable and PivotChart Reports

PivotTable reports are tables that organize and summarize information for easier analysis. PivotChart reports are graphical representations of the same data. PivotTable and PivotChart reports are interactive; you can move information around to compare data and look for trends and relationships. A PivotTable report of the Sales by Quarter data shown earlier in this chapter is displayed in Figure 3-14.

Region	Data	Total
East	Sum of Q1 Sales	300,400
	Sum of Q2 Sales	352,620
	Sum of Q3 Sales	346,700
	Sum of Q4 Sales	
North	Sum of Q1 Sales	466,700
	Sum of Q2 Sales	512,700
	Sum of Q3 Sales	488,550
	Sum of Q4 Sales	
West	Sum of Q1 Sales	496,000
	Sum of Q2 Sales	420,500
	Sum of Q3 Sales	428,475
	Sum of Q4 Sales	
Total Sum of Q1 Sales		1,263,100
Total Sum of Q2 Sales		1,285,820
Total Sum of Q3 Sales		1,263,725
Total Sum of Q4 Sales		

Figure 3-14. *A PivotTable report of the Sales by Quarter data*

There are four areas in a PivotTable report: Data, Rows, Columns, and Page. Numerical data is summarized in the Data Area. Columns that describe the data are placed in the Rows and Columns Areas. Columns used to group data are placed in the Page Area. In the PivotTable report shown in Figure 3-14, the Region field was dropped in the Row Area. The four fields containing sales data (Q1 Sales, Q2 Sales, Q3 Sales, and Q4 Sales) were placed in the Data Area.

As with charts, you can create PivotTables and PivotCharts directly from a SharePoint datasheet view, or create reports with SharePoint data previously exported to Excel. There's a difference between the two methods. When you create PivotTables and PivotCharts using the SharePoint Datasheet view task pane, the query doesn't export the data from the SharePoint list to the Excel workbook. The report is linked directly to the data in the SharePoint list (to create and display PivotTables and PivotCharts on a page in a Share-Point site, see Chapter 9).

Creating a PivotTable Report from SharePoint

To create a PivotTable report directly from SharePoint, follow these steps:

1. Display the list in a datasheet view.

2. Click the **Task Pane** button to display the task pane.

3. Click the **Create Excel PivotTable Report** link in the task pane to launch Excel.

4. When the Opening Query dialog box opens, click **Open** to run the query.

5. In the Import Data dialog box, choose a location for the PivotTable report. The PivotTable, PivotTable Field List, and PivotTable toolbar are automatically displayed, as shown in Figure 3-15.

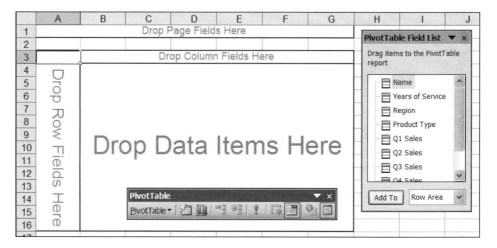

Figure 3-15. *To create a PivotTable, drag fields from the list and drop them in the four areas of the PivotTable.*

6. To create the PivotTable, drag fields from the Field List and drop them in the areas of the PivotTable.

Changing Field Settings

When you drop a field that contains numbers in the Data Area, Excel uses the Sum function to summarize the data in the field. If you drop a field that contains any non-numeric data, Excel uses the Count function to summarize the data. The field names used to describe the fields start with the summarization method (Sum of, Count of), followed by the field name.

To change the summarization method or the field name, right-click the field name and choose **Field Settings** from the context menu to open the PivotTable Field dialog box, shown in Figure 3-16.

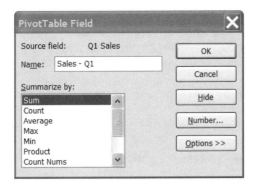

Figure 3-16. *Change the summarization method and other field settings in the PivotTable Field dialog box.*

To change the summarization method, choose another method from the "Summarize by" drop-down list.

To change the field name, enter a new name in the text box. You cannot use the name of a source field. For example, in Figure 3-16, you cannot name the field **Q1 Sales**, but you can rename it **Sales - Q1**.

Pivoting the PivotTable Report

Interactivity is what puts the "pivot" in PivotTable reports. You can rearrange the report by moving fields between the Row, Column, and Page areas. Figure 3-17 shows the Pivot-Table report from Figure 3-14 after the Region field has been dragged from the Row Area to the Column Area.

Data ▾	Region ▾ East	North	West	Grand Total
Sales - Q1	300,400	466,700	496,000	1,263,100
Sales - Q2	352,620	512,700	420,500	1,285,820
Sales - Q3	346,700	488,550	428,475	1,263,725
Sales - Q4				

Figure 3-17. *Drag fields from one area to another to modify the PivotTable report.*

■Note If you're relatively new to PivotTables, you can find more information on creating and manipulating PivotTable reports in Excel. Choose Help ➤ Microsoft Excel Help, then enter **pivot** in the search box. For a quick overview, the Microsoft web site includes a fine demo:

`http://office.microsoft.com/en-us/assistance/HA011989031033.aspx`

It offers a training module as well:

`http://office.microsoft.com/training/training.aspx?AssetID=RC010136191033`

Creating a PivotChart Report

To create a PivotChart from the data in the PivotTable, click the **Chart Wizard** button on the PivotTable toolbar. Excel charts the PivotTable report data in a separate worksheet, as shown in Figure 3-18.

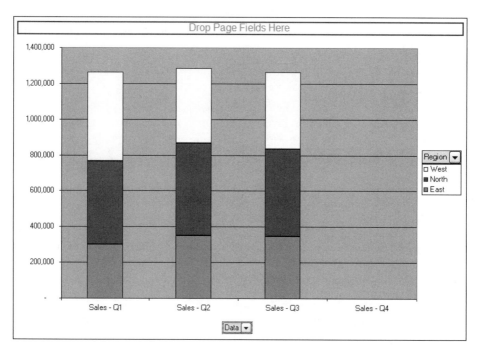

Figure 3-18. *Click the Chart button on the ChartWizard toolbar to create a PivotChart based on the current PivotTable report.*

Refreshing PivotTable and PivotChart Data

The data for the PivotTable report or PivotChart is external data stored on the SharePoint site, not in the Excel workbook. You should occasionally refresh the data to retrieve the latest data from the site. How often you refresh depends on how often the data in the SharePoint list is modified. To retrieve current data from the SharePoint list, click the **Refresh Data** button on the PivotTable toolbar.

Creating a PivotTable Report from Excel Offline Data

To create a PivotTable report using data previously exported to Excel, follow these steps:

1. Select any cell in the list, then choose Data ➤ PivotTable and PivotChart Report to launch the PivotTable and PivotChart Wizard.

2. In the first step of the wizard, choose **Microsoft Office Excel list or database**. Choose the kind of report you want to create and click **Next**.

3. In the second step of the wizard, ensure that the entire list (except the blank row for a new record) is selected. Click **Next**.

4. In the final step of the wizard, choose a location for the PivotTable report and click **Finish** to create the report.

Summary

This chapter focused on reasons you would choose to export SharePoint lists to Excel, and techniques for exporting and synchronizing lists. Offline synchronization provides convenience for road warriors. You have access to PivotTable and PivotChart reports, and other advanced summarization and analysis tools, as soon as you export to Excel. The combination of SharePoint and Excel provides more functionality and a broader feature set for data manipulation and analysis.

■■■

CHAPTER 4

Creating SharePoint Views

One of the most important reasons for importing Excel data into a SharePoint site is the power, flexibility, and control that comes with being able to create and save views of the data. Views make it possible for users to focus on data customized to their unique needs. With views, you can create and save multiple configurations that each display data differently. You can choose which columns to display, and in what order you want to see them. You can change the sort order, group the data differently, and even filter the data to just show records that meet specific criteria. In addition, you can display column totals, designate how many records to show, and choose different layouts.

In this chapter, we'll show you how to create totally customized views of SharePoint lists, and how to change the default view to one that best fits your needs. Then, in Chapter 7, we'll take views to the next level by showing you some practical business solutions using Excel lists and SharePoint views.

■**Note** Throughout this chapter, we'll be referring to creating views of SharePoint lists—it's irrelevant whether a list was created in Excel and imported into SharePoint, or created directly in SharePoint. All the information in the chapter also applies to SharePoint document libraries.

Modifying a SharePoint List

When you create a SharePoint list or import a spreadsheet into SharePoint, SharePoint displays all the columns in the order you create them, or the order in which they appear in the spreadsheet. You can add columns to the list; change the order in which the columns appear on the New Item and Edit Item forms; modify a column's name, description, and other properties; and remove columns from the list.

Adding Columns to a List

In SharePoint, you can create columns that hold single lines of text and others that hold pictures. In all, SharePoint has ten column types available, described fully in the section "Column Types":

- Single line of text

- Multiple lines of text

- Choice (menu to choose from)

- Number (1, 1.0, 100)

- Currency ($, ¥, £)

- Date and Time

- Lookup (information already on this site)

- Yes/No (check box)

- Hyperlink or Picture

- Calculated (calculation based on other columns)

Creating a Column

To create a new column, follow these steps:

1. Open the list on the SharePoint site.

2. Click **Modify Settings and Columns** in the Actions list.

3. Click **Add a Column** in the Column section of the "Customize [list]" page. This opens the Add Column page, a portion of which is shown in Figure 4-1.

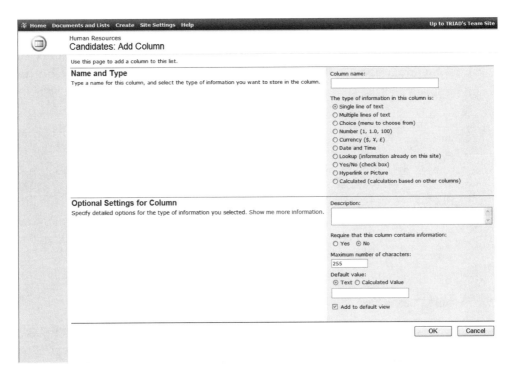

Figure 4-1. *Use the Add Column page to select the type of column you want to create, and to enter required and optional settings for that column.*

When you create a column, you're required to enter a column name and choose a column type. You can then enter optional settings for the column. Regardless of the column type you select, you can enter the following optional settings:

- *A description of the column*: This text appears on the New Item and Edit forms directly underneath the text box for the column.

- *Whether you want to require that the column contain information*: Required columns are designated by an asterisk on the New Item and Edit form. If a user skips a required column and tries to save and close the form, a message pops up that reads, "You must specific a nonblank value for [Column Name]."

- *Whether you want the column added to the default view of the list*: The default view of the list is the view that displays when you open the list. By default, this is set to All Items, but can be changed to any view (see more about creating views in the section "Creating a New View" later in this chapter).

Column Types

Each column type has additional optional settings based on the type you select. To understand each type and when you might use it, we review each of the types in the following sections.

Single Line of Text

Use the **Single line of text** option to enter alphanumeric characters in a text box. The default setting is 255 characters, but you can limit this to fewer characters or expand it to more. However, if you need more than that, you might want to look at the next option. You can also set a default value to save users from having to enter the most common entry. For example, say 90 percent of your employees live in Michigan. You could enter MI in the State column. Those from other states could overwrite the default value.

Multiple Lines of Text

With this column type, you can choose how many lines of text you want to display (5 is the default), but users can enter as much text as they want. You can also choose to allow rich HTML text, which means users can use formatting such as bold, italics, fonts, and so on.

Choice (Menu to Choose From)

You can use this choice to create a drop-down list, radio buttons, or in the case of multiple selections, checkboxes. Enter the choices you want to appear in the "Type each choice on a separate line" text box, as shown in Figure 4-2.

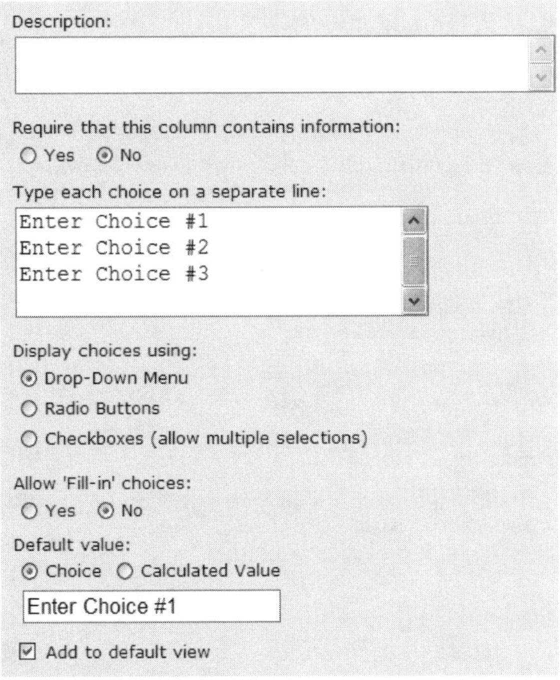

Figure 4-2. *To create choices for users to pick from, enter each choice on a separate line of the text box.*

If you want users to be able to enter items not in the list, select **Yes** under "Allow 'Fill-in' choices." The New Item and Edit forms allow users to enter a different choice, as shown here:

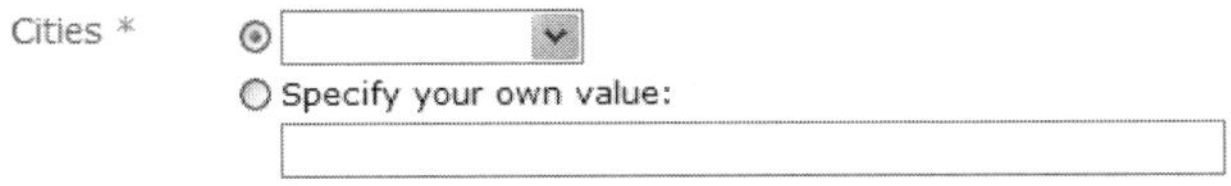

As soon as users select a value from the list, they cannot revert to a blank entry. If you want to allow this option, enter text such as "Select from list . . ." as the first choice. Users can always revert to that choice to indicate they haven't made a selection.

For more information about the Choice column type, see the sidebar "Choice vs. Lookup."

CHOICE VS. LOOKUP

Both the Choice and the Lookup column types allow users to select data from a drop-down list. Either option makes it easier for users to enter data, and gives you better control of your data and more consistency in the responses. What are the criteria for distinguishing which column type to use? Follow these guidelines.

Use Choice if

- the number of options is limited to less than ten. This is a good rule of thumb. You can list many more options than this, but you have to edit the column to modify the list.

- the list is relatively static; Gender, for example.

- you want to display radio buttons rather than a drop-down list.

- you want users to be able to select more than one option using checkboxes.

Use Lookup if

- the list is longer than ten items.

- new items are regularly added to the list.

- you want to be able to select from a list of site members. Rather than re-creating this list, you can create a lookup based on the site's user information.

- you want the column to display *presence information* about site users. Presence information appears next to the column, and lets users know if this person is logged on to Microsoft Windows Messenger for online chats. The status is regularly updated each time the person logs in or out.

- the column is part of a larger list of data already maintained on the site or in an Excel spreadsheet (in the latter case, you have to import the spreadsheet before creating the lookup column).

After you've selected the Choice or Lookup column type, you cannot change to the other type without re-creating the column, so it's useful to evaluate your current and future needs carefully before selecting either of these column types.

Number (1, 1.0, 100)

You can enter any integer in a column of this column type. You can specify a minimum and/or maximum allowed value in the **Min** and **Max** text boxes if you want to validate the column entry. You can also specify the number of decimals you want to display, from 0 to 5. Leave the default choice of **Automatic** if you want to display as many decimal places as are entered. Check the **Show as percentage** checkbox if you'd like the number shown with a percent sign.

Currency ($, ¥, £)

Currency has the same options as Number, except that you can specify a currency format rather than showing the number as a percentage. Select the currency format from the drop-down list of more than 60 available formats.

Date and Time

Use a Date and Time column type for any date-related data. You can choose to display date only, or date and time. If you want to set a default value, you can choose **Today's Date**, a specific date and time you enter, or a calculated date. For example, you can enter =Today+7 to enter a default of a week from the current date (see Chapter 5 for more about calculating dates).

Lookup (Information Already on This Site)

With the Lookup column type (see Figure 4-3), you can create a drop-down list that draws from a list already on the site. For example, you can create a lookup to display site members, and another one to display cities or countries. To use this column type, the list has to be present already on the site. If the list doesn't exist, back up to create or import the list first, and then come back to create this column.

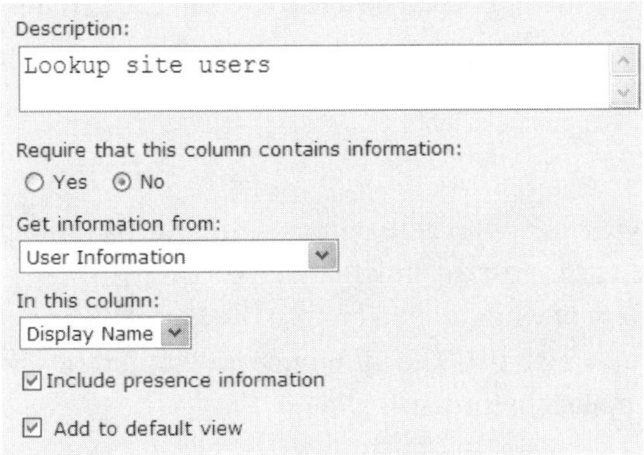

Figure 4-3. *Use the options for Lookup to create a drop-down menu that contains data from another list on the site.*

To select the list you want to use, click the down arrow on the "Get information from" drop-down list and select from the menu of lists on the site. Select **User Information** if you want to select from the site's members. If you select this option, the **Include presence information** checkbox is selected by default. With this option selected, SharePoint monitors whether the user is logged into Microsoft Windows Messenger and is available for online chats. If you don't use Messenger, clear this checkbox.

Regardless of which list you choose, select the column you want to use to populate the drop-down list from the **In this column** menu.

Yes/No (Check Box)

The **Yes/No** checkbox displays as a single checkbox. If the checkbox is selected, the value is Yes. If it's unselected, the value is No.

Use this column type only if you want a default value of Yes or No for the column. If users do nothing, the default value is recorded in the list. For example, let's say new employees are automatically enrolled in the company's health care plan unless they opt out. You could set the default value to Yes to indicate that their enrollment is documented, and then clear the checkbox if an employee opts out.

Documented   ☑

However, if the column documents whether an employee has passed the company's drug test, you probably wouldn't want to set a default value. In this case, use the Choice column type, and then set Yes and No as the choices, with no default value for the column. If the column is blank, you know the information hasn't yet been recorded, and you won't erroneously assume the employee passed or didn't pass just because no one changed the default.

Hyperlink or Picture

With this column type, you can insert a hyperlink or an actual image into the list. The hyperlink can be to any web page, and users can test the link to make sure it works.

Users follow the same process regardless of whether you choose the **Hyperlink** or **Picture** option in the "Format URL as" drop-down list. The difference is whether the actual picture or just a link to the picture appears in the list.

If you plan to use this column type to display photos, create a SharePoint picture library first and upload the pictures you want to use into it. With the **Picture** option selected, the photos are displayed in the list beside the other text fields. For this reason, you probably want to use thumbnails rather than full-size photos. Use a photo editing tool, such as Microsoft Digital Image 2006 or Adobe Photoshop, to save a thumbnail of the photo to the SharePoint picture library.

When users input a new record, they enter a hyperlink to the photo in the picture library, or a hyperlink to the web page into the "Type the Web address" text box, as you can see in Figure 4-4. Encourage them always to test the link by clicking **Click here to test**. The image or web page should open successfully.

■Tip The easiest way for you to insert a hyperlink into a form is to open a second browser window, navigate to the page to which you want to link, and then copy and paste the link into the hyperlink text box on the New Item and Edit forms.

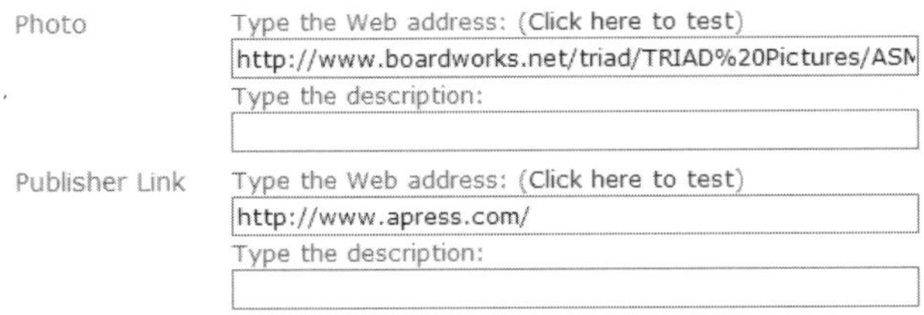

Photo   Type the Web address: (Click here to test)

http://www.boardworks.net/triad/TRIAD%20Pictures/ASN

Type the description:

Publisher Link   Type the Web address: (Click here to test)

http://www.apress.com/

Type the description:

Figure 4-4. *Use the Hyperlink or Picture column type to insert a link to a photo, which is displayed directly in the list or shown as a hyperlink, which users can then click to view the photo or web page.*

Calculated (Calculation Based on Other Columns)

A calculated field is a computation based on other fields in the row. For example, in Figure 4-5, you can see the formula for Total Miles by adding Flight Miles to Bonus Miles.

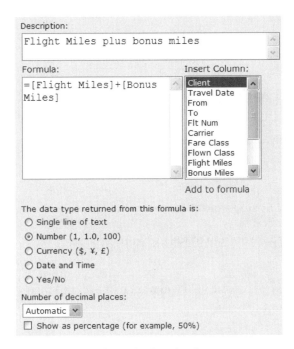

Figure 4-5. *Use the Calculated column type to enter a calculation based on other fields in the row.*

To enter a simple calculation, follow these steps:

1. Double-click the first column you want to include in the calculation.

2. Enter the operator (+, −, *, or /).

3. Double-click the second column you want to include.

4. Repeat steps 2 and 3 until you complete the formula.

5. Choose the data type you'd like to use for the result: **Single line of text**, **Number (1, 1.0, 100)**, **Currency ($, ¥, £)**, **Date and Time**, or **Yes/No**.

6. Select the number of decimal places you want to display.

7. Select the **Show as percentage** checkbox if you want the percent added to the result.

■**Note** You don't need to start the formula with an equal sign (=); SharePoint adds that automatically.

Although formulas aren't as easy to work with in SharePoint as they are in Excel, they're quite powerful. Many of the functions available in Excel are also available in SharePoint. Refer to Chapter 5 for a more detailed explanation of using calculations in SharePoint.

Changing the Order in Which Fields Appear

You can determine the order in which fields appear on the New Item and Edit forms. This can make for easier and more logical data entry, and allows you to group related items together regardless of the order in which you created the columns.

To change the order of fields, follow these steps:

1. Open the list and then click **Modify Settings and Columns** in the Actions list.

2. Click **Change the order of fields** at the bottom of the Columns section of the Customize page.

3. Click the **Position from Top** down arrow on the field you want to move, and then select the new position from the drop-down list.

4. Repeat step 3 until you have all the fields in the order you want them.

In Figure 4-6, Travel Date was changed from position 2 to position 4. This change is reflected in the Columns list on the Customize page, and on the New Item or Edit form for this list. If you're making a lot of changes, you might find it easier to rearrange a few fields, click **OK** to review the changes in the Columns list, and then repeat steps 2–4 for the next group of fields.

Field Name	Position from Top
Client	1
Travel Date	4
From	2
To	3

Figure 4-6. *Use the Position from Top column to rearrange the positon of columns in the New Item or Edit form for a list.*

■**Note** Changing the order of fields doesn't impact the order in which columns appear in the Standard or Datasheet view of the list. To modify the list order, see "Creating a New View" and "Modifying an Existing View" later in this chapter.

Modifying a Column

After a list is in production, it can become apparent that users are confused by column names, are skipping important fields, and are entering data incorrectly in others. We know this probably isn't your users, but just in case you want to give advice to another list manager, you should know that you can change a column's name, its description, its required setting, and in some cases, even the column type. You can also delete columns that you no longer need.

■**Tip** If you'd like to change the name of the list, open the list, click **Modify Settings and Columns** in the Actions list, and then click **Change General Settings** in the General Settings section of the Customize page.

Changing a Column Name and Other Details

To modify a column's name, description, and other properties, click the column in the Columns list on the Customize page of the list (open the list and then click **Modify Settings and Columns** in the Actions list).

Enter changes for the column on the **Change Column** page that opens.

Modifying the Column Type

When you modify a column, you can choose to change the type of the column. However, the choice of available column types is determined by the original type. For example, for Single line of text, Multiple lines of text, Choice, Number, Currency, and Date and Time you can only change to one of these other types. You can no longer choose Lookup, Yes/No, Hyperlink or Picture, or Calculated. To use these column types, you have to create a new column. Table 4-1 summarizes the available choices based on the original column type.

Table 4-1. *Available Choices for Modification Based on Original Column Type*

Original	Single	Multiple	Choice	Number	Currency	Date/Time	Lookup	Yes/No	Hyperlink	Calculated
Single	✓	✓	✓	✓	✓	✓				
Multiple	✓	✓	✓	✓	✓	✓				
Choice	✓	✓	✓	✓	✓	✓				
Number	✓	✓	✓	✓	✓			✓		
Currency	✓	✓	✓	✓	✓			✓		
Date/Time	✓	✓	✓			✓				
Lookup							✓			
Yes/No	✓	✓	✓	✓	✓			✓		
Hyperlink									✓	
Calculated										✓

Deleting Columns from a List

To delete a column that you've created, simply click the **Delete** button at the bottom of the Change Column form. However, be aware that when you delete a column, you'll lose all the data stored in the column.

If SharePoint created a column when you created the list, you might not be able to delete the column (the **Delete** button will be missing). For example, you cannot delete the Last Name column from a contacts list (unless you didn't use the SharePoint Contacts list, but used the Custom List template to create the list in the first place). You can still choose whether to display the column in a list, but it always appears on the New Item and Edit forms. If this presents a problem for users, set the default value to "DO NOT USE" or something similar.

You can create a new view of the list to control whether a column appears in a list view, what position it appears in, how it's sorted, whether it's filtered or grouped, and a number of other options. In the next section, we'll walk through all the options for creating a new view that displays just the data you want to see, in the way that's most useful to you and your users.

Creating a New View

A view is a collection of settings that includes columns displayed, column order, sort order, grouping, filters, totals, item limits, and style. Views can be saved as personal views that only you can see, or public views that are available to all users of the list.

All views, regardless of their individual settings, are based on three view types. These determine the overall structure of the view. Standard and Datasheet views, described in Chapter 2, are interchangeable, whereas Calendar views cannot be changed to another type of view.

If you have date-specific data, a Calendar view lets you see that data displayed on a daily, weekly, or monthly calendar. Let's say you're tracking call data to monitor lulls in activity patterns. By creating a Calendar view of the list, such as the one shown in Figure 4-7, you can quickly identify patterns of high and low activity levels.

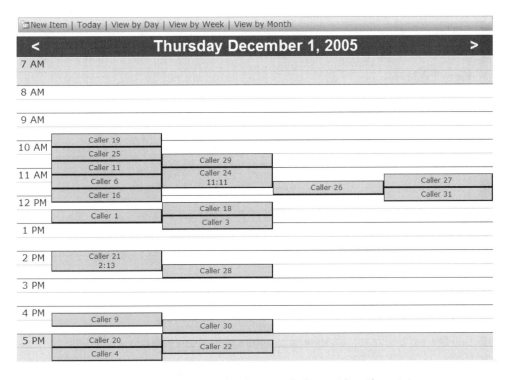

Figure 4-7. *Call data displayed in a Calendar view helps to identify activity patterns.*

Customizing the View

After you've decided what kind of view you want to create, you're ready to customize the view. First, we'll give you an overview of the process for creating a view, and then delve deeper into each of the settings. To create a view, follow these steps:

1. Open the list and click **Modify Settings and Columns** on the Actions list.

2. Click **Create a new view** in the Views section of the Customize page.

3. On the Create View page, select the *type of view* you want to create: **Standard View**, **Datasheet View**, or **Calendar View**. For this example, we'll create a Standard view.

4. Enter the name of the view in the View Name text box. This is what users will see in the list of views, so make it descriptive enough to know what the view shows. "Flights Grouped by Origination" or "December Calls by Call Date" are examples of effective view names.

5. If you want this to be the default view for the list, click the **Make this the default view** checkbox.

6. Select an **Audience**. Personal views are intended for just your use, and can be created by anyone with Contributor rights or higher; Public views are for everyone who has access to the list, and must be created by a user with Web Designer or higher rights to the list.

■**Caution** Personal views aren't secure. If another user knows the URL of one of your personal views, they can use, modify, or even delete the view.

---

7. Select the *columns* you want to display and the order in which you want to display them.

8. Select an ascending or descending *sort order*. You can sort two levels deep.

9. Add any *filters* to limit the data return to specific criteria.

10. To *group* the data, identify a column on which to group and, if desired, to subgroup the data.

11. Add *totals*, including counts, to any columns.

12. Select a *style* for the list.

13. Determine the number of records, or *item limit*, you want to display on a single page.

14. Click **OK** to save the view, and then click **Go back to [List name]** at the top of the Customize page to return to the list.

If you didn't make the new view the default view, you need to select it from the Select a View list to apply the view.

Now that you know the overall steps to creating a view, the following sections will tell you more about each of the settings on the Create View page.

Displaying and Positioning Columns

When you select columns to display in the view, you might notice columns that weren't part of the list you created. Every list SharePoint creates has the following six additional system fields that cannot be modified:

- *ID*: A unique identifier autonumber field

- *Attachments*: A field that indicates if an item has an attachment

- *Created*: The date and time an item was created

- *Created By*: The user who created the item

- *Modified*: The date and time an item was last modified

- *Modified By*: The user who last modified the item

If you'd like to display these system fields, select the corresponding checkbox in the Display column.

▮Tip Even though the attachment field is available for all lists, only lists based on certain templates—Announcements, Contacts, Events, Issues, and Tasks—give you the ability to add attachments to list items by default (click the **Attach File** button on the New Item toolbar). If you'd like to attach files to list items in custom lists you create, open the General Settings for the list, click **Change General Settings**, and verify that **Enabled** is selected under "Attachments to this list are" in the Attachments section.

You might also notice that one field in the list, such as the Client field shown here, is listed three different ways:

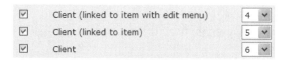

The first option in this example—**Client (linked to item with edit menu)**—puts a hyperlink on the item so users can click to go to the detailed item. It also adds a drop-down edit menu with options to **View Item**, **Edit Item**, **Delete Item**, and **Alert Me**.

The second option—**Client (linked to item)**—puts the hyperlink on the item but doesn't include an edit menu. Use this option if the list is read-only but you want users to be able to see the item detail.

The third option—**Client**—has no link and no edit menu. Use this option if you want users to see only the columns and records displayed in the view, without the option to see the full item detail.

You also have the option of displaying a column called Edit. This column, shown here, displays an **Edit** icon that users can click to open the item.

Edit

After you decide which fields you want to display, select the order in which you'd like them displayed.

Sorting Data

Select the sort order by first choosing a column to sort, and then by selecting a direction: *ascending* or *descending*. You can sort up to two levels deep; for example, by last name and then by first name. However, you cannot sort three or more levels deep, so you cannot sort by organization, then by last name, then by first name. If you need more than two levels, use Group By.

Filtering Data

Filters are one of the most powerful tools in creating custom views. Rather than wading through hundreds of records, you can narrow a list down pretty quickly to just the few records that meet the criteria you set. By saving a filter as part of a view, users can quickly switch from all records to an identified subset of the records faster than they can say "wow."

To create a filter, follow these steps:

1. Select the column you want to filter on in the "Show the items when column" drop-down list. (SharePoint automatically switches the radio button from **Show all items in this view** to **Show items only when the following is true**).

2. Select the qualifier from the list of choices shown here:

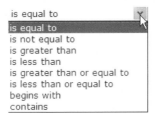

3. Enter the value you're comparing to in the Value text box.

4. To enter additional filter criteria, select **And** or **Or**, and then repeat steps 1–3.

For example, if you'd like to display flights that occurred between November 1 and November 30, 2005, enter the filter as shown in Figure 4-8.

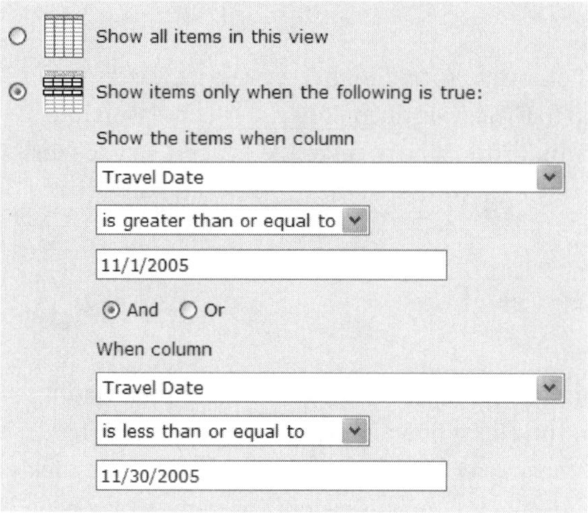

Figure 4-8. *Use And to join two filters to display dates within a range of dates.*

If you want to identify blank or nonblank values, select **is equal to** or **is not equal to**, and then leave the Value text box empty.

■Tip If you're uncertain whether to select **And** or **Or** to join two filter criteria, ask yourself this simple question: "Do I want to display items than meet both criteria or items that meet either one?" If the answer is "both," choose **And**; if the answer is "either," choose **Or**.

You can add as many filters to a list as you deem appropriate. Just click **Show More Columns** at the bottom of the Filter section to add more filter criteria.

Grouping Data

With grouping, you can expand and collapse data within specified categories. Figure 4-9 shows data grouped by origination point (From); all the groups are collapsed except for Flint (FNT), so you can focus on just those trips.

To set grouping, select the first column you want to group by. Grouping automatically sorts by that column, so select whether you want the groups to appear in Ascending or Descending order. Set a second grouping level if you want to create a subgroup. Figure 4-10 shows flights grouped by origination (From) and then by Fare Class.

	Edit	Travel Date	Client		From	To	Flt Num	Carrier	Fare Class	Flown Class	Flight Miles
	📝 New Item | 🔲 Filter | 📝 Edit in Datasheet										
⊞ **From : BOS** (5)											
⊞ **From : DTW** (8)											
⊟ **From : FNT** (3)											
	📝	11/13/2005	BCG !NEW	FNT	DTW	NW 2888		NW	M	M	500
	📝	12/5/2005	FIN !NEW	FNT	MSP	NW 3611		NW	B	B	500
	📝	12/9/2005	BCG !NEW	FNT	DTW	NW 3358		NW	Q	Q	500
⊞ **From : IND** (1)											
⊞ **From : MSP** (2)											
⊞ **From : YQR** (1)											

Figure 4-9. *With grouped data, you can expand and collapse the groups to focus on the data you want to see.*

	Edit	Travel Date	Client		From	To	Flt Num	Carrier	Fare Class	Flown Class	Flight Miles
	📝 New Item | 🔲 Filter | 📝 Edit in Datasheet										
⊟ **From : BOS** (5)											
⊟ Fare Class : B (3)											
	📝	10/30/2005	CUC !NEW	BOS	DTW	NW 0393		NW	B	B	632
	📝	11/23/2005	CUC !NEW	BOS	DTW	NW 0393		NW	B	B	632
	📝	12/17/2005	UUA !NEW	BOS	DTW	NW 0853		NW	B	B	632
⊞ Fare Class : F (1)											
⊞ Fare Class : M (1)											
⊟ **From : DTW** (8)											
⊟ Fare Class : B (2)											
	📝	10/18/2005	UUA !NEW	DTW	BOS	NW 0392		NW	B	B	632
	📝	11/2/2005	CUC !NEW	DTW	BOS	NW 0429		NW	B	B	632

Figure 4-10. *Use two levels of grouping to display groups within groups.*

Adding Totals

You can add totals to any of the columns in a list. You can use any of seven summation functions: Count, Average, Maximum, Minimum, Sum, Std Deviation, and Variance. Select the function you want to use on the drop-down list adjacent to the column to which you want it applied.

If you're using Group By, SharePoint positions the total at the top of the group. Figure 4-11 shows totals for the entire column (Flight Miles), for the group (From), and for the subgroup (Fare Class).

Flight Miles	Bonus Miles
Sum = 11,500	Sum = 1,816
Sum = 3,160	Sum = 316
Sum = 1,896	Sum = 0
632	0
632	0
632	0

Figure 4-11. *By adding a total to a grouped list, you can generate sums for the entire column, for the group, and for the subgroup.*

To remove a total from a column, select **None** from the Totals drop-down list for that column.

■Tip If you'd rather display the totals at the bottom of the list, you can edit the page in Microsoft FrontPage, and then move the totals where you want them.

Selecting a Style

Styles determine how a list appears on the page. The default style is pretty basic. However, you have your choice of **Boxed, no labels**; **Boxed**; **Newsletter**; **Newsletter, no lines**; **Shaded**; and **Default**. Figure 4-12 shows an example of the Boxed style. This style is particularly useful if you want users to concentrate on one item at a time and then move on to the next. For example, we've used it to display a list of training classes so that users could read the descriptions of each class before moving on to the next.

New Item | Filter | Edit in Datasheet

Start Time	Caller 1 !NEW		Start Time	Caller 2 !NEW
Date	12/1/2005 12:34 PM		Date	12/1/2005 6:20 PM
Number	555-478-7878		Number	517-456-4697
Minutes	1		Minutes	1

Start Time	Caller 3 !NEW		Start Time	Caller 4 !NEW
Date	12/1/2005 12:46 PM		Date	12/1/2005 5:30 PM
Number	555-218-3133		Number	555-218-3133
Minutes	1		Minutes	1

Start Time	Caller 5 !NEW		Start Time	Caller 6 !NEW
Date	12/1/2005 9:16 PM		Date	12/1/2005 11:21 AM
Number	555-218-3133		Number	555-642-6780
Minutes	1		Minutes	1

Figure 4-12. *The Boxed style creates a completely different look for a list.*

If you want to change the look of a list, we recommend you try out each of these styles. Some look better with some lists and some with others.

Setting Item Limits

Item limits determine how many items that display on a page. If you have a long list, it might take too long to load, so limiting the items helps to manage this for the users. The default limit is 100 items. When you reach the hundredth item, you see a link to direct you to the next 100, as shown here:

(Items 1 to 100) Next ►

If you want to load more or fewer items at one time, you can set the number of items to display. You can also limit the total number of items returned to a specific number. In this case, users would see the top items in the list and not have access to any additional items.

Modifying an Existing View

After you've created several views, you might find the need to modify them. To modify an existing view, follow these steps:

1. Open the list and then click **Modify Settings and Columns** in the Actions list.

2. Click the view you want to modify in the Views section of the Customize page.

3. Modify the list using the same tools you used to create it.

4. Click **OK** to save the modified view.

One important reason for modifying an existing view is to change its URL or web address. SharePoint addresses have a limit of 256 characters. It doesn't take long to reach that limit on most enterprise servers. Although you want to make the view names friendly and descriptive, by editing the web address of the view, you can greatly reduce the number of characters in the address. Figure 4-13 shows the web address of a view we created for this chapter. If you modify the view name to DecCallsByCallDate.aspx, you save nine spaces right off the top. Not a bad result for minimal effort.

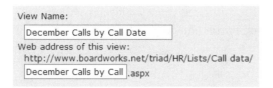

Figure 4-13. *Rename the web address of the view to remove extra spaces. This saves characters and makes the path easier to read.*

Summary

Whether you start with an Excel worksheet or with a SharePoint list template, by customizing lists you can make them work to meet your particular needs. In this chapter, we showed you how to modify an existing list by adding columns and changing the order of columns. We explored the various types of columns that are available in SharePoint, and the strengths of each one. We also examined the world of views, and how views can change your perspective in data. By showing and hiding columns; sorting, filtering, and grouping data; adding totals; selecting a style; and setting item limits, you can create a series of dynamic and useful views that give users entirely new ways to work with data.

In Chapter 5, we're going to delve into calculations in SharePoint. Although they're not as flexible and easy to work with as Excel calculations, you'll find plenty of power to meet many of your calculation needs. And you if can't do what you need to do, you can always go back and review Chapter 3, which tells you how to export SharePoint lists to Excel.

CHAPTER 5

Creating Custom Calculations in SharePoint

SharePoint lists are surprisingly versatile. Not only can you add various types of columns (see Chapter 4), you can also create columns that contain simple or complex formulas. You can do standard operations such as addition and subtraction, or make use of SharePoint's long list of available functions. Many of the Excel functions you've grown to know and love are available for use in SharePoint lists. You can create calculated columns—that is, formulas based on columns in a row—or you can display column totals. The best part is that you can export formulas created in a SharePoint list for use in Excel. (Unfortunately, the reverse isn't true—Excel formulas are converted to values when an Excel worksheet is imported to a SharePoint list.) In this chapter, we'll show you how to create formulas in a SharePoint list, and we'll explore many of the most useful functions available to you.

Working with Formulas

Formulas in SharePoint take a little more effort to create than in Excel because you have to create a calculated column, and then create the formula for the column. However, once you do that, the column is locked so users cannot inadvertently overwrite the formula, as they might do in Excel.

Creating Formulas

When you create a formula in a SharePoint list, you can include the following:

- *References*: References are column names, and refer to a cell in the current row in the datasheet. If the column name includes spaces, you must enclose the name in square brackets: [Flight Miles], for example. You can use references for columns that are formatted as **Single line of text**, **Number**, **Currency**, **Date and Time**, **Choice**, **Yes/No**, and **Calculated**. You cannot reference a cell in a row other than the current row.

- *Operators*: You can use any of the standard math, comparison, and logical operators, such as +, −, /, *, %, ^, >, <, >=, <=, <>, &, OR, NOR, and XOR.

- *Constants*: You can include four different type of constants:

  - *String*: Strings must be enclosed in quotes and can be up to 255 characters. An example of a string constant might be (=[Origination] or ="DTW").

  - *Numeric*: Numeric constants can be positive or negative and can include decimals; for example, =[Flight Miles]*.10.

  - *Date constants*: Dates can be presented with or without delimiters; for example, 1/23/06 or 012306.

  - *Boolean constants*: You can use Boolean constants in logical expressions such as IF statements. For more about IF statements, see IF in the section "Applying Logical Functions" later in this chapter.

- *Functions*: Functions are predefined formulas. SUM is a simple function. It performs a predefined operation based on identified arguments or specified values, such as column references. See "Incorporating Functions into Formulas" later in this chapter.

■**Caution** You can create up to eight calculated columns in a SharePoint list. If you try to exceed that number, SharePoint returns an error:

```
Column Limit Exceeded: There are too many columns of the specified data type.
Please delete some other columns first. Note that some column types like numbers
and currency use the same data type.
```

Although it isn't clear from the message, this refers to calculated columns. You can exceed this limit for non-calculated columns.

When you create a formula in SharePoint that contains several operators, you need to be aware of the order in which SharePoint evaluates the formula. Knowing the order of operations can protect you from costly errors. For example, the result of the following formula, =2+3*6, is 20 (3*6=18+2=20) and not 30 (2+3=5*6=30). SharePoint evaluates the multiplication first and then adds 2 to the product, rather than adding first and then multiplying.

If a formula has two operators at the same level—addition and subtraction, for example—SharePoint evaluates the formula from left to right. So, for example, in the formula =4*5/4, SharePoint first multiplies 4 times 5 (20), and then divides by 4 for a result of 5. Table 5-1 shows the order of operations for SharePoint formulas.

Table 5-1. *Order of Operations for SharePoint Formulas*

Operator	Description
–	Negation (as in –1)
%	Percent
^	Exponentiation
* and /	Multiplication and division
+ and –	Addition and subtraction
&	Connects two strings of text (concatenation)
=, <, >, <=, >=, <>	Comparison

If you need to change the order of operations, use parentheses to enclose the part of the formula you want to calculate first. For example, if you wanted to calculate 2+3 and then multiply the result by 6, you could do that by enclosing the 2+3 in parentheses; for example, (2+3)*6.

Creating Calculated Columns Using Column References

To add a calculated column, follow the steps described in Chapter 4 for adding a new column to a list (see "Creating a Column" in Chapter 4). Enter a name for the column and choose **Calculated** from the list of available column types. Then follow these steps to modify the Optional Settings for the column:

1. Enter a description of the column.

2. Double-click the first column you want to use in the formula.

3. Enter an operator.

4. Double-click a second column to follow the operator.

5. Continue until you've completed the formula.

6. Select a data type that will be returned from the formula: **Single line of text**, **Number**, **Currency**, **Date and Time**, or **Yes/No**.

7. If you select **Number**, **Currency**, or **Date and Time**, select additional options for that data type:

- *Number*: **Number of decimal places** and **Show as percentage**

- *Currency*: **Number of decimal places** and **Currency Format**

- *Date and Time*: **Date Only** or **Date & Time**

8. Clear the **Add to default view** checkbox if you don't want the column added to the default view.

By applying these steps, you can create simple and complex formulas using any of the allowed operators: references, constants, and functions. SharePoint creates the column and inserts the resulting calculations. So, for example, if you enter the formula `[Flight Miles]+[Bonus Miles]` in the column called Total Miles, SharePoint inserts the column and displays the results in the new column. By using column references, such as column names, you avoid the issue that a cell in a SharePoint list doesn't have a cell address, unlike in Excel.

■**Note** You don't have to enter the equal sign (=) to begin a formula in SharePoint. SharePoint adds it automatically when you save the column. You also don't have to enclose column names in brackets unless the column name includes spaces, but you might find it useful in clarifying formulas as you create them. If the column name doesn't include spaces, SharePoint removes the brackets after you save the column.

Creating Common Formulas

By combining operators with references and constants, you can create countless formulas in SharePoint lists. Table 5-2 demonstrates common formulas using standard operators.

Calculating Column Totals

Formulas in SharePoint lists are limited to formulas related to columns in a single row. For example, you cannot create a formula to calculate the variance from the average where you compare a cell in a column to the average of the column. However, you can include column and group totals using the COUNT, AVERAGE, MAXIMUM, MINIMUM,

SUM, STD DEVIATION, and VARIANCE functions. Adding column and group totals is functionality that's built into SharePoint lists—it doesn't require you to create a formula. To add column totals, refer to "Adding Totals" in the section "Creating a New View" in Chapter 4.

Table 5-2. *Common SharePoint Formulas*

Description	Formula	Example	Result
Add the values in three columns	=Column1+Column2+Column3	=[FlightMiles]+[BonusMiles]+ [PromoMiles]	Calculates total miles
Subtract the values in two columns	=Column1-Column2	=[Price]-[Discount]	Calculates price minus discount
Multiply the values in columns	=Column1*Columns2	=[Price]*[DiscountPercent]	Calculates the amount of the discount (DiscountPercent column must be formatted as a percentage)
Divide the values in two columns	=Column1/Column2	=[TotalCost]/[Quantity]	Calculates cost per item
Multiply the values in two columns and subtract the product from the first column	=Column1-Column2*Column3	=Price-[Price]* [DiscountPercent]	Calculates the discounted price
Multiply the value in a column by a constant	=Column1*10/100	=[Cost]*10/100	Calculates 10 percent of the cost
Add the value in two columns and multiply by a third	=(Column1+Column2)*Column3	=[FlightMiles+BonusMiles]*2	Doubles total miles
Subtract one date from another	=Column1-Column2	=[StartDate]-[EndDate]	Calculates how many days between the start and end dates
Compare the values in two columns	=Column1>Column2	=[ProposedCost]>[ActualCost]	Returns Yes if the proposed cost is greater than the actual cost

Incorporating Functions into Formulas

Just like in Excel, functions make it possible to evaluate text and data in ways that return useful results. Functions are predefined formulas that use a specific structure to perform calculations. With functions, you can perform simple and complex operations with little effort. For example, you can use the AVERAGE function to determine the average of a group of values, rather than using the two-step process of summing the values and dividing by the number of values. You can apply other functions, such as CONCATENATE, to text values to combine the values into one. For example, you can combine the [FirstName] column and the [LastName] column to become [LastName, FirstName] or [FirstName LastName].

SharePoint provides you with approximately 150 functions from which to choose, in 8 different categories. These include the following:

- *Date and Time*: Use these functions to calculate dates; for example, seven days from today, the number of days between today and a future date, or to calculate the Julian date.

- *Financial*: With financial functions, you can compute the future value of an investment, the interest payment for given period, the payment for a loan, and other similar values.

- *Information*: Use the IS information functions to test the type of a value or column reference. For example, is a field blank, or does it contain a number or text?

- *Logical*: With the logical functions, you can conduct tests on values and formulas, such as evaluating if a value is greater than another.

- *Lookup and Reference*: Use this function to look up a value from a list.

- *Math and Trigonometry*: This category contains everything from everyday math functions, such as SUM, to rounding functions and high-level geometric functions.

- *Statistical*: The largest category of functions, statistical functions include common functions such as AVERAGE and STDEV (Standard Deviation), and more obscure functions such as FISHER and HYPGEOMDIST (Hypergeometric Distribution).

- *Text and Data*: Use Text and Data functions to manipulate text, combine text fields, convert text to numbers, and compare text strings, among other things.

To use a function in SharePoint, you follow the same steps for creating any formula, and enter the function where appropriate. You must manually type the name of the function into the Formula box, as shown in Figure 5-1. Although typing the function name in upper case isn't required, it's good practice, so you can distinguish the functions from column references easily.

Figure 5-1. *Type the function into the Formula box, then build the formula using column references.*

As you enter the function, make sure the arguments of the function are enclosed in parentheses. If you need to include other parentheses in the formula to clarify the order of operations, add enough parentheses to complete the formula. For example, say you enter the following formula:

```
=[Column1]*(100+SUM([Column2],[Column3],[Column4]))
```

You need to insert a closed parenthesis to close the SUM function, and another one to add 100 to the SUM before multiplying by Column1. Although SharePoint automatically adds a closed parenthesis to an expression that contains a function, it might add it incorrectly without invoking an error. Look at the following example:

```
SUM(5,5,5*10
```

If SharePoint adds the closing parenthesis at the end of the expression, the result is 60:

```
5*10=50+5+5=60
```

However, if you add the closing parenthesis after the third 5, the result is much different:

```
5+5+5=15*10=150
```

If you enter a formula incorrectly, SharePoint returns an error page that says the following:

```
The formula contains a syntax error or is not supported.
```

Don't bother clicking the link that displays "Troubleshoot issues with Windows SharePoint Services." It won't help you. Instead, click the **Back** button to return to the formula and figure out what you're missing.

The only way to become familiar with all SharePoint's functions is to explore them one by one. Depending on your work requirements, you might be surprised to find functions that do exactly what you need to have done. No doubt, you'll find some functions that have no meaning or value to you. If you or members of your team are new to functions, copy and paste the Help documentation for functions you think have value to you and your team into a Word document. Then, post the document to a library on the SharePoint site for an easy-to-access reference.

■**Note** For a complete list of available functions, see SharePoint Help. Click **Help** on the top navigation bar, then click **Home** on the Help window that opens. Scroll down to click **Formulas and Functions**, then click **Functions**.

In the rest of this chapter, we'll explore many of the most common and most useful functions available in SharePoint. Rather than discussing them in alphabetical order based on category, we've chosen to discuss them in the order of complexity and frequency of use. This order is somewhat subjective, but you should be able to move from one category to the next with relative ease. If you find functions you think might be useful, practice using them by creating formulas with your own SharePoint lists.

■**Tip** To create formulas and use functions, you need to know the column names of the list you're working with. A simple way to reference this list is to print it. On the Customize [List Name] page (click **Modify Settings and Columns** of the list you want to modify), select the Columns list and then print the selection. This gives you painless access to column names and types to help you create formulas quickly and easily.

Calculating with Math Functions

In the Math and Trigonometry category, SharePoint includes 39 functions that range from simple functions such as SUM to functions that calculate the inverse hyperbolic cosine of a number (ACOSH). In this section, we'll review SUM, PRODUCT, and MOD, then move on to a few of the rounding functions: ROUND, ROUNDUP, ROUNDDOWN, EVEN, and ODD.

Standard Math Functions

You can use math functions such as SUM and PRODUCT in place of the standard operators. For example, instead of `=Column1+Column2+Column3`, you can use the following SUM
function:

`=SUM(Column1,Column2,Column3)`

As you can see, the SUM function doesn't simplify data entry in SharePoint as it does in
Excel, because you don't have the ability to enter cell ranges. In Excel, you could enter
`SUM(Column1:Column3)` to add all three columns. In SharePoint, you must list the individual
columns, separated by commas. However, the SUM function is still useful, especially in
complex formulas and formulas with nested functions (see the section "Nesting Functions
for Maximum Efficiency" later in this chapter).

PRODUCT works similarly to SUM, but for multiplication. Following is an example of
a formula with the PRODUCT function:

`=PRODUCT([Rate],[Quantity])`

The PRODUCT function `=PRODUCT(384,50)` gives you a result of 19200.

MOD is a function that's used commonly in warehousing and interestingly enough,
in vending machines. With MOD, you can know how many are left over—how many
boxes are left over after filling pallets; how many nickels, dimes, and quarters are left over
after paying for a candy bar with a dollar bill. The syntax for the MOD function is
`=MOD(n,d)`, where `n` is the number and `d` is the divisor.

Let's say you have 384 boxes to ship, and each pallet holds 50 boxes. How many boxes
will be left over after you fill as many pallets as you can? If you simply divide 384 by 50,
you know you'll fill 7.68 pallets. But how many boxes does .68 represent? The MOD function, `=MOD(384,50)`, gives you a result of 34. That tells you that the eighth pallet will
contain only 34 boxes. You can then decide if you want to ship a partial pallet, ship the
remaining boxes another way, increase the shipment by 16 boxes `(50-34)`, or reduce the
shipment by 34 boxes.

Rounding Functions

At first glance, it might appear that rounding functions give you control over how many
decimal places you want to display in a list. However, rounding a value and changing its
format to display fewer decimals are fundamentally different. A value of 52.25 can be displayed as 52 or 52.2, but the value used in calculations is still 52.25. With the rounding
functions, the actual value can be changed to 52, 53, 52.2, or 52.3, depending on which
function you choose and how you choose to apply it.

SharePoint has a number of rounding functions in addition to the basic math functions. Table 5-3 describes several of the most commonly used rounding functions.

Table 5-3. *These Math and Rounding Functions Round Numbers Up or Down*

Function	Syntax	Description	Example	Result
SUM	`SUM([Column1], [Column2],[Column3])`	Totals the identified columns.	`=SUM([Small], [Medium],[Large], [Extra Large]`	Returns the total number of all sizes in inventory.
PRODUCT	`PRODUCT([Column1], [Column2])`	Multiplies the values.	`=PRODUCT([Rate], [Hours])`	The product of rate times hours.
MOD	`MOD(n,d)`	Returns the remainder after the number is divided.	`=MOD(384,50)`	The number that remains after dividing 384 by 50 is 34.
ROUND	`ROUND(number, num_digits)`	Number is the number or column reference you want to round. Num_digits is how many places to which you want to round the number. ROUND rounds numbers 5 and over up, and under 5 down.	`ROUND([Price], 2)`	Rounds the value in the Price column to two decimal digits.
ROUNDUP	`ROUNDUP(number, num_digits)`	Works the same as ROUND, but always rounds up.	`ROUNDUP([Price],0)`	Rounds the value in the Price column to the next highest integer.
ROUNDDOWN	`ROUNDDOWN(number, num_digits)`	Works the same as ROUND but always rounds down.	`ROUNDUP([Price],0)`	Rounds the value in the Price column to the next lowest integer.
EVEN AND ODD	`EVEN(Number); ODD(Number)`	Rounds numbers up to the nearest even or odd integer.	`EVEN([PRICE]); ODD([Price])`	Rounds the value in the Price column to the next even or odd integer. If the value is even, no rounding occurs with the EVEN function. If the value is odd, it isn't rounded with the ODD function.

■**Note** When a part of the syntax appears in bold, it is required. The part that is not bold is optional.

Using Statistical Functions

Even if you called your statistics class Sadistics instead, you probably need a few of SharePoint's statistical functions in your work with lists. Let's say you've created an inventory of logo wear items that employees can purchase from the company. The list, shown in Figure 5-2, displays how many items are in stock for each product in each of five sizes. The Total column uses the SUM function, discussed earlier under math functions. The column to the right of Total uses the AVERAGE function to show you the average number of each item you have. The Min and Max columns point to how low the inventory is in one area and how high it is in another. The Count column tells you how many different sizes you have available for each item.

Human Resources
Logo Wear Inventory

New Item | Filter | Edit in Datasheet | | | | | **Calculated Columns**

Item	Small	Medium	Large	XLarge	2X	Total	Average	Min	Max	Count
Black Warm-up Jacket	37	23	34	45	12	151	30	12	45	5
Blue T-Shirt	53	45	67	45	23	233	47	23	67	5
Baseball cap	34	34	34	87		189	47	34	87	4
Steel Blue Polar Fleece Sweater	56	23	45	34	45	203	41	23	56	5
White Golf Shirt	6	10	4	45		65	16	4	45	4

Figure 5-2. *Using Math functions such as SUM, and Statistical functions such as AVERAGE, MIN, MAX, and COUNT adds important information to this list.*

Table 5-4 shows you more about these functions, and describes several additional statistical functions.

Table 5-4. *Statistical Functions Analyze Data*

Function	Syntax	Description	Example	Result
AVERAGE	`AVERAGE([Column1],` `[Column2],[Column3])`	Returns the arithmetic mean of the arguments	`=AVERAGE([Small],` `[Medium],[Large],` `[Extra Large], [2X])`	Tells you the average number of items in stock.
COUNT	`COUNT([Column1],` `[Column2],[Column3])`	Counts the number of arguments that contain numbers	`=COUNT([Small],` `[Medium],[Large],` `[Extra Large], [2X])`	Counts how many different sizes are available.
COUNTA	`COUNTA([Column1],` `[Column2],[Column3])`	Counts the number of arguments that are not empty, including text and logical values	`=COUNTA([PART1],` `[PART2],[PART3],` `[PART4])`	Counts how many different parts each component has.
MAX	`MAX([Column1],` `[Column2],[Column3])`	Returns the largest value among the arguments	`=MAX([Small],` `[Medium],[Large],` `[Extra Large], [2X])`	Identifies the largest quantity of any one item in stock.
MEDIAN	`MEDIAN([Column1],` `[Column2],[Column3])`	Returns the middle value in a set of numbers	`=MEDIAN([Small],` `[Medium],[Large],` `[Extra Large], [2X])`	Because there is an odd number of values, it returns the middle value. If there were an even number, it would average to the two middle values.
MIN	`MIN([Column1],` `[Column2],[Column3])`	Returns the smallest value among the arguments	`=MIN([Small],` `[Medium],[Large],` `[Extra Large], [2X])`	Identifies the smallest quantity of any one item in stock.
MODE	`MODE([Column1],` `[Column2],[Column3])`	Returns the most frequently recurring value among the arguments	`=MODE([Small],` `[Medium],[Large],` `[Extra Large], [2X])`	Identifies the most frequently recurring value. If no value repeats, it returns #N/A.
STDEV	`STDEV([Column1],` `[Column2],[Column3])`	Gives an estimate of standard deviation, or how widely values are dispersed from the average	`=STDEV([Small],` `[Medium],[Large],` `[Extra Large], [2X])`	Tells you the amount of variance in the numbers of items in stock, by size. A large number might be an indication that you need to sell off some stock.

Applying Date Functions

Date functions are some of the most widely used functions available for use in SharePoint lists. With date functions, you can subtract dates to find out the difference in days; you can calculate what weekday a specific date is; and you can extract year, month, day, hour, minute, and second values from dates and times. With these functions, you can do analyses and projections based on date data. For example, let's say an expense must be submitted by the fifth day of the month after the expense was incurred in order to be paid that month. Using the MONTH function, you could automatically calculate the next month based on the expense date.

Table 5-5 shows you more about the date and time functions.

Table 5-5. *Calculate Dates with Date and Time Functions*

Function	Syntax	Description	Example	Result
DATE	DATE([Year], [Month],[Day])	Returns a particular date based on year, month, and day columns.	=DATE([Year], [Month],[Day])	39021 or 10/31/2006
WEEKDAY	WEEKDAY([Column1])	Returns an integer corresponding to the day of the week using Sunday (1) through Saturday (7) as the default. For Monday (1) through Sunday (7), use =WEEKDAY ([Column1],2); for Monday (0) through Sunday (6), use =WEEKDAY ([Column1],3).	=WEEKDAY ([CloseDate],2)	Day of the week, with numbers 1 (Monday) through 7 (Sunday)
YEAR	YEAR([Column1])	Extracts the year from a date.	=YEAR ([CloseDate])	2006
MONTH	MONTH([Column1])	Extracts the month from a date.	=MONTH ([CloseDate])	Month 1–12
DAY	DAY([Column1])	Extracts the day from a date.	=DAY ([CloseDate])	Day 1–31
TIME	TIME([Hour], [Minute],[Second])	Decimal representation of the time of day.	=TIME([Column1], [Column2], [Column3])	12:00:00 p.m. is represented as .5
HOUR	HOUR([Column1])	Extracts the hour from a date value.	=HOUR ([CloseDate])	Integer 0–23
MINUTE	MINUTE([Column1])	Extracts the minutes from a date value.	=MINUTE ([CloseDate])	Integer 0–59
SECOND	SECOND([Column1])	Extracts the seconds from a date value.	=SECOND ([CloseDate])	Integer 0–59

CALCULATING WITH DATES AND TIMES

In addition to using date functions, you can also create other kinds of formulas based on date and time values. For example, say items must be shipped from the warehouse three days after an order is confirmed. You can create a calculated column to display the expected ship date based on the order confirmation date. Create the following formula:

```
=[OrderConDate}+3
```

SharePoint automatically calculates the expected ship date. Similarly, you can subtract a constant from a date, as in =[ShipDate]-3. If you want the number of days between two dates, create a calculated column to subtract the two dates; for example:

```
=[OrderConDate]-[ShipDate]
```

The result is returned in days.

To understand how to construct formulas using date functions, it's helpful to know how SharePoint calculates functions based on dates. All dates, regardless of how they're formatted, are stored as sequential serial numbers. By default, December 31,1899 is serial number 1, and January 1, 2006 is serial number 38718, because it's 38,718 days after January 1, 1900. When you add or subtract dates, SharePoint is using the dates' serial numbers to do the calculation. For example, to discover how many days are between 6/4/2006 and 12/4/2006, SharePoint subtracts 38872 from 39055 and returns 183. To discover the serial representation of a date, use the DATEVALUE function:

```
=DATEVALUE(10/1/2006)
```

You can also use time values directly in calculations. With time, hours range from 1 to 24, minutes range from 1 to 60, and seconds range from 1 to 60. Decimal representations of time are based on date value, so 12:00 noon is .5, or one-half of a day. Likewise, 1:30 a.m. is 0.072917 of a day, and 1:30 p.m. is 0.572917. Use the TIMEVALUE function to discover the decimal representation of a time:

```
=TIMEVALUE(2:36 PM)
```

The TODAY function is another type of date and time function. Being able to display a calculation based on the TODAY function is useful in a number of situations. For example, you might need to review issues that were submitted to a list within the last seven days. However, the TODAY function is available only as a default value, and isn't available for use in calculations. A workaround can get you by this limitation. To use the TODAY function, follow these steps:

1. Create a column and name it "Today." The data type you choose isn't relevant, so choose any type.

2. Create a second column that references the [TODAY] column as if it were the TODAY function. For example, create a formula such as =[TODAY]-7. Choose Date and Time as the data type for the formula results. (Note that the value that appears in the new column will be incorrect until you complete the next step, so don't panic.)

3. Delete the [TODAY] column. The value in the new column shows the correct date, seven days prior to today. You can then compare this date to the submitted date to identify those issues that were submitted in the last seven days.

Because this is a workaround, you cannot modify the column in any way without receiving an error that the TODAY function isn't supported. If you do this, you'll have to delete the new column and follow all the steps again.

Using Text and Data Functions

Text and data functions give you the ability to manipulate and evaluate data in text fields. The most commonly used text function is CONCATENATE, which combines text from more than one column. For example, you can combine the [FirstName] and [LastName] columns into a [FullName] column that contains First Name, Last Name or Last Name, First Name.

You can use other text functions, such as LEFT and RIGHT, to extract text from text strings. Let's say you have a list of properties, such as the one shown in Figure 5-3, that includes a column for property codes. Each number is made up of a two-digit location code, a four-digit unique identifier, and a three-digit type code. For example, a residential property in Traverse City, Michigan might have a code of 55-4567-333, where 55 represents the city, 4567 is the unique identifier, and 333 designates it as a residential property.

New Item	Filter	Edit in Datasheet			
Property	PropertyCode	TypeCode	CityCode
2345 Green Lake Rd. !NEW	55-4567-333	55	333

Figure 5-3. *In the list, the property code was dissected into two additional columns with the LEFT and RIGHT functions so that the list can be easily filtered.*

Using the text functions LEFT and RIGHT, you can dissect the property code shown in Figure 5-3 into three distinct parts, and then easily create filtered views based on the location and property type. With SEARCH and REPLACE, you can search for text in a text string and replace it with other text.

Using REPLACE by itself, you can substitute text based on its position, including appending text to the beginning of a text string. For example, if you wanted to add a brand name to precede names of products in a list, as shown in Figure 5-4, you could use REPLACE. The following formula inserts "FabWear " (note the space after the brand name) in the first position (1), replacing no text (0):

```
=REPLACE([Item],1,0,"FabWear ")
```

Item	REPLACE
New Item | Filter | Edit in Datasheet	
Black Warm-up Jacket	FabWear Black Warm-up Jacket
Blue T-Shirt	FabWear Blue T-Shirt
Baseball cap	FabWear Baseball cap
Steel Blue Polar Fleece Sweater	FabWear Steel Blue Polar Fleece Sweater
White Golf Shirt	FabWear White Golf Shirt

Figure 5-4. *Using the REPLACE function, you can add the brand name "FabWear" to the item names.*

With other text functions, such as UPPER, LOWER, and PROPER, you can convert text from one case to another; for example, "residential" to "RESIDENTIAL," or "Residential."

Table 5-6 describes several of the most useful text and data functions.

■**Tip** You can concatenate fields without using the CONCATENATE function by building the formula yourself. For example, to combine [FirstName] and [LastName] into a [FullName] column displaying Last name, First name, you can create the following formula:

```
=[LastName]&" ,"&[FirstName]
```

The ampersand character joins the fields, and anything enclosed in parentheses appears as text; in this case, a space and a comma.

Table 5-6. *Text and Data Functions Manipulate Text Strings*

Function	Syntax	Description	Example	Result
CONCATENATE	`CONCATENATE (text1,text2,...)`	Joins two or more text strings into one.	`=CONCATENATE (Holm, Aidan)`	Aidan Holm
LEFT	`LEFT([Column1],2)`	Extracts the left two characters from the string.	`=LEFT ([PropertyCode],2)`	Returns the first two characters of the code
RIGHT	`RIGHT([Column1],3)`	Extracts the right three characters from the string.	`=LEFT ([PropertyCode],3)`	Returns the last three characters of the code
TRIM	`TRIM([Column1]`	Removes all extra spaces from text except single spaces between words.	`=TRIM ([" baseball  cap"]`	Changes " baseball cap " to "baseball cap"
LEN	`LEN([Column1])`	Returns the number of characters in a text string.	`=LEN([Item])`	Returns the length of the text string
LOWER	`LOWER([Column1])`	Converts characters to lower case.	`=LOWER[(Boston)]`	"BOSTON" becomes "boston"
UPPER	`UPPER([Column1])`	Converts characters to upper case.	`=UPPER[(Boston)]`	"boston" becomes "BOSTON"
PROPER	`PROPER([Column1])`	Converts characters to proper case	`=PROPER[(Boston)]`	"BOSTON" or "boston" becomes "Boston"
SEARCH	`SEARCH(find_txt, within_txt, Start_num)`	Returns the number of characters where a character or text string is first found. Find_txt is text you want to find; within_txt is the location (that is, [Column1]); Start_num is the number of characters in the string you want to start searching (optional).	`=SEARCH("cap", "baseball cap", [10])`	In string "baseball cap," returns 10
REPLACE	`REPLACE(old_text, start_num, num_chars, new_text)`	Replaces original text (old_text) with new text (new_text) based on the position of the first character (start_num), and the number of characters (num_chars) you want to replace.	`=REPLACE([Item],1, 0,"FabWear ")`	Inserts "FabWear " in the first position (1), replacing no text (0)

Applying Logical Functions

You use logical functions to create conditional formulas. You can use logical functions to test whether conditions are true or false, and to make logical comparisons between expressions. For example, using the IF function, you can test if the value in one column is greater or less than a specific value. If it evaluates as true, you could apply a formula to the value; if not, leave it as is.

In practical terms, let's say you want to discount all the items in a store's inventory that had been in stock prior to January 1. You could use the IF function to examine the DateAcquired column to determine if an item was acquired prior to January 1. If it was, you would apply the discount; if it wasn't, you'd leave it at the current price. The formula might look like the following:

```
=IF([DateAcquired]>1/1/2006,[Price]-[Price]*30%,[Price])
```

With an IF function, the first part of the statement sets up the condition: is [DateAcquired]>1/1/2006? The second part of the statement, after the first comma, says to do this if the condition is true. In this case, you'd discount the item by 30 percent. The third part of the statement, after the second comma, says to do this is the condition is false. In this example, you'd keep the price as it is. The syntax for an IF function is as follows:

```
=IF(logical_test,value_if_true,value_if_false)
```

You can use AND, OR, and NOT functions to combine conditions and set up different conditions. For example, let's say in the preceding example, you want to apply a 30 percent discount if the item was acquired between 10/1/2005 and 1/1/2006, and a 50 percent discount if it was older than 10/1/2006. You could do this with the AND function. The following formula contains an AND function (AND(logical1,logical2,...)) that sets up the condition of dates between 10/1/2005 and 12/31/2006 (<1/1/2006) and a nested IF:

```
=IF(AND([DateAquired]<1/1/2006,>=10/1/2005),[Price]-[Price]*30%,
IF([DateAcquired]<10/1/2005,[Price]-[Price]*50%,[Price]))
```

These two IF statements are dependent on each other (for more about nested functions, see "Nesting Functions for Maximum Efficiency" later in this chapter).

Use AND when you want the condition to meet both criteria. You can use OR if you want the condition to meet either criteria; for example, if you acquired the item prior to 1/1/2006 OR the item is damaged. You could also use NOT to include only items that haven't been damaged:

```
 =NOT([Condition]="Damaged"
```

When creating formulas with logical functions, you can often find more than one way to develop the formula. The key is to create an accurate formula that makes sense to you. As long as it meets those criteria, it doesn't matter which functions you choose to do it.

Table 5-7 describes the logical functions.

Table 5-7. *Logical Functions Test for Conditions*

Function	Syntax	Description	Example	Result
IF	IF(logical_test, value_if_true, value_if_false)	Tests to see if a condition is true. If it is, the formula sets the first value. If it isn't, it sets the second.	=IF[FlightMiles]<500, [FlightMiles]*50%+ [FlightMiles], [FlightMiles]	Evaluates whether a flight is less than 500 miles. If it is, adds a 50 percent miles bonus.
AND	AND(logical1, logical2,...)	Evaluates criteria that evaluates as other than true or false.	=AND ([FlightMiles]>500, [FlightMiles]<1000	Evaluates to true when a flight is more than 500 and less than 1,000 miles.
OR	OR(logical1, logical2,...)	Evaluates criteria that evaluates as other than true or false.	=OR ([FlightMiles]>500, [Destination]= "Los Angeles"	Evaluates to true when a flight is more than 500 miles or the destination is Los Angeles.
NOT	NOT(logical)	Evaluates whether something is false.	NOT ([Destination]="Detroit")	Anywhere but Detroit.

■**Note** TRUE and FALSE are also logical functions. However, you can type TRUE and FALSE directly into formulas without using the functions. For example, you could enter a formula that evaluated whether a statement was TRUE and if so, apply a calculation to it.

Using Information Functions

Information functions give you information about the values in a list. For example, ISBLANK looks at whether a cell in a list is blank. The information functions are particularly useful when combined with the IF function. Let's say you want to look at clothing items in the store's inventory and apply a different brand name depending on what the item is. If the item is a cap, you want the brand name "FabWear" to precede the item; every other item should be branded "TopWear." By combining text, logical, and information functions, you can create a formula that accomplishes this task. It's easiest to start with creating a column, Caps, that identifies the caps in the list. Use the SEARCH function to search the [Item] column for the text "cap." The following formula returns "cap" if it finds it, and #VALUE! if it doesn't:

```
=SEARCH("cap",[Item])
```

You're now ready to create the calculated Brand column using the following formula:

```
=IF(ISERROR([Caps]),REPLACE([Item],1,0,"TopWear "),REPLACE([Item],1,0,"FabWear "))
```

This formula starts with an IF statement that evaluates if the Caps column displays an error, using the ISERROR function (this error is represented by #VALUE!). If it does, the formula uses the REPLACE function to insert "TopWear" at the first position in the string. If it doesn't, it inserts "FabWear" into the first position of the string. Figure 5-5 shows the results of this formula.

Item	Caps	Brand :
Black Warm-up Jacket	#VALUE!	TopWear Black Warm-up Jacket
Blue T-Shirt	#VALUE!	TopWear Blue T-Shirt
Baseball cap	10	FabWear Baseball cap
Steel Blue Polar Fleece Sweater	#VALUE!	TopWear Steel Blue Polar Fleece Sweater
White Golf Shirt	#VALUE!	TopWear White Golf Shirt

New Item | Filter | Edit in Datasheet

Figure 5-5. *In this list, the Caps columns identifies the items that contain the text string "cap," and the Brand column shows the results of applying the appropriate brand names to the items.*

Tip If you create a column solely for the purpose of calculations, create a custom view that doesn't display the column. See Chapter 4 for more about creating views.

Table 5-8 details the most common information functions.

Table 5-8. *Information Functions Give You Information About Values*

Function	Syntax	Description	Example	Result
ISBLANK	`ISBLANK(value)`	Identifies an empty cell.	`=ISBLANK([MiddleName])`	Evaluates as true if the MiddleName column is empty.
ISERR	`ISERR(value)`	Refers to any error value except #N/A.	`=ISERR([MiddleName])`	Evaluates as true if the cell contains any value except #N/A.
ISERROR	`ISERROR(value)`	Refers to any error value (#N/A, #VALUE!, #REF!, #DIV/0!, #NUM!, #NAME?, or #NULL!).	`=ISERROR([CAPS])`	Evaluates as true if an error value displays in the cell.
ISNA	`ISNA(value)`	Refers to the #N/A (value not available) error value.	`=ISNA([MiddleName])`	Evaluates as true if the cell contains #N/A.
ISNONTEXT	`ISNONTEXT(value)`	Refers to any item that isn't text. (This function returns TRUE if the value refers to a blank cell.)	`=ISNONTEXT([FlightMiles])`	Evaluates as true if the cell is blank or contains a value that is not text.
ISNUMBER	`ISNUMBER(value)`	Refers to a number.	`=ISNUMBER([FlightMiles])`	Evaluates as true if the cell contains a number.
ISTEXT	`ISTEXT(value)`	Refers to text.	`=ISTEXT([FlightMiles])`	Evaluates as true if the cell contains text.

Nesting Functions for Maximum Efficiency

Although it's possible to create multiple columns to create formulas that are based on the results of a function, you can also nest functions into one formula. SharePoint supports up to eight levels of nested functions. To nest a function, you include a secondary function inside the primary function. For example, if you want to sum three columns and then round the result, you'd create a formula similar to the following:

```
=ROUND(SUM[Column1],[Column2],[Column3]))
```

Using the order of operations, this sums the three columns and then applies the ROUND function to the result.

SharePoint isn't very helpful in suggesting where an error exists in a formula. When creating formulas with nested functions, you might want to create them in stages, testing each part of the formula as you go along. In the example in the previous paragraph, you could create the SUM function and review the results in the column. If it's correct, you could then add the ROUND function to the formula. In this way, you can narrow down the possible errors as you go along.

■**Note** The most common error when creating nesting formulas is omitting the closing parentheses at the end of each function. Excel automatically prompts you to fix this error; SharePoint does not. You have to figure out the error for yourself.

Summary

Formulas add extra functionality to a SharePoint list. The list is no longer a static data repository, but an active part of your collaboration work with your team. Much of the same functionality you have in Excel is available in SharePoint lists. You can apply formulas using references, operators, constants, and functions. SharePoint offers 150 functions, from simple math functions such as SUM to complex statistical functions such as DEVSQ (returns the sum of squares of deviations of data points from their sample mean). In this chapter, we identified many of the most commonly used and most helpful functions.

In a SharePoint list, you can add column totals to a list, but you cannot create formulas based on these totals. Formulas can be based only on data within a row, not on column data. To combine multiple functions into one formula, you can create nested functions. SharePoint isn't helpful in identifying the possible source of an error in a formula, so by constructing the formula in steps, you can test each part of the formula as you go along.

In Chapter 6, we'll look at options for publishing Excel workbooks as web pages to a SharePoint site.

CHAPTER 6

■■■

Publishing Excel Web Pages for SharePoint

In previous chapters, we've shown you how to take advantage of the built-in integration between SharePoint lists and Excel lists. If all the data stored in Excel workbooks was stored in lists, this book would have only five chapters. But Excel is so much more—and so is SharePoint. SharePoint is a great platform for Excel reports, whether the data you want to share is a chart, a table, or an entire workbook. In this chapter, we'll show you how to publish Excel information as HTML, and then use this file in on your SharePoint site. Using Excel's web tools, you can publish workbooks, worksheets, charts, and pivot tables.

When you save or publish Excel worksheets as web pages, the pages you create are either static or interactive. Static pages are simple stationary pages you could publish in every version of Excel since Excel 97. Interactive pages include the Office Web Components, which empower users by letting them work directly with Excel data in their browser using Excel tools, turning the web page into a decent ad hoc report and analysis tool. Interactive web pages let users add formulas, sort and filter data, analyze data, and edit charts.

Creating a Web Page in Excel

Not every report user is an Excel user. A workbook saved as a web page is friendlier and more accessible for users than an Excel workbook, and practically foolproof. All users can view the web page, even if they're viewing it on a Mac, or on a PC that doesn't have Excel installed.

Saving an entire workbook as a static web page is an easy process: open the workbook, check the workbook's formatting, set the page title, then save it as a web page.

Formatting the Workbook Before Saving

Review the workbook's the column widths, alignment, and other formatting, and adjust formatting if appropriate. You can't easily modify formatting in the saved web page. In the file shown in Figure 6-1, there's no space between the ID numbers in column 1 and the names in column 2. The column heading in the third column, Years of Service, is truncated. These are examples of issues that are most easily corrected in Excel prior to saving the web page.

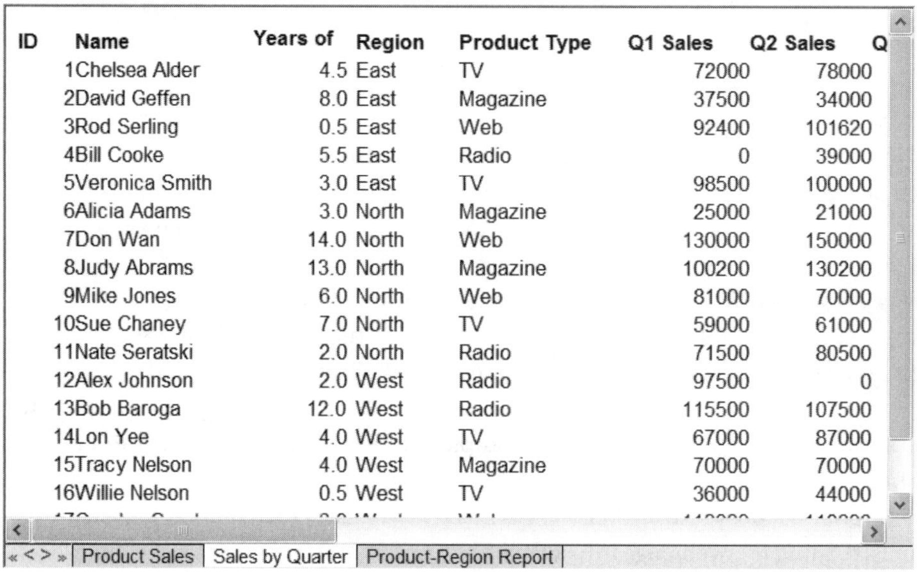

ID	Name	Years of	Region	Product Type	Q1 Sales	Q2 Sales	Q
	1Chelsea Alder	4.5	East	TV	72000	78000	
	2David Geffen	8.0	East	Magazine	37500	34000	
	3Rod Serling	0.5	East	Web	92400	101620	
	4Bill Cooke	5.5	East	Radio	0	39000	
	5Veronica Smith	3.0	East	TV	98500	100000	
	6Alicia Adams	3.0	North	Magazine	25000	21000	
	7Don Wan	14.0	North	Web	130000	150000	
	8Judy Abrams	13.0	North	Magazine	100200	130200	
	9Mike Jones	6.0	North	Web	81000	70000	
	10Sue Chaney	7.0	North	TV	59000	61000	
	11Nate Seratski	2.0	North	Radio	71500	80500	
	12Alex Johnson	2.0	West	Radio	97500	0	
	13Bob Baroga	12.0	West	Radio	115500	107500	
	14Lon Yee	4.0	West	TV	67000	87000	
	15Tracy Nelson	4.0	West	Magazine	70000	70000	
	16Willie Nelson	0.5	West	TV	36000	44000	

« < > » | Product Sales | Sales by Quarter | Product-Region Report |

Figure 6-1. *Adjust column widths, text wrapping, and numeric formatting before saving the workbook as a web page.*

In Excel, apply a numeric format (not General) to all numbers, even a column of simple integers, such as those in the first column of Figure 6-1. Edit long column headings to make them shorter, and align column headings to reflect the alignment of the data in the column. To see the difference a few simple formatting changes can make in the published web page, see Figure 6-4 later in this chapter.

If your workbook includes workbook or worksheet protection, you must remove it before saving the workbook as a web page. Otherwise, it can't be saved (a warning message appears when you try to save a protected workbook as a web page).

Saving the Workbook As a Web Page

To save the entire workbook as a web page, select any single cell in the workbook. Do not select a range of cells. Choose File ➤ Save as Web Page to open the Save As dialog box, shown in Figure 6-2.

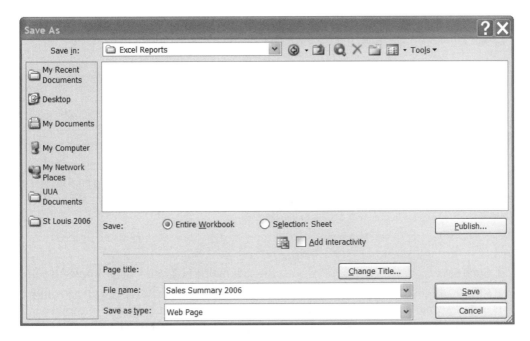

Figure 6-2. *Use the Save As dialog box to create a static or interactive web page to display Excel data.*

Make sure you select the Save **Entire Workbook** option. The default file name for the web page is the workbook name with an HTM extension. It's good practice to edit the file name to remove spaces.

■**Note** In a URL, each space is replaced with **%20**, so each space adds three characters to the length of the URL. URLs are limited to 255 characters. If there are spaces in site names, folder names, and library names, you can easily exceed this limit when you save the HTML file on your SharePoint site.

Choose your file location with care. When you create the web page, Excel will create a main file and a folder with supporting files. SharePoint's file upload doesn't support uploading folders, so moving the file and folder to SharePoint later isn't impossible, but it's a bit complex. It's best if you save the web page on your SharePoint site.

■**Tip** We create a document library named "webpages" in every Windows SharePoint Services site. All web pages displayed on the site, including pages created in Excel, are saved in the webpages document library. The webpages library isn't listed on the Quick Launch bar.

The Title will appear in the browser title bar when the page is displayed. Click the **Change Title** button to open the Set Page Title dialog box and enter a title for the page.

■**Tip** If you intend to display this web page within another page (for example, the home page on your SharePoint site), don't include a title. You can title the web part that displays the page, saving precious real estate on your page. For more information on displaying web pages within other pages, see the section "Displaying HTML Pages in SharePoint" later in this chapter.

Click **Save** to create the web page and close the dialog box. You'll be prompted if your workbook contains features that aren't supported in HTML. Discarded features include lists, views, scenarios, and shared workbook features, such as tracking. The message box in Figure 6-3 indicates that the workbook includes lists that won't be saved. The data in the lists will be published, but the web page won't include the Excel list functionality, such as sorting and the New Record row. Click **Yes** to continue and create the web page.

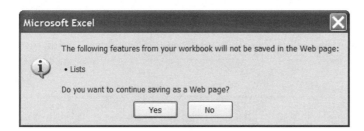

Figure 6-3. *The HTML page won't support Excel's list features.*

You can open the web page in either Excel or Internet Explorer (IE). To open the page, open the HTML file. The file opens as a regular workbook in Excel. The web page is shown in the IE browser in Figure 6-4. The page is formatted much like the workbook, including sheet tabs. You can edit this page using FrontPage, or any other application that can edit HTML.

ID	Name	Years of Service	Region	Product Type	Q1 Sales	Q2 Sales	Q
1	Chelsea Alder	4.5	East	TV	72000	78000	
2	David Geffen	8	East	Magazine	37500	34000	
3	Rod Serling	0.5	East	Web	92400	101620	
4	Bill Cooke	5.5	East	Radio	0	39000	
5	Veronica Smith	3	East	TV	98500	100000	
6	Alicia Adams	3	North	Magazine	25000	21000	
7	Don Wan	14	North	Web	130000	150000	
8	Judy Abrams	13	North	Magazine	100200	130200	
9	Mike Jones	6	North	Web	81000	70000	
10	Sue Chaney	7	North	TV	59000	61000	
11	Nate Seratski	2	North	Radio	71500	80500	
12	Alex Johnson	2	West	Radio	97500	0	
13	Bob Baroga	12	West	Radio	115500	107500	
14	Lon Yee	4	West	TV	67000	87000	
15	Tracy Nelson	4	West	Magazine	70000	70000	

« ‹ › » | Product Sales | Sales by Quarter | Product-Region Report |

Figure 6-4. *The Excel workbook saved as an HTML web page*

If your workbook contains only one worksheet with data, Excel creates a single HTML file. If the Excel workbook has more than one worksheet with data, Excel creates a number of files. There's an HTML file with the file name you specified. Other files are stored in a folder with the same name as the HTML file, with _files appended:

- The filelist.xml file, which references all the files in this folder and the main HTML file

- One HTML document for each worksheet

- A cascading stylesheet specifying how the workbook should be displayed in a browser

- The tabstrip file containing the sheet tabs

There will be additional files if your workbook contains other objects, such as charts or PivotTable reports.

Displaying the Web Page in SharePoint

When you're ready to post the page on your SharePoint site, don't use SharePoint's Upload Files utility. You must move both the HTML page and the folder; SharePoint's upload feature doesn't upload folders, only files. To easily move the HTML file and folder contents to SharePoint, select and copy the file and the corresponding folder. Open the document library where you want to save the files, and click the Explorer View link on the left side of the page to switch to Explorer View. Paste the file and folder.

To provide access to the web page, create a link to the HTML file. You can add links to a Links list, or place links anywhere on a SharePoint web part page using the Content Editor Web Part.

Saving a Selection As a Web Page

You have more options, including automatic republishing and interactivity, when you save a selection as a web page. To save a selection, open the workbook and then select the content you wish to save as a web page. Valid selections include the following:

- A worksheet (select any single cell on the sheet)

- A range

- A chart

- A PivotTable report (select the entire pivot table)

Select the cells, PivotTable report, or chart that you want to save as a web page, then choose File ➤ Save as Web Page. In the Save options, choose **Selection** instead of **Entire Workbook**. Edit the file name if you wish. Click the **Publish** button to open the Publish as Web Page dialog box, shown in Figure 6-5.

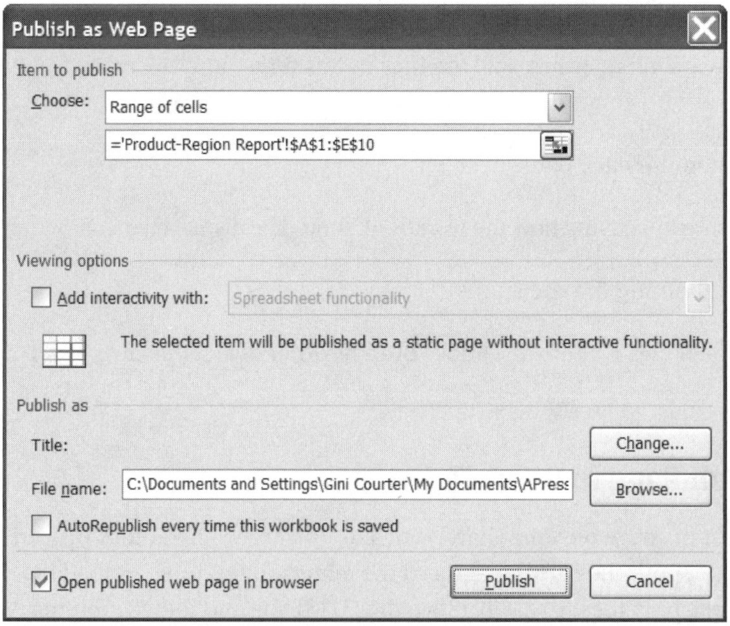

Figure 6-5. *Use the Publish as Web Page dialog box settings to set options, including automatic republishing.*

Republishing Web Pages Automatically

In the "Publish as" section of the Publish as Web Page dialog box, you have another chance to designate a page title. Here's an important option: select the **AutoRepublish every time this workbook is saved** checkbox to take the hassle out of republishing. Excel will automatically republish the worksheet every time any user saves changes, provided he or she has permission to write to the SharePoint folder or network folder where you publish the web page. If you're going to republish automatically, you need to save the web page in its final destination: a folder on your SharePoint site (see the sidebar "Adding SharePoint Sites to My Places"). Click **Browse** to choose a file location. (See the section "Automatically Republishing Web Pages" later in this chapter for more information on republishing.)

Click the **View in Web Browser** button before you click **Publish** to view your page in IE immediately. When you're ready to publish, click the **Publish** button to create the web page.

ADDING SHAREPOINT SITES TO MY PLACES

While you're working intensely on a SharePoint site, you can save time by adding frequently used web folders to the My Places bar in Excel. Follow these steps to add shortcuts to Excel's common dialog boxes:

1. In IE, copy the URL for your SharePoint folder.

2. In Excel (or any other Office application), open the Open or Save As dialog box.

3. Paste the URL in the Filename text box and press Enter.

4. Choose **Tools** from the dialog box toolbar, and then choose **Add to My Places** to add the folder to the My Places bar.

5. Close the Open or Save As dialog box.

Creating Interactive Web Pages

Excel includes three Office Web Components, and each supports specific kinds of interactivity. They're called Office Web Components (OWCs) instead of Excel Web Components because they can be used in web pages created with other Office applications, but the functionality is all Excel.

- The Spreadsheet component inserts a spreadsheet where users can add formulas, sort and filter data, and format the worksheet. Use the Spreadsheet component to present unsummarized data.

- The Chart component is linked to data in the Spreadsheet component, so that the chart can display changes when the data in the spreadsheet changes.

- The PivotTable component lets users analyze database information using most of the sorting, filtering, grouping, and subtotaling features of PivotTable reports.

There's a fourth component that works in the background: the Data Source component, the data retriever for the PivotTable and Chart components. Figure 6-6 shows an interactive web page using the PivotTable component. The toolbar at the top of the pivot table allows the user to sort, filter, show or hide the field list, and export the table to Excel for offline use.

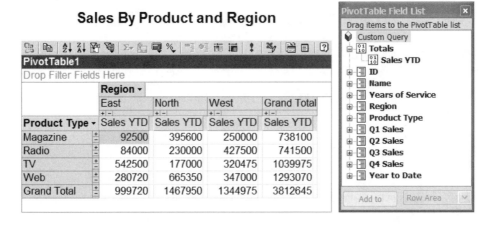

Figure 6-6. *Add interactivity to give your users the ability to analyze data.*

UNDERSTANDING OFFICE WEB COMPONENTS

The Office Web Components (OWCs) are a set of ActiveX components. With the components, you don't need to learn Java to create the slick interactive interface your users are asking for. The OWCs are supported by Excel and Access 2000, 2002, and 2003; they rely on Internet Explorer, starting with version 5.01 with SP2 or higher.

The OWCs are only interactive if the user's browser supports ActiveX components. If users have an older browser, they'll still see the spreadsheet, chart, or pivot table, but they won't be able to manipulate it in their browser. The OWCs have two other requirements: your users must have a Microsoft Office license to use the components, and the OWCs must be installed on your SharePoint server. (To download the components, go to `http://www.microsoft.com/downloads` and search for owc11.exe.) The Office licensing and browser requirements make the OWCs a better choice for an intranet, where they were intended to be used, rather than the Internet.

By default, IE blocks unsigned ActiveX components. When you or your users open a web page that includes ActiveX components, you'll need to click the Information Bar that appears at the top of your browser window and choose **Allow Blocked Content**. Depending on your settings, you might also have to okay one or two message boxes as part of this process. Don't let this IE behavior dissuade you from using the OWCs (or encourage you to dumb down your browser security settings). The active content won't be blocked when you view the web pages as part of a SharePoint site. SharePoint is wall-to-wall trusted ActiveX web parts.

To create an interactive page, follow these steps:

1. Open the workbook that contains the sheet.

2. Remember to remove protection from protected workbooks, sheets, or ranges in the workbook, even if the protection doesn't apply to the sheet or selection you wish to publish. If Excel trips over password protection in your workbook, you'll see this message box, and will need to remove protection and begin the Save process again.

3. Select the sheet, range, pivot table, or chart that you want to publish.

4. Choose File ➤ Save as Web Page to open the Save As dialog box.

5. Enable the **Add Interactivity** checkbox, then click the **Publish** button to open the Publish as Web Page dialog box, shown previously in Figure 6-5.

6. Choose the component you wish to use from the drop-down list by selecting the kind of functionality you want users to have: spreadsheet, chart, or pivot table. If you select an Excel data range, you can choose either the Spreadsheet or PivotTable component.

Excel creates the PivotTable. Excel isn't as facile with charts; the Chart component is only available if you selected a chart object before opening the Save As dialog box.

Publishing and Using the Spreadsheet Component

The Spreadsheet component includes about as much spreadsheet functionality as you can pack into a browser window. With the static page, users had only one report available in the browser. With the interactive page, they have a report tool with sorting, filtering, and formatting capabilities. Changes users make are retained during the browser session so they can switch from the browser to other applications while they work with the spreadsheet.

Excel users will immediately know how to use most of the buttons on the Spreadsheet component toolbar, shown in Figure 6-7, although the folks in our office were disappointed that the **AutoSum** button doesn't have a drop-down list!

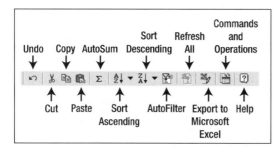

Figure 6-7. *The Spreadsheet component toolbar provides spreadsheet functionality in a browser window.*

Two buttons aren't standard in Excel: the **Export To Excel** button and the **Commands and Options** button. The **Export To Excel** button, familiar to SharePoint users, creates the Excel worksheet in a user-specified folder so users can manipulate a copy of the data as much as they wish without changing the original data in the web page.

The **Commands and Options** button opens the Commands and Options dialog box, which includes additional user tools (see Figure 6-8). Make sure your users know about this dialog box, because it's filled with power: the power to change the format of a worksheet, work with formulas in the worksheet, find worksheet data, and change worksheet and workbook options.

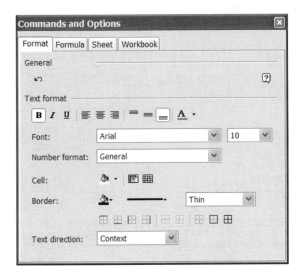

Figure 6-8. *You use the Commands and Options dialog box to format and modify the data displayed in the Spreadsheet component.*

The Spreadsheet component doesn't support all the features and functionality of Excel. Table 6-1 describes worksheet properties and features that the component doesn't support.

Table 6-1. *Features and Formatting Not Supported by the Spreadsheet Component*

Feature	Description
Comments	Discarded.
Conditional formatting	Not supported. Cells display as formatted when the page is published.
Graphics	Not displayed.
Group and outline symbols	Not supported.
Indented text	Not supported. Displays without indents.
Links to other worksheets, workbooks, and web queries	Discarded. Cells display with values when the page is published.
Outlined ranges	Collapsed rows are hidden.
Precedent and dependent arrows	Discarded.
Print settings, including rows to repeat, columns to repeat, and print area	Discarded.
Rotated text	Not supported. Text is reset to horizontal.
Shared workbook information	Discarded.
Validation rules and error alerts	Discarded.

Because data values persist during a browser session, another good use of the Spreadsheet component is to create a small application that collects values from a user and performs a few calculations.

Publishing and Using the Chart Component

The Chart component displays both the chart and the underlying data, as shown in Figure 6-9. Users modify the data to change the chart, just as they would in Excel.

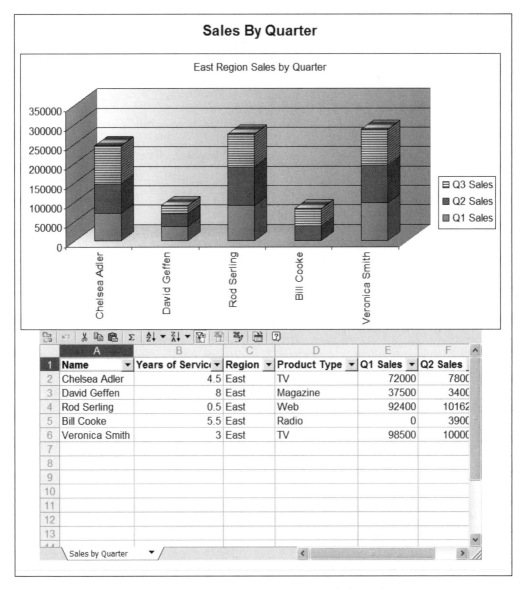

Figure 6-9. *The Chart component reflects changes in the underlying data.*

To publish a chart with interactivity, select the chart area before choosing File ➤ Save as Web Page. Don't spend a lot of time formatting your chart before publishing it. The Chart component supports most chart features, but doesn't support drawing objects (such as callouts and other annotations) and the placement of chart elements. For example, if you've neatly positioned the title and data labels and resized the plot area, you've wasted your time. They'll all snap back to their default positions in the Chart component. Table 6-2 describes the chart features that the Chart component doesn't support.

Table 6-2. *Features Not Supported by the Chart Component*

Feature	Description
Surface charts	Not supported.
Graphics and drawing objects in chart	Discarded.
Semi-transparent fills	Discarded.
Series lines	Discarded.
Chart element placement	Titles, legend, and other elements return to their default locations.
Plot visible cells only	Ignored. All data is plotted.
Error bars based on a calculation	Discarded.

The data table is only included on the web page when you include interactivity. If you don't want the data table, publish the chart without interactivity.

Publishing and Using the PivotTable Component

The PivotTable component is underused. Many competent Excel users don't create pivot tables, often because they don't know where to begin. If you create the pivot table and publish it as a web page, users will figure out how to use it. Unlike an Excel PivotTable, the Office PivotTable component is almost foolproof. If users make a serious mistake, they can close IE to discard their changes, fire IE back up, and start again. The web page in Figure 6-10 works like the Excel PivotTable report, with zones for a row area, column area, data area, and page area.

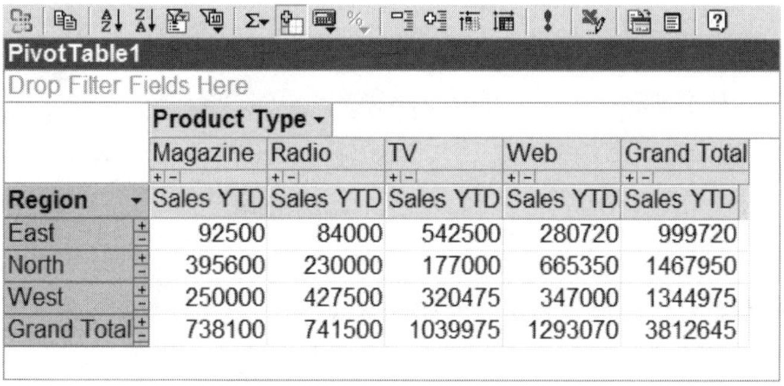

Figure 6-10. *The PivotTable component lets users interactively analyze data.*

To create the web page using the PivotTable component, follow these steps:

1. Create the pivot table in Excel and apply appropriate formatting to the labels and numeric data, add calculated fields, and set field options.

2. Each pivot table has a default name. The first pivot table in a workbook is named PivotTable1. While you're working in Excel, you don't need to pay attention to the name because it's invisible. This isn't true in the web page, where the name is proudly displayed directly beneath the toolbar:

   To change the name of the pivot table, right-click any cell and choose **Table Options** from the context menu to open the PivotTable Options dialog box. Enter a name for the pivot table and click **OK**.

3. Select the table. A tip if you're new to pivot tables: start in the lower right corner; the cell in the upper left corner contains a button. If there is no data in the Page area, don't include the page area in the selection. With the table selected, choose File ➤ Save as Web Page to open the Save As dialog box.

4. Choose **Selection: PivotTable** and enable the **Interactivity** checkbox. If the Selection shows a range (for example, $B$2:$J$8) instead of PivotTable, cancel and start again with the pivot table selection.

5. Click the **Publish** button and set your options in the Publish as Web Page dialog box (see Figure 6-5).

You don't need to include every field from the data source in the pivot table. The component includes a **Field List** button. Clicking the button opens the PivotTable Field List dialog box (shown previously in Figure 6-6), so users can add and remove fields from the table just as they would in Excel.

The PivotTable component doesn't support every PivotTable report feature. Table 6-3 describes the features that aren't supported.

Table 6-3. *Features Not Supported by the PivotTable Component*

Feature	Description
Background refresh settings	Discarded.
Calculated fields	Not supported. Converted to summary functions.
Calculated items	Discarded.
Custom calculations	Discarded.
Custom number formats	Discarded.
Custom sort orders	Discarded.
Error value and empty cell options	Discarded. Both errors and empty cells are displayed as blanks.
Indents	Discarded.
Numeric formatting of individual table cells	Discarded.
Print settings	Discarded.

Appending to an Existing Web Page

If you have a published spreadsheet and you'd like to add another web component, such as a chart or a pivot table to it, you can append the data to the existing page. To place a second component on a page, follow these steps:

1. Choose File ➤ Save as Web Page and then click **Publish** to reopen the Publish as Web Page dialog box.

2. Select the existing HTML file.

3. When you click **Publish**, you're prompted to replace or add to the page. Choose **Add To File** to display more than one component on the page.

This is a useful technique, but before you decide to put multiple components on a single page, skip forward to the section "Displaying HTML Pages in SharePoint" to see how you can use SharePoint web parts to display multiple web parts in a single page.

Automatically Republishing Web Pages

If you change data used to create a web page, you can resave or republish the data to keep the web page up to date. To have Excel automatically republish data when you save changes to the original workbook, check the **AutoRepublish every time this workbook is saved** checkbox in the Publish As Web Page dialog box. When you save the workbook, Excel displays the dialog box shown in Figure 6-11.

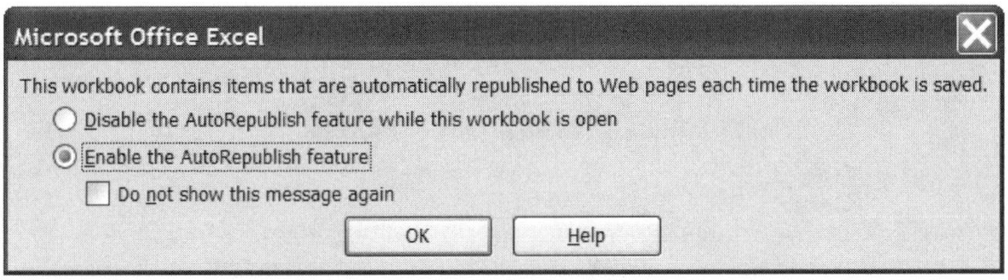

Figure 6-11. *You're prompted to republish when the workbook is saved.*

Normally you'll choose the second option: **Enable the AutoRepublish feature**. If you choose to enable AutoRepublish, you can also instruct Excel to bypass the human element in the future by enabling the **Do not show this message again** checkbox. "Do not show this message again" is Microsoft-speak for "Click here and you'll never find this option again." There might be times that you won't want to republish a file automatically. For example, AutoRepublish is very inconvenient when you're working offline with a file that has been saved as a web page, or you're entering "what if" data or an incredibly sensitive piece of information that's not supposed to be published.

If you don't enable the **Do not show this message again** checkbox, you'll always be prompted to approve the republish operation. If you choose the first option, **Disable the AutoRepublish feature while this workbook is open**, you won't be prompted to republish again until you close, reopen, and save the workbook.

To turn off AutoRepublish, follow these steps:

1. Choose File ➤ Save as Web Page and then click **Publish** to open the Publish as Web Page dialog box.

2. In the Choose drop-down list, select **Previously Published Items**. Select the previously published item for which you want to disable AutoRepublish, and click the **Remove** button.

3. Close the dialog box and save the workbook.

Displaying HTML Pages in SharePoint

Excel creates an HTML page, not a web part. SharePoint's Page Viewer Web Part lets you move your charts, tables, and spreadsheet pages front and center. You use the Page Viewer to display data from an existing HTML page, such as the pages we created previously in this chapter.

You can use the Page Viewer Web Part on any page. If you want to display several web pages on a single page (like a dashboard), begin by creating a web part page. Figure 6-12 shows a portion of a web part page that serves as a sales dashboard.

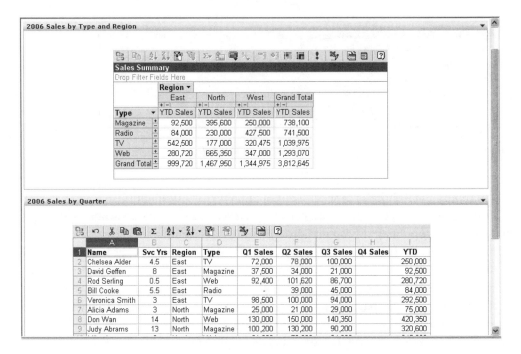

Figure 6-12. *This web part page includes two instances of the Page Viewer Web Part.*

The first Page Viewer Web Part displays an interactive web page with pivot table functionality. The second Page Viewer Web Part displays a page created using the interactive Spreadsheet component. Users can sort, filter, pivot, and format the two components to create their own analyses and reports.

Creating a Web Part Page

To create a web part page, follow these steps:

1. In SharePoint, click **Create** on the menu.

2. On the Create page, scroll to the bottom and choose **Web Part Page** to open the New Web Part Page customization page, shown in Figure 6-13.

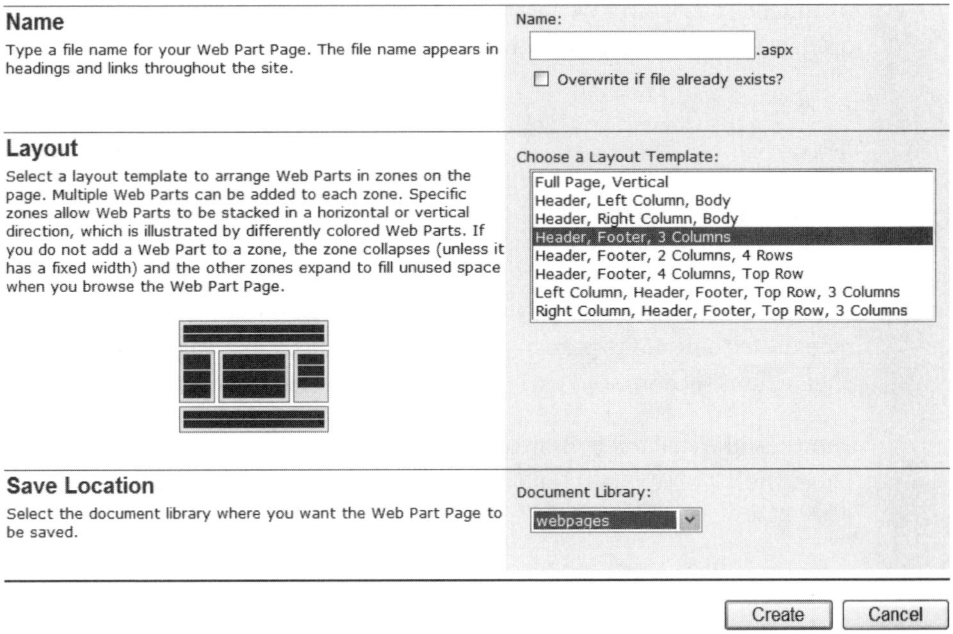

Name

Type a file name for your Web Part Page. The file name appears in headings and links throughout the site.

Name:

[   ] .aspx

☐ Overwrite if file already exists?

Layout

Select a layout template to arrange Web Parts in zones on the page. Multiple Web Parts can be added to each zone. Specific zones allow Web Parts to be stacked in a horizontal or vertical direction, which is illustrated by differently colored Web Parts. If you do not add a Web Part to a zone, the zone collapses (unless it has a fixed width) and the other zones expand to fill unused space when you browse the Web Part Page.

Choose a Layout Template:

Full Page, Vertical
Header, Left Column, Body
Header, Right Column, Body
Header, Footer, 3 Columns
Header, Footer, 2 Columns, 4 Rows
Header, Footer, 4 Columns, Top Row
Left Column, Header, Footer, Top Row, 3 Columns
Right Column, Header, Footer, Top Row, 3 Columns

Save Location

Select the document library where you want the Web Part Page to be saved.

Document Library:

webpages ▼

[Create]   [Cancel]

Figure 6-13. *Create a web part page to display the HTML pages you created in Excel.*

3. Enter a file name and choose a page layout. Choose your layout carefully. There's no "Change my page layout" button. If you want to change the layout after you click **Create** you'll need to use FrontPage.

4. Select a save location for your web page. If you created a webpages folder, this is a good time to use it. Click **Create** to create and open the web part page in Design view so you can add web parts.

■**Tip** The SharePoint Quick Launch bar is reserved for libraries and lists, so you aren't asked whether the web part page should be added to the Quick Launch bar. Add a link to the web part page somewhere in your site to provide easy access for your users.

Adding and Modifying the Page Viewer Web Part

You use SharePoint's Page Viewer Web Part to display the contents of a web page. The Page Viewer Web Part is dynamic; when the user opens or refreshes the page, the web part contents are refreshed.

To add the Page Viewer Web Part to a page, click the **Modify Shared Page** button in the top right corner of the browser window to open the menu.

Modify Shared Page ▾

- If the button shown is the **Modify My View** button, click the button and choose **Shared View** from the menu. If you can't choose **Shared View**, you don't have permission to edit the page.

- In SharePoint Portal Server, you must click the **Edit Page** link in the Actions menu on the left side of the page to display the Modify Shared Page link. If you don't have an Actions section, you don't have permission to edit the page.

Choose Add Web Parts ➤ Browse as shown in Figure 6-14 to open the Add Web Parts task pane. The list of Web Part Galleries appears at the top of the task pane.

Figure 6-14. *Use the Modify Shared Page menu to add web parts to the page.*

Understanding SharePoint Web Part Galleries

SharePoint includes four collections of web parts that you can use to customize your web site. The four Web Part Galleries are as follows:

- *Online Gallery*: The set of web parts that are installed and deployed by the site or site collection administrator and available throughout the site collection.

- *SharePoint Site Web Part Gallery*: The set of web parts that are available in a specific site, including the built-in web parts (such as Announcements), as well as web parts automatically created by SharePoint when you create libraries or lists. The name of this gallery varies.

- *Virtual Server Gallery*: The "global" collection of web parts that are available for all sites on the server.

- *Web Part Page Gallery*: The collection of web parts for the current page. This gallery is populated dynamically, and contains every web part that's associated with the page, even if the web part isn't currently displayed. To add a web part to the gallery, choose it from the Add Web Parts task pane. To remove a web part from the gallery, place the web part on the page, then choose **Delete** from the web part menu.

Some of these galleries might be empty. For example, in the task pane shown in Figure 6-15 the Online Gallery has no web parts. You can browse any of these galleries for parts that you can use on the web pages on your site. Choose the gallery in the top half of the task pane, then browse the list of web parts.

Figure 6-15. *Browse the Web Part Galleries to locate the Page Viewer Web Part.*

Browse to locate the Page Viewer Web Part. Either drag the web part and drop it into one of the zones on your page, or choose the zone in the "Add to" drop-down list at the bottom of the task pane (see Figure 6-15) and click **Add** to add the part to the zone.

The web part is incredibly unimpressive until you modify it to add content. Click the **Open the Tool Pane** link in the web part to display the Page Viewer Web Part task pane shown in Figure 6-16.

Figure 6-16. *Configure the Page Viewer Web Part in the task pane.*

Customizing the Page Viewer Web Part

Most web parts have four sets of properties: views (or content), appearance, layout, and advanced. You use the properties to modify the web part:

- *Views/Content*: Choose a view for a list or specify the content to be displayed in the web part.

- *Appearance*: Change the web part's title, height, width, frame style, and frame state.

- *Layout*: Hide the web part or change its position on the page or within the zone.

- *Advanced*: Lock down the web part so users can't move it, close it, or minimize it.

Before you set the properties for the Page Viewer Web Part, make sure that the web page you wish to display (the page you created earlier in Excel) is stored in a shared location, preferably in a folder on the SharePoint site. If you're moving the page from another location, make sure you also move the related folder (if any) that Excel created when you saved a workbook, chart, or pivot table as a web page. With all the files in their final location, follow these steps to customize the Page Viewer Web Part:

1. In IE, open the HTML page you created in Excel and copy the URL from the IE address bar.

2. In the SharePoint Page Viewer Web Part task pane, leave the default option, **Web Page**.

3. Paste the URL (copied in step 1) into the Link text box.

4. Click the **Test Link** hyperlink to make sure it opens the correct file.

5. Expand the Appearance properties section. Enter a title for the web part.

6. Click **OK** to view the web part.

You'll usually need to tweak the Appearance settings for the Page Viewer Web Part to accommodate the contents of the web page you're displaying. If the height or width of the content area of the HTML page is greater than that height of the web part, the content will be cut off, and the web part will include a scroll bar. The web part's height and width are Appearance properties. Click the down arrow on the right end of the web part's title bar and choose **Modify Shared Web Parts** to reopen the task pane.

Expand the Appearance section and set the height (as shown in Figure 6-17) and/or the width. Click **Apply** to check your changes. Click **OK** when you're finished.

Figure 6-17. *Adjust the height and width of the web part to fit the content.*

Summary

This chapter has focused on two kinds of HTML tools. With Excel's HTML web publishing features, you can create Excel reports, charts, and pivot tables for use on the web. Users can access an HTML page directly from SharePoint if you simply add a link from the HTML page to a SharePoint link list. To display your HTML pages on a page with other SharePoint content, use the Page Viewer Web Part.

CHAPTER 7

■■■

Building Out-of-the-Box Business Solutions

In this chapter, we'll use the features discussed in the previous chapters to build two Windows SharePoint Services and Excel solutions that solve real-world business challenges. The solutions include the following elements:

- Excel lists (described in Chapter 2)

- SharePoint lists (described in Chapter 3)

- SharePoint views (described in Chapter 4)

- Custom calculations (described in Chapter 5)

- Excel Spreadsheet, PivotTable, and PivotChart components (described in Chapter 6)

- SharePoint Page Viewer and Content Editor Web Parts (described in Chapter 6)

As you read through the chapter, if you need additional information about creating or using a specific element or web part, refer to the chapter listed for each element.

Business Solutions Using Lists and Views

You can build myriad business solutions using nothing more than lists and views, and you often don't need to build the solutions from scratch. Almost every organization has an Excel workbook that would be better presented as one or more SharePoint lists: one person maintains the workbook, and other team members need to e-mail the workbook's owner to edit the workbook or get details about current data. If you publish this buttoned-down Excel workbook as one or more SharePoint lists and make it available for other team members to use, the team will be more efficient and much happier. In short, you'll be a hero. This heroism isn't on the same scale as saving a rainforest, but you'll still feel good about delivering business value by saving time and improving team morale.

> *... that is the whole meaning of life*
> *To be able to look to the heavens*
> *And scream "I have lived. I have lived" —*
> *To have carved epic lives from ordinary moments.*
>
> — George David Miller, "Before I Read This Poem"

In this section, we'll provide an overview of a solution we've created for corporate clients: a quick and dirty software issue-and-resolution tracking system. We'll explain the business scenario (names have been changed to protect the innocent) and build the Share-Point solution using the Excel workbook that the team was already using to manage its data.

The Project Issue Tracking Scenario

The Custom Order System (COS) project is in danger of missing its deadline. During user acceptance testing (UAT), the team discovered that some of the system requirements documentation had been lost during a staffing transition. As a result, COS is missing key functionality. UAT has now been suspended and a "tiger team" is being assembled to design, code, and test the missing screens quickly.

Brian, the project manager, has always used Excel to track issues identified during testing. When a tester needs to log an issue, he or she e-mails the issue to Brian, who enters it in the workbook, shown in Figure 7-1. At the end of each day, Brian e-mails the workbook to developers, who indicate the issues they'll work on the next day. As a developer resolves an issue, he or she sends an e-mail to the testers and copies Brian, who updates the worksheet. It's a cumbersome system. Brian has considered sharing the workbook, but updating the log helps Brian keep a "finger on the pulse" of unresolved issues, and he often does some quick analysis using sorting and filters.

	A	B	C	D	E	F	G	H	I	J	K	
1	ID	Priority	Status	Area	Desc	Version	Tester	Reported	EstCompl	ComplDat	Dev	Re
2	1	High	Completed	Client Info	Business Category dropdown should display only categories for the selected Business	1.0.1	NC	8/9/2005	8/9/2005	8/9/2005	RJ	
3	2	Low	Active	Client Info	Add checkbox to Research Required	1.0.1	KD	8/9/2005				
4	3	High	In Process	Client Info	Sales should be a drop down with the salespeople listed. On user choice, populate	1.0.1	EZ	8/9/2005	8/12/2005		RJ	NC
5	4	Medium	Active	Client Info	Sales Leader should show name, not ID	1.0.1	NC	8/9/2005				
6	5	Medium	In Process	Client Info	Account Type - display the description, not the type code	1.0.1	EZ	8/9/2005	8/11/2005		RJ	EZ
7	6	Medium	Active	Client Info	No decimal places for number of versions	1.0.1	SC	8/9/2005				
8	7	High	Completed	Client Info	Multiple versions: Add Y/N dropdown	1.0.1	SC	8/9/2005	8/9/2005	8/10/2005	CV	NC
9	8	High	Active	Marketing	Date missing	1.0.1	SC	8/9/2005				
10	9	High	Active	Marketing	Many labels missing	1.0.1	SC	8/9/2005				
	10	High	Active	Marketing	Under Preference,	1.0.1	SC	8/9/2005				

Figure 7-1. *The Excel issue tracking worksheet*

When UAT was suspended, testers had already logged 55 issues. Brian is also swamped with e-mails from COS stakeholders who want to be kept up to date on the progress of the project. Brian's Excel issue tracking worksheet is no longer sufficient.

Building the SharePoint Issue Tracking Solution

Simply publishing the issue tracking worksheet as an Excel list would make it easy for testers and developers to enter their information directly. However, built-in functionality in SharePoint Tasks lists would be useful for the COS project team, including the My Tasks, Due Today, and Active Tasks views, and preconfigured alerts for task assignment. Because each issue is a task, it makes sense to modify the existing Tasks list to match Brian's worksheet, then copy and paste the worksheet data into the Tasks list.

Site permissions will be used to provide stakeholders with read-only information and prevent them from modifying the issue tracking list. Views can be created for stakeholders, developers, and testers to take the load off Brian's Inbox.

Here are the high-level activities required to build the issue tracking solution:

1. Create a Windows SharePoint Services site—the COS site—for the project team.

2. Modify the columns in the Tasks list to match Brian's issue tracking worksheet.

3. Modify the All Contacts view to include Job Title.

4. Add testers and developers to the Contacts list.

5. Add tester and developer users to the site, either using copy and paste to grab e-mail addresses from the Contacts list, or using the Outlook address book.

6. Create additional list views:

   • Paste a datasheet view used once for importing data

   • Completed issues

   • High priority issues

7. Import the data from the issue tracking worksheet using copy and paste.

8. Modify the home page and launch the site.

Modifying the Tasks List

You need to modify both the Excel list and the Tasks list so that the data can be copied and pasted. This type of preparation is often necessary when you're creating a new SharePoint site that will include existing Excel data, so we'll walk through the steps needed to prepare and complete the copy and paste operation.

In Excel, use the Replace feature to change the data in the Priority column to match the choices in SharePoint: Replace High with (1) High, Medium with (2) Medium, and so on. Also, replace the tester and developer initials with the users' names from the Manage Users page—the same names that will appear in the drop-down lists when users add new tasks to the list (see Figure 7-2).

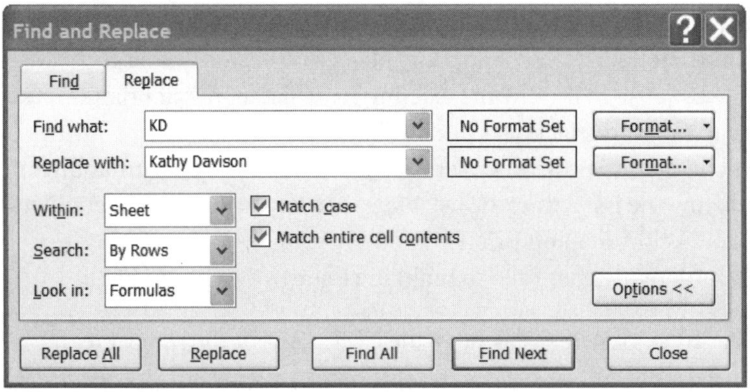

Figure 7-2. *Use the Find and Replace dialog box to replace initials with names.*

In SharePoint, rename the Title column to Area. Rename the Due Date to match the Est Compl field in Excel. Remember that the Tasks list has a view called Due Today, which uses the Due Date field. You need to rename Due Date because you want the Due Today view to show tasks where the Est Compl (Estimated Completion) is today.

Delete the % Complete column and add other columns from the Excel list. You need to modify the SharePoint Status column choices to replace Deferred with On Hold, and Not Started with Active.

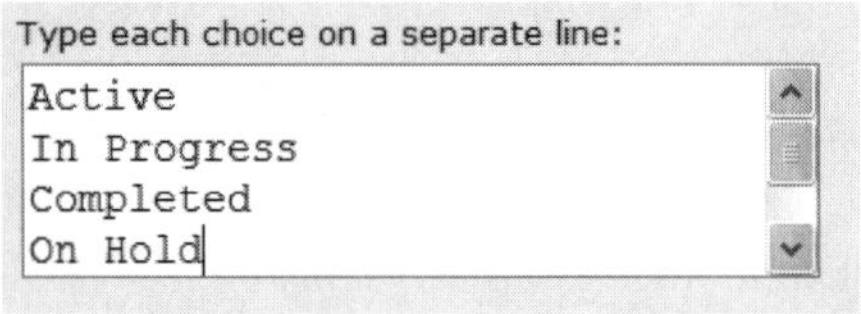

Change the Assigned To column name to Developer, and add a new lookup column, Tester, to the list (see Figure 7-3). You need to add the users to the site to populate these two columns before you import the data from Excel.

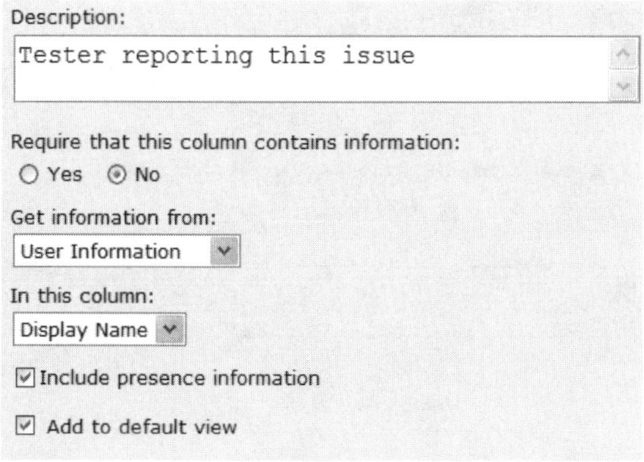

Description:

```
Tester reporting this issue
```

Require that this column contains information:
○ Yes ◉ No

Get information from:
| User Information ∨ |

In this column:
| Display Name ∨ |

☑ Include presence information

☑ Add to default view

Figure 7-3. *Adding a Tester column with user names from the SharePoint site*

Finally, you need to create a Paste view, omitting unneeded columns, and with columns in the same order as in the Excel workbook (see Figure 7-4). In the Excel Issue Tracking log, the user has filled in an Issue ID. SharePoint will automatically assign an ID to each task. With Brian's agreement, you aren't going to import the ID numbers from the issue tracking worksheet, because the team will use the ID numbers that SharePoint assigns in the future. Therefore, the ID column won't be included in the Paste view (because you're not pasting ID data from Excel), but it will be displayed in all other views.

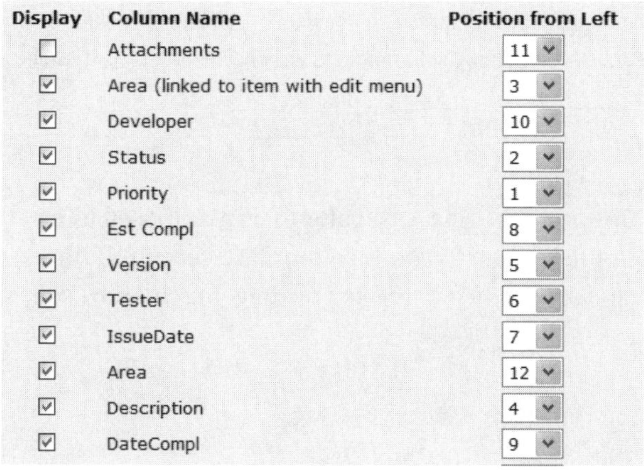

Display	Column Name	Position from Left
☐	Attachments	11 ∨
☑	Area (linked to item with edit menu)	3 ∨
☑	Developer	10 ∨
☑	Status	2 ∨
☑	Priority	1 ∨
☑	Est Compl	8 ∨
☑	Version	5 ∨
☑	Tester	6 ∨
☑	IssueDate	7 ∨
☑	Area	12 ∨
☑	Description	4 ∨
☑	DateCompl	9 ∨

Figure 7-4. *The Paste view will be used once to import data from Excel.*

Importing Data Using Copy and Paste

With the Tasks list Paste view open in Datasheet view, you're now ready to select and copy the data records from Excel, then select the first cell in row 1 and choose **Paste**. The data doesn't match precisely (see Figure 7-5).

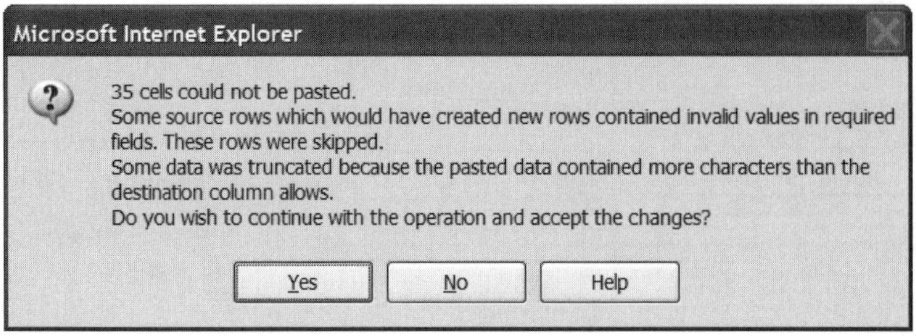

Figure 7-5. *Paste error message box*

The message box lists two kinds of errors:

- *New rows containing invalid values*: Either your fields don't match, or you didn't replace all the Developer, Tester, Priority, and Status values in Excel with the new values that SharePoint requires.

- *Truncated data*: At least one of the Excel cells has more than 255 characters.

If you choose **Yes** to continue with the operation, you'll learn more about the problem. You can look at the data, then discard it, fix the problem, and try again.

Note There's only one downside to continuing. SharePoint gives each new task a unique ID, including rows that are later deleted. When you paste the second time, the ID numbers will begin with the next available number, rather than beginning with 1.

Figure 7-6 shows the invalid values problem. The Area column was supposed to be the third column, but it's at the end of the list (the fifteenth column), so columns four through fifteen are in the wrong place. This can be easily fixed by dragging the Area column header to its correct position.

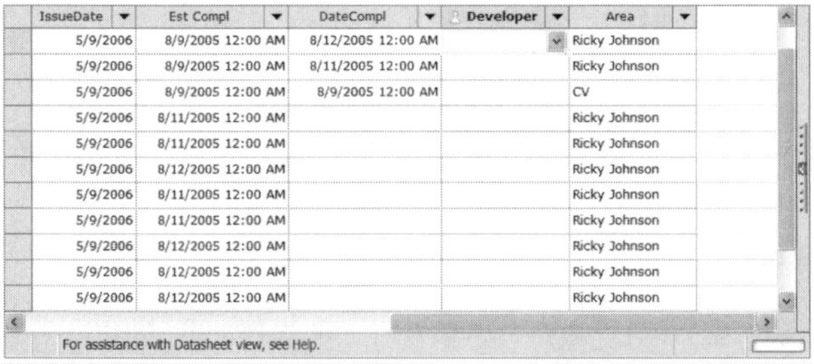

Figure 7-6. *The Area column was out of place, and caused the paste error.*

One of the Descriptions was truncated. You need to check all the Excel descriptions to make sure they're 255 characters or less. You can use Excel's LEN function to identify the descriptions that are too long.

There's a third problem that SharePoint didn't notify us about. The Issue Date column has a default setting of Today's Date. When the data was pasted, SharePoint used the default, not the date from the Excel list. For now, you need to change the default setting for the Issue Date column to None. After you've pasted the data from Excel, you can change the default back to Today's Date.

After fixing these issues, copy and paste the Tasks data again.

Modifying the Home Page

You want to turn the home page of the COS site into a dashboard focusing primarily on the information needs of the project's stakeholders. If business users and managers can get the information they need from the site, they'll feel more informed and have more confidence in the project team. Project announcements can be posted on the site, allowing the team to handle stakeholder communications proactively rather than reactively in response to individual e-mail requests. Brian will spend less time managing stakeholders and will have more time to manage the project. You're putting the stakeholder information on the home page so the team doesn't need to spend time training stakeholders so they can navigate the site.

The home page will meet some developer and tester needs as well. Team members will be able to add and update tasks on the home page. However, team members will primarily use the Quick Launch bar to access custom views, such as My Tasks.

Here are the modifications to the home page:

- Close the Calendar web part—stakeholders don't need it.

- The COS team doesn't have a logo, so also close the Site Image web part.

- Change the General settings for Shared Documents and Contacts to remove their links on the Quick Launch bar (Site Settings ➤ Modify Site Content ➤ Customize).

- Add a Contacts web part to display a list of team members and roles.

- Create an easy way for stakeholders to send e-mail to the team by adding a mailto hyperlink.

- Add three views of the Tasks list to the site's home page: Active Tasks, Completed Tasks, and Due Today.

Creating the Mailto Link

It's easy to repurpose the Links list to provide a way for users to contact the team. To create a mailto link, enter **mailto:**, followed by the e-mail address as the URL (see Figure 7-7). When you test the link, it should open an e-mail message form with the e-mail address in the To text box. Provide descriptive text for the link, then click **Save and Close**.

Figure 7-7. *Creating a hyperlink that opens an e-mail message form*

Make two modifications to the Links web part: change the Toolbar Type to **No Toolbar** so that users can't add a link, and change the title to invite users to click the link to contact the team (see Figure 7-8).

Figure 7-8. *Modify the Links web part to hide the toolbar.*

Alternatively, you can change the frame style to **None**, which omits the title bar and leaves a freestanding link on the page:

▪ Click here to email the COS
  Team.

Adding Views to the Home Page

Choose Modify Shared Page ➤ Add Web Parts ➤ Browse to open the Add Web Parts task pane. Drag and drop the Tasks web part into the left zone three times (see Figure 7-9).

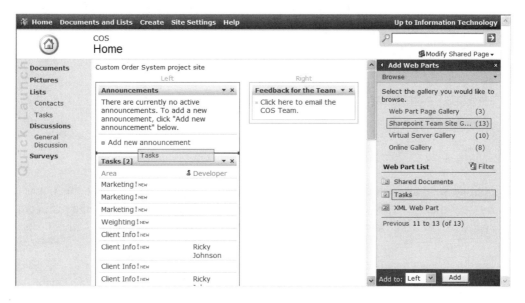

Figure 7-9. *Add three Tasks web parts to the home page.*

Select the top Tasks web part. Follow these steps to modify the web part to show today's tasks:

1. Click the down arrow on the top Tasks view and choose **Modify Shared Web Part** from the menu.

2. In the Selected View drop-down list, choose **Due Today**. A message box warns that you'll lose the changes made to this view. Click **OK**.

3. Click the **Edit the current view** link (right under the drop-down list) and modify the column selection to include, in order, the following fields:

   - Area (linked to item with edit menu)

   - Description

   - Status

   - Priority

   - Developer

Display	Column Name	Position from Left
☑	Area (linked to item with edit menu)	1 ⌄
☑	Developer	6 ⌄
☑	Status	3 ⌄
☑	Priority	4 ⌄
☐	Area	5 ⌄
☑	Description	2 ⌄

4. Click **OK** to return to the Modify Web Part task pane.

5. Change the Title to **Tasks Due Today**.

6. Click **OK**.

Similarly, modify the second Tasks web part to show Active Tasks. Choose the Active Tasks view, then edit the view to include the Est Compl column. However, you don't need to include Status (the view is filtered for Status = Active). Name the web part Active Tasks.

Display	Column Name	Position from Left
☑	Area (linked to item with edit menu)	1 ⌄
☑	Description	2 ⌄
☑	Priority	3 ⌄
☑	Est Compl	4 ⌄
☑	Developer	5 ⌄

Modify the third Tasks web part to show Completed Tasks. Choose the Active Tasks view (there is no Completed Tasks view), then edit the view to include the Date Compl column. Change the filter to Status = Complete. Name the web part Completed Tasks.

Finalizing and Launching the Site

Two views are left to create for the Tasks list: Completed Issues and High Priority Issues. These views will be accessed from the Tasks list, not the home page. After creating the views, there are two more tasks to complete before launch: have Brian add an announcement about the purpose of the site, and add the stakeholders as read-only users. The completed SharePoint site shown in Figure 7-10 provides a complete issue tracking solution for Brian and the COS team.

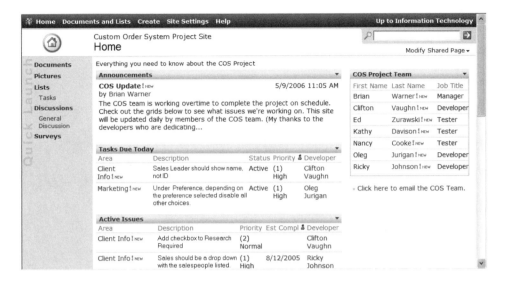

Figure 7-10. *The home page of the COS Issue Tracking SharePoint site*

Extending the Solution

After we created the site, Brian reported that his team was using the site proficiently, and his e-mail volume had ramped way down. However, Brian was still receiving e-mails asking about the scheduling of issues. Specifically, managers wanted to know what tasks were scheduled to be completed in the next three days so they could ensure that subject matter experts would be available if the developers had last-minute questions. A Tasks in the Next Three Days view would lower anxiety.

This view requires two filter criteria. The estimated completion date, Est Compl, needs to be greater than or equal to today, and less than or equal to the date three days from now (today + 3). You can't use [TODAY] in a filter calculation such as the following:

```
Est Compl <= [TODAY]+3
```

To create this view, you must first create a calculated column that subtracts three days from Est Compl. Figure 7-11 shows the formula and settings for the ThreeDays calculated column.

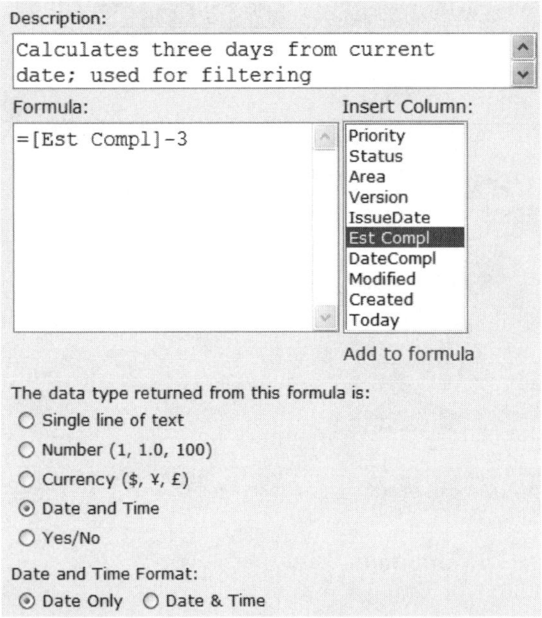

Figure 7-11. *Creating a column to calculate three days prior to the estimated completion date*

■**Note** For more information on TODAY, see the section "Applying Date Functions" in Chapter 5.

Now you can create a filtered view with two criteria: is the estimated completion date on or after today? If so, is ThreeDays on or before today? Figure 7-12 shows the filter criteria for the NextThreeDays view, which will replace Today's Tasks on the home page.

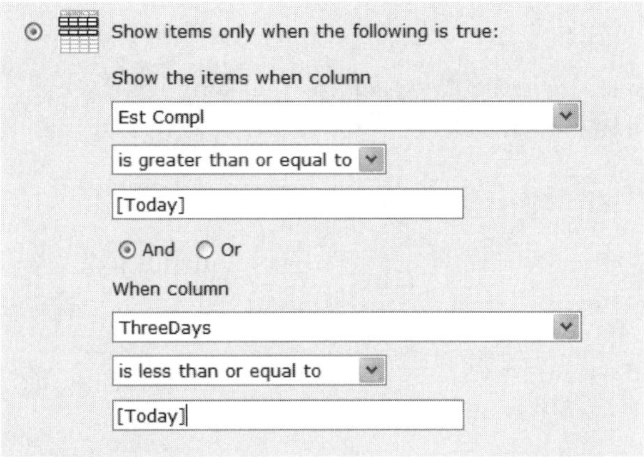

Figure 7-12. *Using the ThreeDays calculation in a filter*

The Issue Tracking site features a customized list (Tasks, in this example) maintained by an individual or a team, and a home page that provides other users with transparent access to the list. You could create similar sites for a wide variety of business uses, including the following:

- Help desk ticket resolution

- Maintenance requests

- Inventory; items on hand

- Expense reimbursement tracking

- Proposals to be reviewed by a team

- Order tracking

Wherever you find a team member or manager who spends way too much time answering questions from an Excel list, think SharePoint.

Business Solutions Using Charts and Tables

The Issue Tracking site is a decent reporting interface. Stakeholders can get the information they need by reviewing the Tasks list web parts. The next step in SharePoint reporting is a dashboard—a web page used to report summary information about one or more aspects of a business. Dashboards are used in every area of organizational life. In this solution, you'll create a Sales Performance dashboard.

The Sales Performance Scenario

Kim works in sales analysis, summarizing information about sales performance by sales person, region, and product line. As in many organizations, the sales people that Kim supports earn a commission, and the commission is designed to provide incentives for meeting specific sales goals. For example, this year, all sales people are guaranteed a 3 percent commission on their sales. In every region that meets or exceed its goal, sales commissions will be increased from 3 percent to 5 percent: a 66 percent increase. The sales force has real skin in the game. Kim knows all the sales people; they call her frequently to inquire about the current totals for regional sales, national sales, and sales by category during special promotions.

Information about sales is entered in an Excel spreadsheet. The data includes the name of the client and the client's current and expected orders. For some clients, there's an agreement that only the client's sales people will have access to their data, so sharing the workbook is not an option. Kim needs to control the workbook, and publish parts of the workbook on a SharePoint site that provides the aggregate information that sales people require. Figure 7-13 shows the first few rows in the Excel worksheet.

	Sales Person	Region	Order N	Order Da	Customer	Category	Order Amou	Contract Recd	Commission
1	Order Summary 2006								
4	BBS	Northwest	33-463405	1/1/2006	Bridal Specialties	Laundry	$39,000.00	Yes	$1,170.00
5	DAR	Southwest	33-458195	1/1/2006	Ora-Olay	Household Cleaners	$12,000.00	Yes	$360.00
6	DAR	Southwest	33-497941	1/1/2006	NoTell	Household Cleaners	$35,500.00	Yes	$1,065.00
7	DAR	Southwest	33-487501	1/1/2006	Williams Services	Household Cleaners	$44,556.00	Yes	$1,336.68
8	DAR	Southwest	33-487499	1/1/2006	Johnson Retail	Household Cleaners	$34,300.00	Yes	$1,029.00
9	EMS	Southeast	33-441880	1/1/2006	Bridal Specialties	Baby Care	$3,500.00	Yes	$105.00
10	EMS	Southeast	33-485139	1/1/2006	Econo-Tel	Laundry	$3,780.00	Yes	$113.40
11	EMS	Southeast	33-448666	1/1/2006	Happy Days Laundry	Laundry	$4,100.00	Yes	$123.00
12	EMS	Southeast	33-484425	1/1/2006	Baby Factory	Household Cleaners	$4,412.00	Yes	$132.36
13	EMS	Southeast	33-520666	1/1/2006	Econo-Tel	Baby Care	$4,412.00	Yes	$132.36
14	KJJ	Northwest	33-502968	1/1/2006	Mommy's Talkin'	Household Cleaners	$34,025.00	Yes	$1,020.75
15	KLR	Great Lakes	33-409786	1/1/2006	7-Eleven	Household Cleaners	$78,840.00	Yes	$2,365.20
16	TRW	Northwest	33-457376	1/1/2006	Johnson Retail	Perfume	$2,000.00	Yes	$60.00
17	TRW	Northwest	33-506530	1/1/2006	NoTell	Household Cleaners	$13,039.60	Yes	$391.19
18	TRW	Northwest	33-506556	1/1/2006	NoTell	Household Cleaners	$22,210.00	Yes	$666.30
19	TRW	Northwest	33-466415	1/1/2006	Econo-Tel	Skin Care	$31,165.00	Yes	$934.95

Figure 7-13. *The Excel worksheet currently used to track sales orders*

The workbook includes a number of other worksheets that Kim uses for analysis. She's most frequently asked about these three sheets:

- *Sales Target*: Sales goals for each of the five sales regions and a chart of current sales against the goals (see Figure 7-14).

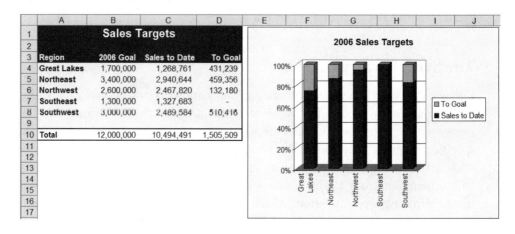

Figure 7-14. *The Sales Target worksheet includes a table and a chart*

- *Category Sales*: PivotChart of sales by category (see Figure 7-15).

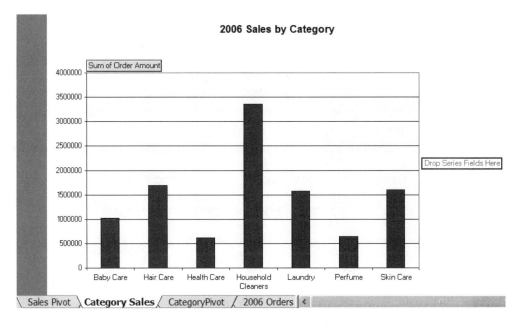

Figure 7-15. *The Category Sales PivotChart report worksheet*

- *Sales Pivot*: A pivot table showing sales by region and product category (see Figure 7-16).

	A	B	C	D	E	F	G
1	**2006 Sales By Category and Sales Region**						
2							
3	Order Amount	Region ▾					
4	**Category** ▾	**Great Lakes**	**Northeast**	**Northwest**	**Southeast**	**Southwest**	**Grand Total**
5	Baby Care	189,731	234,866	228,677	371,944		1,025,218
6	Hair Care	78,140	98,956	77,328	193,983	1,241,015	1,689,422
7	Health Care		609,993				609,993
8	Household Cleaners	384,211	992,071	884,723	410,502	688,637	3,360,142
9	Laundry	119,487	262,921	846,884	66,438	272,771	1,568,501
10	Perfume	91,593	274,544	123,859	76,190	77,415	643,601
11	Skin Care	405,598	467,294	306,349	208,627	209,747	1,597,614
12	**Grand Total**	**1,268,761**	**2,940,644**	**2,467,820**	**1,327,683**	**2,489,584**	**10,494,491**

Figure 7-16. *The Sales Pivot worksheet's pivot table shows sales by region and category.*

The tables and charts on these three worksheets are the objects you'll publish and use to create the Sales Performance dashboard.

Building the SharePoint Sales Performance Dashboard

In this solution, you'll publish the charts and tables from Kim's Excel workbook to create HTML pages, then use the Page Viewer Web Part to display the pages on the sales team's SharePoint site. Sales people already use the site, so Kim won't have to do much marketing of the site to the sales group.

Here are the high-level activities required to build the Sales Performance dashboard:

1. Save the table on the Sales Target worksheet as a web page.

2. Save the chart on the Sales Target worksheet as a web page.

3. Save the PivotChart on the Category Sales worksheet as a web page.

4. Save the PivotTable on the Sales Pivot worksheet as a web page.

5. Create a web part page to display the Category Sales and Sales Pivot HTML pages using the Page Viewer Web Part.

6. Add descriptive text and a heading to the web part page with the Content Editor Web Part.

7. Add all four web pages to the sales teams' SharePoint site using the Page Viewer Web Part.

8. Add a link to the web part page on the home page.

Saving the Selections as Web Pages

You could save the entire Sales Target worksheet as a web page, but the worksheet contains two different but related objects: a table and a chart (see Figure 7-14). The table is the most critical of the four web pages because it summarizes the information that's most frequently requested. Publishing the table and the chart separately provides more layout flexibility when you add the web parts to the SharePoint site.

Note Before you start saving web pages, create a SharePoint library called webpages to store the web pages. (This library shouldn't be listed on the Quick Launch bar.) Also add the webpages library to My Network Places so you can save the web pages directly to the library.

To save the table as a web page, follow these steps:

1. Select the table, then choose File ➤ Save as Web Page from the menu to open the Save As dialog box.

2. Choose the **Selection** option to save only the selected table.

3. Enter a file name (SalesTargetsTable).

4. Click the **Publish** button to open the Publish as Web Page dialog box (see Figure 7-17).

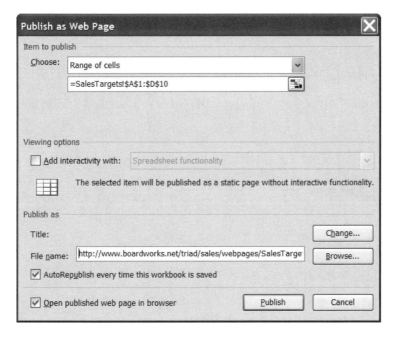

Figure 7-17. *Set publishing options in the Publish as Web Page dialog box.*

5. Leave the Title blank. The Excel table already has a title.

6. Browse and select the webpages folder on the SharePoint site as the file location.

7. Enable the **AutoRepublish every time this workbook is saved** checkbox.

8. Leave the **Open published web page in browser** checkbox enabled.

9. Click the **Publish** button to publish and view the web page.

Follow the same steps to publish the chart, PivotChart, and PivotTable.

■**Note** See Chapter 6 for more information on publishing Excel objects and selections as web pages.

Tips for Publishing PivotTable and PivotChart Reports

When you publish the PivotTable, the labels for the Order Amount and Region fields appear in the HTML file:

Order Amount	Region
Category	**Great Lakes**
Baby Care	189,731
Hair Care	78,140
Health Care	
Household Cleaners	384,211
Laundry	119,487
Perfume	91,593
Skin Care	405,598
Grand Total	**1,268,761**

You can't delete the Order Amount and Region labels; they're part of the pivot table. You can, however, change the font color for these two cells to white. Save the workbook, and Excel will autorepublish the web page without the labels.

That trick won't work with the PivotChart buttons. There's a different and better way to hide the buttons and gain more territory for your chart. Right-click any of the PivotChart field buttons and choose **Hide PivotChart Field Buttons** from the context menu:

Charts that are located on their own chart sheets often present difficulties. The resulting HTML pages often are monster charts, over a thousand pixels wide, that are impossible to use (except, perhaps, as wallpaper). You can solve this problem by changing the chart's location, making it an object on a worksheet. Insert a worksheet, then select the chart sheet and choose Chart ➤ Location from the menu. Choose the **As object in** option and select the new worksheet. You'll need to spend a few minutes adjusting the chart size, font size, and plot area, but when you publish the chart object as a web page, you'll have a usable chart.

Using the Page Viewer Web Part to Display the Charts and Tables

All four web pages are created. It's time to display them on the SharePoint site. Put the Sales Target table and chart on the home page. The other two web parts will be displayed on the separate web part page.

1. Open the SharePoint site in your browser.

2. Choose Modify Shared Page ➤ Add Web Parts ➤ Browse to open the Add Web Parts task pane.

3. Drag a Page Viewer Web Part from the gallery and drop it in the larger zone on the page. Do it again so you have two Page Viewer Web Parts on the page.

4. Launch another instance of Internet Explorer. Navigate to the webpages folder on the SharePoint site.

5. Open the SalesTargetsTable.html web page. Copy the address for the page from the address bar.

6. Switch back to the browser window that's displaying the home page of the Share-Point site.

7. Click the **Open the Tool Pane** link in the first web part.

8. Paste the URL in the Link text box. Test the link.

9. In the Appearance section, change the Frame Style to **None**.

10. Enter a title. Even though the title won't be displayed on the web part (with no frame, there's no title bar), the title is displayed on menus when you're modifying the page.

11. Click **Apply**.

12. Repeat steps 5–11 for the second instance of the Page Viewer Web Part with the SalesTargetChart web page.

13. Click **OK** to close the Add Web Parts task pane.

It's unlikely that both parts will display well on the page without some additional tweaking. Modify the parts' height and width to accommodate the table and chart. Work with the wider part first—the width of the zone is the width of the widest part in the zone. If you tweak the part that needs the most width in pixels first, you won't need to set the width on the other part.

■**Note** For more information on tweaking the Page Viewer Web Part, see the section "Displaying HTML Pages in SharePoint" in Chapter 6.

Creating the Web Part Page

The web part page will be used primarily to display other tables and charts, starting with the Category Sales chart and Sales pivot table. If other charts are added in the future, the page will get too lengthy. Users don't like to scroll more than a couple screens. Therefore, it would be good to choose a format that has at least two zones: one for the Page Viewer Web Parts, and another narrower zone for explanatory text and a future Links list.

1. In SharePoint, choose **Create** from the top menu, then scroll to the bottom of the page and choose **Web Part Page** to go to the page for the New Web Part Page (see Figure 7-18).

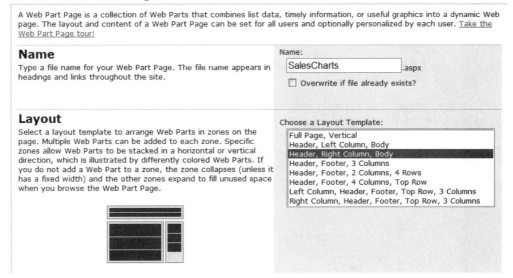

Figure 7-18. *Choose a web part page layout that will accommodate your charts and tables.*

2. Enter a name for the page. The name will be used as the title at the top of the web part page, so you might choose to include spaces in the name.

Tip If you have FrontPage, you can give the web part page a short name, then edit the Title Bar web part in FrontPage. To edit the page in FrontPage, open the webpages library, select the web part page, then click the **Edit in FrontPage** button. Alternatively, display the page in Internet Explorer and choose File ➤ Edit with Microsoft Office FrontPage from the IE menu.

---

3. Choose the **Header, Right Column, Body** web part page layout.

4. Select the webpages document library as the Save Location.

5. Click **Create** to create and open the web part page.

6. Add a Content Editor Web Part in the right column.

7. Click the **Rich Text Editor** link in the Content Editor Web Part. Enter brief descriptive text (for example, "Charts and tables on this page are updated daily"). Click **Apply**.

8. Add two Page Viewer Web Parts to the body, as shown in Figure 7-19.

9. Change the properties on the Page Viewer Web Parts to display the HTML pages for the Category Sales chart and the Sales pivot table.

You can tweak the web part layout and appearance settings as needed.

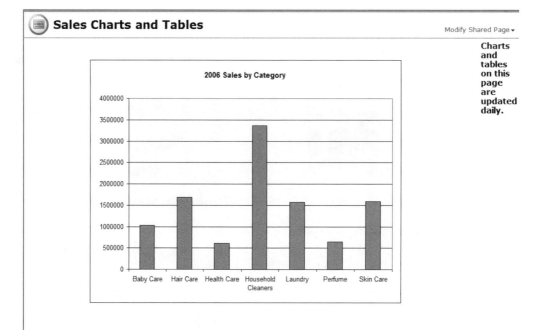

Figure 7-19. *The Sales Performance web part page*

Some Final Tasks

You're missing one navigation tool: a link from the home page to the web part page. If the Links library isn't being used, you can add a single link, turn off the toolbar, and choose **None** as the frame style to create the link. Alternatively, you can use a Content Editor Web Part and add a hyperlink to the web part page. Figure 7-20 shows the new home page for the sales team.

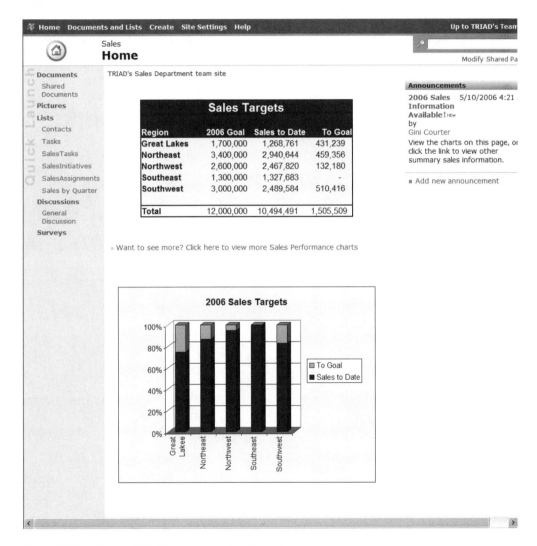

Figure 7-20. *The modified home page for the sales team*

Maintaining the charts and tables is easy. Each time Kim saves the Excel workbook, all four HTML pages are automatically republished. Kim will need to find a new reason to stay in touch with the sales staff.

Summary

You don't need an ASP.NET developer to build web-based reporting and dashboard solutions. You can use Excel worksheets and SharePoint's custom lists, views, and web parts right out of the box to address business challenges. In the next three chapters, we'll show you some customizing tools and special add-ins to extend the power of Excel and SharePoint integration.

■ ■ ■

CHAPTER 8

Using Excel to Query SharePoint

With the Excel Web Query feature (available in Excel 2002 and 2003), you can retrieve data from any table on an intranet or the Internet, including tables and lists in SharePoint. Windows SharePoint Services back-end lists (for example, the Site Collection users list) don't include tools to export to Excel. If your WSS sites aren't part of an SPS solution, a number of third-party add-ins, from shareware apps to web parts bundled as expensive "suites," return or display data from SharePoint's back-end lists.

Other third-party apps capture and archive the current state of site lists. But you don't need add-ins to retrieve SharePoint list data. An Excel web query is just the implement you need to harvest the banquet of data available on a SharePoint site, even the data that's stored in the less accessible back-end lists. You can retrieve SharePoint information as static data, or create a refreshable web query.

Creating a Static Query

Create a static query when you want to capture a snapshot of the current state of a list or library on your SharePoint site. For example, at the end of each month you might want to capture the modified date for the documents in a library so you can have aged documents updated by the appropriate members of your team. With Excel, you can create a static web query that includes the hyperlinks to the library documents.

Here's another scenario: you might want to document progress on uploading documents before launching a site. This query might be more useful with the hyperlinks removed.

To create a static web query of a library, follow these steps:

1. Open the library (or list) in your browser.

2. Select the data you want to copy to Excel.

3. Choose Edit ➤ Copy from the Internet Explorer menu.

4. Open Excel.

5. Select a cell and paste the data.

6. Before you deselect the pasted range, click the **Paste Options** button to open the options menu (see Figure 8-1).

Figure 8-1. *Choose an option to retain or remove hyperlinks.*

7. To create a static web query with hyperlinks, choose **Keep Source Formatting** (see Figure 8-2).

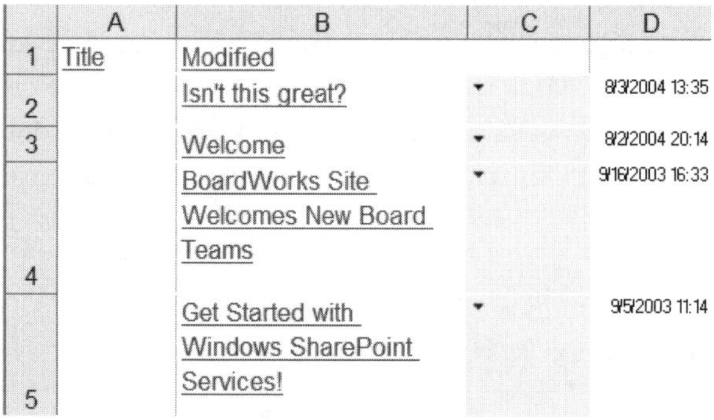

	A	B	C	D
1	Title	Modified		
2		Isn't this great?	▼	8/3/2004 13:35
3		Welcome	▼	8/2/2004 20:14
4		BoardWorks Site Welcomes New Board Teams	▼	9/16/2003 16:33
5		Get Started with Windows SharePoint Services!	▼	9/5/2003 11:14

Figure 8-2. *A static web query, including hyperlinks back to the SharePoint site*

8. To remove the hyperlinks, choose **Match Destination Formatting** (see Figure 8-3).

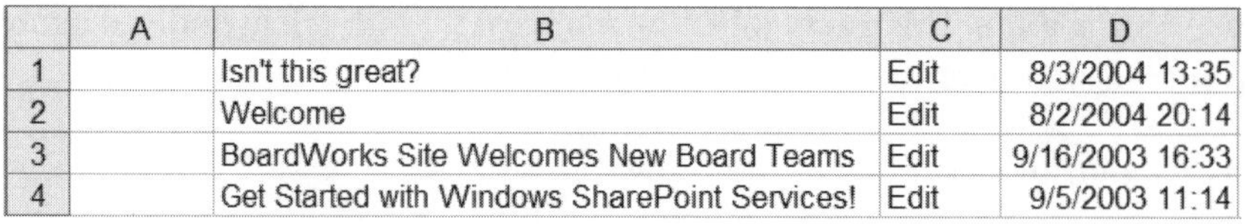

	A	B	C	D
1		Isn't this great?	Edit	8/3/2004 13:35
2		Welcome	Edit	8/2/2004 20:14
3		BoardWorks Site Welcomes New Board Teams	Edit	9/16/2003 16:33
4		Get Started with Windows SharePoint Services!	Edit	9/5/2003 11:14

Figure 8-3. *The same static web query with the hyperlinks removed*

■**Note** In Figure 8-3, column A is empty. The list view included a column for attachments, which the web query can't return. To avoid empty columns, create a view that only includes the information you want in the query. For more information on creating views, see Chapter 4.

---

9. Adjust column widths as necessary.

We'll discuss the third option on the options menu, **Create Refreshable Web Query**, in the next section.

Creating a Refreshable Web Query

In a refreshable web query, the data is updated either automatically or when you manually refresh the query. Refreshable web queries can return three different kinds of data, all of which are found in SharePoint: a single table (such as a library or list), multiple tables (from a page with multiple web parts), or formatted or plain text.

To create a refreshable web query from SharePoint, follow these steps:

1. Open the SharePoint library (or list) in your browser.

2. Select the data you want to query in Excel.

3. Choose Edit ➤ Copy from the Internet Explorer menu.

4. Open Excel.

5. Select a cell and paste the data.

6. Before you deselect the pasted range, click the **Paste Options** button to open the options menu.

7. Choose **Create Refreshable Web Query** to open the New Web Query dialog box (see Figure 8-4).

Figure 8-4. *Use the New Web Query dialog box to identify the data you want to return to Excel.*

8. Move the pointer to the yellow table-selection icon at the upper left corner of the data table you want to import. A border appears around the data that will be imported. Click the icon to select the data (see Figure 8-5). The icon changes to a green check mark. You can select multiple ranges for a single query. For more control over positioning, create multiple queries in one worksheet.

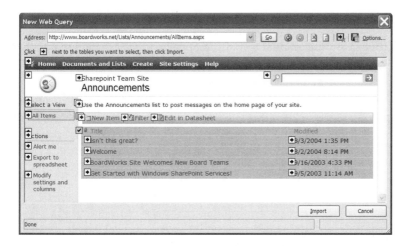

Figure 8-5. *Click the icon to select the range you wish to import.*

9. Click **Import** to open the Import Data dialog box.

10. Choose a location for the query results and click **OK** to create the query and return the data to Excel.

The External Data toolbar appears when a web query is open in Excel (see Figure 8-6).

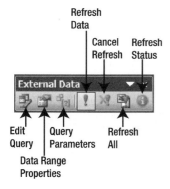

Figure 8-6. *Use the External Data toolbar to set query options.*

■**Tip** If you prefer, you can choose Data ➤ Import External Data ➤ New Web Query to open the New Web Query dialog box directly, then navigate to the page using the address bar at the top of the dialog box.

Refreshing Query Data

You can refresh the query data manually or automatically. To refresh data manually, select any cell in the refreshable query results and click the **Refresh Data** button on the External Data toolbar. If the Refresh Data dialog box opens, click **OK**.

To have your query update automatically, click the **Data Range Properties** button on the External Data toolbar to open the External Data Range Properties dialog box (see Figure 8-7).

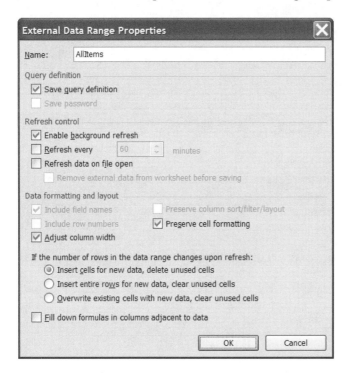

Figure 8-7. *Set automatic refresh in the External Data Range Properties dialog box.*

- In the "Refresh control" section of the dialog box, leave the default **Enable background refresh** setting if you want to be able to work in Excel while the query data is being refreshed.

- To have Excel automatically refresh the data, enable the **Refresh every** checkbox and set the refresh frequency using the spin box "minutes" control.

- If your query returns a large data set, you can reduce the file size by setting the query refresh options. Have Excel refresh the query data when you open the file, then discard the data when you save the workbook. In the External Data Range Properties dialog box, enable the **Refresh data on file open** checkbox. Enable the **Remove external data from worksheet before saving** checkbox to discard the query results when you save the workbook.

You can choose more than one refresh option. For example, you might choose all three options to refresh the query when you open the workbook, then background refresh every 30 minutes while you have the file open. When you're finished setting the refresh options, click **OK** to apply the options to the web query.

Caution Do not uncheck the **Save query definition** checkbox. You won't lose the data, but you'll lose the query definition, so it will no longer be refreshable.

Modifying a Web Query

You can change the data your query returns by editing the query. You can modify the following:

- The web page used by the query

- The data table or text returned by the query

- The type of formatting: rich text, HTML, or none

To edit the query, select any cell within the data returned by the query, then click the **Edit Query** button on the External Data toolbar to open the Edit Web Query dialog box, which looks a lot like the New Web Query dialog box. To change the web page or data returned by the query, simply choose a different page or data, as you did when you created the query.

Setting Formatting Options

To change formatting, click the **Options** button in the upper right corner of the Edit Web Query dialog box to open the Web Query Options dialog box (see Figure 8-8).

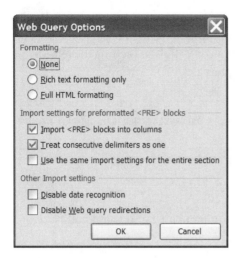

Figure 8-8. *Choose formatting options in the Web Query Options dialog box.*

The default formatting is **None**. Some HTML formatting, such as merged cells, creates problems for data analysis in Excel. If you want to use the query results in pivot tables or charts, choose the **None** option. Choose **Rich text formatting only** or **Full HTML formatting** if you don't need to analyze the data and want to retain the formatting from the web site.

These formatting options are generic options for use with web pages. When you query a list from a SharePoint site, don't bother to change formatting. Your query doesn't actually retrieve the text from the web site. SharePoint list pages include a custom HTML tag that redirects the query to the list's data source, so you're retrieving XML data in plain text, directly from SharePoint's database.

Preserving Formatting Applied in Excel

After you run the query for the first time, you'll want to apply some formatting. However, the default settings discard formatting applied to the cells included in the query results when the query is refreshed. Column formatting—for example, column widths—is retained. To keep the formatting you've applied to cells so you don't need to reapply formatting every time the query refreshes, enable the **Preserve cell formatting** checkbox in the "Data formatting and layout" section of the External Data Range Properties dialog box.

Setting Date Recognition Options

With the default settings, Excel automatically interprets dates in the query results and presents them in short form. If you have non-date text entries such as 11-12, and you don't want Excel to convert them to November 12, check the **Disable date recognition** checkbox.

Setting Redirection Options

As noted earlier, when you query a SharePoint list, SharePoint automatically redirects the query to the data source. When the query shown in Figure 8-5 runs with redirection enabled (the default setting), it returns the data set in Figure 8-9 to Excel.

	A	B	C
1	Attachments	Title	Modified
2	FALSE	Isn't this great?	8/3/2004
3	FALSE	Welcome	8/2/2004
4	FALSE	BoardWorks Site Welcomes New Board Teams	9/16/2003
5	FALSE	Get Started with Windows SharePoint Services!	9/5/2003

Figure 8-9. *Query results from SharePoint with redirection enabled*

With redirection disabled, the query can't be redirected to the SharePoint data source for the list. Instead, the query returns data directly from the page, as shown in Figure 8-10.

	A	B	C	D
1		Title		Modified
2		Isn't this great?		8/3/2004 1:35 PM
3		Welcome		8/2/2004 8:14 PM
4		BoardWorks Site Welcomes New Board Teams		9/16/2003 4:33 PM
5		Get Started with Windows SharePoint Services!		9/5/2003 11:14 AM

Figure 8-10. *Query results from SharePoint with redirection disabled*

After you've edited the query, Excel automatically refreshes the query using the new options and settings.

REDIRECTING WEB QUERIES ON YOUR SHAREPOINT SITE

If you include web pages of data on your SharePoint site that weren't created using SharePoint web parts, you can build redirection into your pages and tables the same way SharePoint does. There are two steps to redirection:

1. In the opening HTML tag of your web page, include the following Microsoft Office namespace declaration:

```
<HTML xmlns:o="urn:schemas-microsoft-com:office:office">
```

2. Add the `WebQuerySourceHRef` attribute to the opening tag of each table you want to redirect (`http://datasource` is the URL for your data source):

```
<TABLE ... o:WebQuerySourceHRef="http://datasource">
```

Saving the Query

If you want to use the web query elsewhere in your workbook, you can copy and paste the query range. To save the query for future use in other workbooks, follow these steps while creating the query:

1. With the New Web Query dialog box open, click the **Options** button and set any options you want to save as part of the query.

2. Click the **Save Query** button (on the left of the **Options** button) to open the Save Query dialog box.

Excel automatically selects the Queries folder for the file location.

3. Enter a file name for the query. Click **Save** to save the query and return to the New Web Query dialog box.

To use the query in another Excel workbook, choose Data ➤ Import External Data ➤ Import Data to open the Select Data Source dialog box. Choose the query and click **Open**. Choose a location in the Import Data dialog box and click **OK** to add the query to the workbook.

Using Web Queries to Manage SharePoint Site Users

Excel is a useful management tool for SharePoint sites, both internal and external. The management of externally hosted SharePoint sites presents its own challenges. If you have a number of SharePoint sites that other users administer, it's easy to lose track of the number of users on each site. Administrators might forget to remove users when they no longer need access to the site. When a contractor or employee leaves and must be removed from the externally hosted sites, you must remove that person from each site, as well as from the site collection.

You can use Excel's refreshable web query feature to monitor a collection of up to 255 sites in a single workbook. The Excel worksheet shown in Figure 8-11 retrieves user information from a Windows SharePoint Services web site. The worksheet also includes a hyperlink to the web site and a calculation showing the total number of users.

	A	B	C	D	E
1	Team Site:	**Human Resources**			
2	URL:	http://www.boardworks.net/triad/HR/default.aspx			
3	Total Users:	10			
4					
5		**Users**	**User Name**	**Site Groups**	
6		Aidan W. Holm	APPTIX\aholm16	Contributor	
7		Annette Marquis	APPTIX\amarquis6	Administrator	
8		Charlotte Cowtan	APPTIX\ccowtan6	Web Designer	
9		Clifton Vaughn	APPTIX\cvaughn	Reader	
10		D. Keith Holm	APPTIX\dkholm	Contributor	
11		Gini Courter	APPTIX\gcourter74	Administrator	
12		Helio Fred Garcia	APPTIX\hfgarcia	Reader	
13		Jagan Annadi	APPTIX\jannadi	Reader	
14		Leonardo Brito	APPTIX\lbrito	Contributor	
15		Robb Morse	APPTIX\rmorse	Contributor	
16					
17					
18					
19					
20					

Figure 8-11. *Site management workbook for the human resources web site*

You can't create a web query to a page you don't have permission to view, so you must be an administrator or have permission to manage the SharePoint web sites that you need to add to the workbook. Follow these steps to create an Excel worksheet that uses a refreshable web query to report the users on a SharePoint site:

1. Navigate to your Windows SharePoint site's home page.

2. Click the **Site Settings** link on the top navigation bar to open the Site Settings page. (If there is no Site Settings link, you don't have permission to manage the site.)

3. In the Administration section of the Site Settings page, click the **Manage users** link (see Figure 8-12).

Human Resources
Site Settings

Use the links on this page to manage site settings and update your personal information on this Microsoft Windows SharePoint Services 2.0 (6.0.2.6568) site.

Administration

Use the links in this section to add or remove users, add or remove sites, or navigate to other site administration features.

   ▫ Manage users
   ▫ Manage sites and workspaces
   ▫ Configure Site and Workspace Creation
   ▫ Go to Site Administration

Figure 8-12. *The Administration section of the Site Settings page*

4. Select the table of users, user names, and site groups. (Select with the mouse; don't just click the **Select All** checkbox.)

5. Choose Edit ➤ Copy from Internet Explorer menu.

6. In Excel, open a new workbook. Create headings for the Team Site, URL, and Total Users, as shown in Figure 8-11.

7. Paste the SharePoint data below the headings in column A.

▓**Note** The selected table on the Manage Users page has a checkbox in the first column, so column A of the Excel workbook will be blank. The three columns of data will be returned to columns B, C, and D.

---

8. Click the **Paste Options** button and choose **Create Refreshable Web Query** to open the New Web Query dialog box.

9. Choose the table selection icon just below the **Select All** checkbox to select the user table (see Figure 8-13).

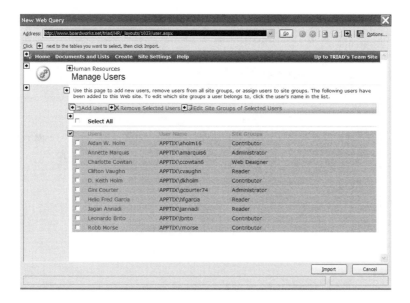

Figure 8-13. *Select the user table using the table selection icon.*

10. Click the **Option** button and select **None** in the Formatting section of the Web Query Options dialog box. Click **OK** to return to the New Web Query dialog box.

11. Click **Import** to return the user data to Excel.

12. Enter the team's name in cell B1.

■**Note** You can link from Excel to any page in the SharePoint site. Choose the page you want to link to (usually either the Manage Users page or the site's home page) to use as a hyperlink in the Excel worksheet.

---

13. Switch to the SharePoint site and navigate to the page you want to link to from the Excel worksheet. Select the URL in the IE address bar, then right-click and choose **Copy** from the context menu.

14. Switch to Excel and select cell B2.

15. Choose Insert ➤ Hyperlink from the Excel menu, or hold Ctrl and press K to open the Insert Hyperlink dialog box. Paste the URL into the Address text box (it will be copied to the Text to Display text box) and click **OK** to insert the URL as a hyperlink (see Figure 8-14).

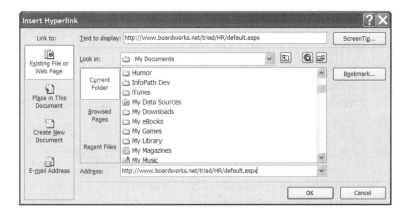

Figure 8-14. *Format the URL as a hyperlink for easy access to the site.*

16. In cell B3, create a formula to count the users or user names in column B or C. The names are text, not numbers, so use the COUNTA function. For example, in our worksheet, the names returned by the query start in cell C6, so the formula is =COUNTA(C6:C65536).

17. Double-click the worksheet tab and name the sheet the same as the site name (in cell B1).

18. Adjust column widths to accommodate the query results. Apply formatting, if you wish, to the column headings in the query.

19. Right-click any cell in the query results and choose **Data Range Properties** from the context menu to open the External Data Range Properties dialog box.

20. Enable the **Preserve cell formatting** checkbox in the "Data formatting and layout" section. Click **OK**.

21. Save the workbook.

With the default settings, you must manually refresh the user list, so you can examine the current user count, then refresh the query to see if there have been any changes. Click the **Refresh Data** button on the External Data toolbar, or right-click anywhere in the list and choose **Refresh Data** from the context menu. If you prefer, you can set the refresh options so the query will update automatically.

Now, make a copy of this worksheet for each SharePoint site you manage. Modify the query and heading data for each site's worksheet, and give the worksheet the same name as the site name in B1. If you wish, you can create a summary worksheet that includes the heading information from each worksheet, so you can view all the sites and their user counts on one sheet.

When you need to remove a user from one or more SharePoint sites, follow these steps to find every site of which the user is a member:

1. Open the Excel workbook. Click in the results for one of the queries.

2. Click the **Refresh All** button on the External Data toolbar to update all queries. You can watch the refresh progress at the left end of the status bar.

3. When all queries are updated, choose Edit ➤ Find on the menu, or press Ctrl+F to open the Find and Replace dialog box (see Figure 8-15).

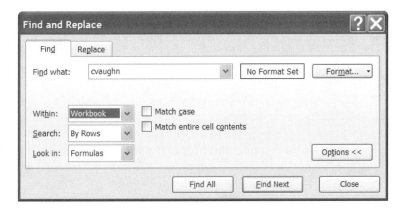

Figure 8-15. *Use the Find and Replace dialog box to locfate the sites for the specified user.*

4. Enter the user name in the "Find what" text box.

5. Click the **Options** button.

6. Choose **Workbook** from the Within drop-down list.

7. Click **Find All** to return the list of all sites that include this user.

The results in the Find All dialog box are links, so you can click any link to go to the site worksheet. Click the hyperlink at the top of the worksheet to go to the SharePoint site.

Summary

In this chapter, we put Excel's Web Query feature—created for use with HTML pages—to work returning XML data from SharePoint. If you're willing to color outside the lines just a bit, web queries can be an invaluable tool for capturing SharePoint data for analysis or presentation.

CHAPTER 9

■■■

Using SharePoint's Office Web Parts

In earlier chapters, we explored three ways to make Excel data available to SharePoint users:

- In Chapter 1, we discussed uploading a workbook to a SharePoint document library and letting users open it directly in Excel. Although this certainly works, it means that worksheet data is one step removed from the SharePoint site—users do their work in Excel and then resave to the SharePoint site.

- In Chapter 2, we showed you how to publish an Excel list to SharePoint. Although dynamically linked Excel lists are extremely useful with spreadsheets filled with text data, they're more challenging if you need to include calculations. As you saw in Chapter 5, it's possible to add calculations to a SharePoint list, but the process isn't as flexible or as intuitive as in Excel.

- In Chapter 6, we demonstrated how to save a worksheet as a web page and upload to a SharePoint site. This gives users access to Excel data but restricts them from editing. It presents a static view of the data.

If none of these options give you exactly what you need, you might want to explore adding an Office web part to a SharePoint page. The Office web parts, which include Office Spreadsheet, Office Datasheet, Office PivotTable, Office PivotChart, and Office PivotView Web Parts, give you Excel functionality right on a SharePoint page. You can use the Office web parts to create dynamic dashboards, such as the one shown in Figure 9-1, based on data housed in one of three places:

- In an existing SharePoint list

- In an external data source, such as a SQL Server or Access database

- Entered directly into the Spreadsheet Web Part

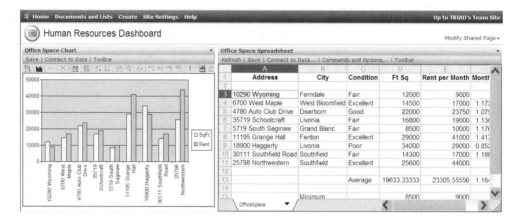

Figure 9-1. *A business dashboard can put critical information at the fingertips of the people who need it. Data entered into the spreadsheet is immediately reflected in the adjacent chart.*

See "Connecting Web Parts to Data" later in this chapter for more about connecting to an existing SharePoint list and to external data sources.

In this chapter, we'll take at look at each of the Office web parts, how to use them, how to connect them to external data, and how to modify them.

■**Note** The Office 2003 web parts add-in, which includes the Office web parts discussed in this chapter, isn't installed with the typical installation of Microsoft SharePoint. To make the web parts available, your server administrator can download and install Microsoft Office Web Parts and Components from the Microsoft Download Center (http://www.microsoft.com/downloads). Search for STSTPKPL.EXE.

Using the Office Spreadsheet Web Part

An Office Spreadsheet Web Part, such as the one shown in Figure 9-2, is the closest thing to Excel you can get without opening Excel itself. Users with Contributor rights can enter data into multiple worksheets, add formulas, format worksheets, and sort and filter data. If they want to work with the data offline, users can export the workbook to Excel.

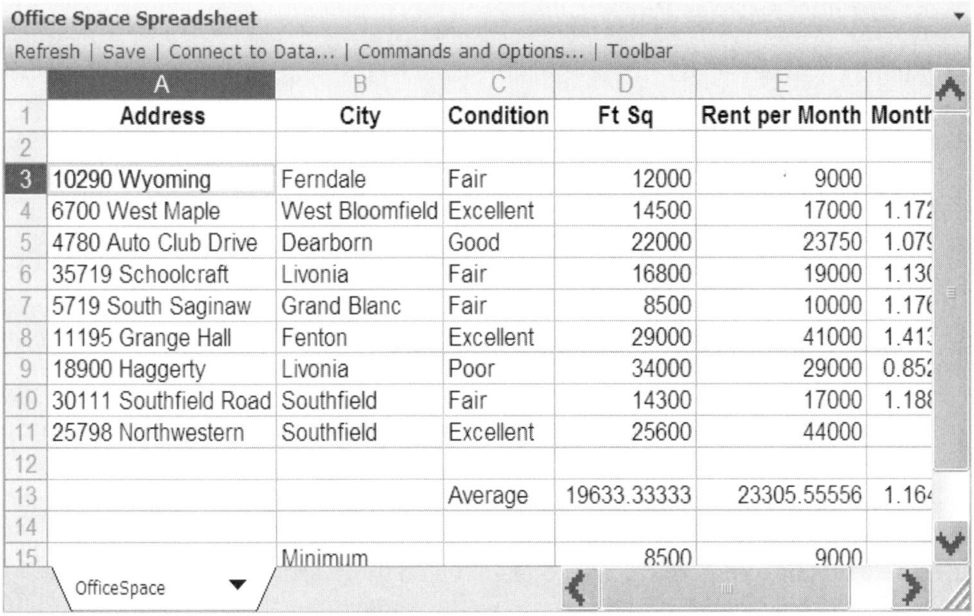

Figure 9-2. *An Office Spreadsheet Web Part gives you Excel-like functionality right in SharePoint.*

An Office Spreadsheet Web Part has some limitations. For example, you cannot use Fill to copy formulas, and there is no formula bar. However, it's so similar to Excel that most Excel users can learn to use it without too much difficulty. It's an easy way to have multiple people entering data into a central worksheet where everyone can access and work with it without having to launch Excel.

Web parts, as described in Chapter 1, are components designed to display specific information such as an announcements list, a calendar, a document library, or in this case, a spreadsheet. A *web part page* is a web page that contains preestablished zones where web parts can be positioned. You can add the Office Spreadsheet Web Part to the home page or to any other web page on a SharePoint Portal or in a WSS site. However, some features are restricted if you place the Office web parts on a page that isn't specifically a web part page.

Let's first look at creating a web part page; then we'll add an Office Spreadsheet Web Part to the page.

Creating a Web Part Page

A web part page is one of the elements available on the Create page, along with libraries, lists, custom lists, discussion boards, surveys, and web pages. To access the Create page, follow these steps:

1. Click **Create** on the top navigation bar on a WSS site or on an SPS page.

2. Click **Manage Content** in the Actions menu.

3. Click **Create**. On the Create page, under Web Pages, click **Web Part Page**. This opens a new web part page.

From here, you enter a name for the page and select a layout template. Selecting the right layout template can be a bit tricky. Each of the rectangles in the template preview represents a web part zone. If you plan to add only one Spreadsheet Web Part to the page, then Full Page, Vertical might be perfect for you. It has only one zone. You can put more than one web part in a zone depending on the design of the zone. In other words, you can place a web part in a column above another web part in a single zone, as in the Full Page, Vertical web part page. However, if you want to place two web parts side by side, you need to start with a template that has either side-by-side zones or that has rows, which allow for multiple web parts. Header, Footer, 2 Columns, 4 Rows, shown in Figure 9-3, is an example of a template that allows for side-by-side web parts.

Figure 9-3. *Using this web part page template—Header, Footer, 2 Columns, 4 Rows—you can add multiple web parts side by side and in each of the other identified zones.*

Web parts expand to fill unused space on the page, so too many web part zones is generally less of a problem than not enough. You cannot add web part zones that don't already exist in the template, so if you decide you need to position a web part where no zone is available, you might need to re-create the entire page to choose a different template.

Follow these steps to create a web part page:

1. Scroll to the bottom of the Create page and under Web Pages, click **Web Part Page**.

2. Enter a name for the web part page. Because this is the actual file name, it is best, but not required, to create a short name with no spaces.

3. Choose a layout template from the available templates. Pick a layout that's close to what you envision you want your page to look like when you're finished.

4. Select the document library where you want to save the web page in the Save Location.

5. Click **Create**. SharePoint creates the page and takes you to the design view of the page, which displays the available zones, as shown earlier in Figure 9-3.

Adding the Office Spreadsheet Web Part to a Page

Now that you have a web part page, you can add an Office Spreadsheet Web Part, or any other type of available web part to the page. To add the Office Spreadsheet Web Part, follow these steps:

1. From the upper right-hand corner of the page, click Modify Shared Page ➤ Add Web Parts ➤ Browse. This opens the Add Web Parts task pane.

2. You can find the Office Spreadsheet Web Part in the Virtual Server Gallery. Click **Virtual Server Gallery** to display the list of available web parts.

3. Point to and drag the Office Spreadsheet Web Part to one of the available web part zones on the page. When you drag the web part into a zone, a blue line appears to indicate where the top or the left side of the web part will line up. Drop the web part where you want it to appear. Figure 9-4 shows an Office Spreadsheet Web Part in the left zone of a Header, Footer, 2 Columns, 4 Rows template.

Figure 9-4. *Drag the Office Spreadsheet Web Part from the gallery and drop it in a zone on the web part page.*

If you decide you don't like where the web part ended up, you can move it to another zone or position within a zone. Point to the title bar of the web part, and when the pointer changes to a four-headed arrow, click and drag the web part to another location.

■**Note** In the case of web part pages, Header and Footer don't have the conventional significance, such as a location where page numbering or date and time appear on a hard copy of an Excel worksheet. On a web part page, the terms merely refer to zones at the top and bottom of the page. The Header and Footer zones span the width of a web part page, so use them for web parts that are too wide to display in the left, center, and right zones.

Although you can start adding content to an Office Spreadsheet Web Part while the page is still in design view, it's a good practice to switch out of design view before you start working with it. First, click the **Close** button (×) on the Add Web Parts task pane to close the task pane. You're prompted to save or discard the changes to the web page. Click **OK** to save them. When the page refreshes, you're still in design view, but your changes are saved. Now, click **Modify Shared Page** at the top right of the page again. Then, click **Design this Page** to toggle it off (it should have a check mark in front of it when you're in design view). When the page refreshes, you should be in the normal view of the page. You'll know it because you can no longer see the zones.

■**Note** When you click **Modify Shared Page**, if you find that **Design this Page** is dimmed, double-check to make sure that the Add Web Parts or any other task panes are closed. This needs to happen in order to generate the prompt to save or discard changes before you can switch out of design view.

Working with the Office Spreadsheet Web Part

Entering data into an Office Spreadsheet Web Part isn't much different than entering data into an Excel worksheet. Click in the first cell in which you want to enter something, and start typing. You can use the tab, arrow, Home, and End keys to navigate around the sheet just like in Excel. By the way, there are 262,144 rows and 18,278 columns (A to ZZZ) in an Office Spreadsheet Web Part's sheet, as compared to Excel's paltry 65,536 rows and 256 columns (A to IV). This web part should handle most of your everyday data needs!

Just like in an Excel workbook, each web part can contain multiple worksheets. Click the sheet tab to switch to another sheet (see "Setting Worksheet and Workbook Options" later in this chapter to see how to add, delete, and rearrange sheets).

To access common tools such as Undo, Cut, Copy, and Paste, click the **Toolbar** button on the toolstrip that's visible at the top of the web part. The **Toolbar** button toggles a modified version of Excel's Standard toolbar. Table 9-1 identifies the buttons on the toolbar. You'll be familiar with many of their Excel counterparts.

Table 9-1. *The Office Spreadsheet Web Part Toolbar*

Button Name	Description
About	Contains licensing information about Microsoft Office Web Components.
Undo	Negates the last action taken. Can be used multiple times.
Cut, Copy, and Paste	Moves and copies contents of cells or groups of cells.
AutoSum	Enters a SUM formula in the active cell for values above or to the left.
Sort Ascending	Sorts the column that contains that active cell in A–Z or 1–9 order. Click the down arrow on the button to select another column to sort by.
Sort Descending	Sorts the column that contains that active cell in Z–A or 9–1 order. Click the down arrow on the button to select another column to sort by.
AutoFilter	Activates **AutoFilter** buttons to filter data in the columns.
Refresh All	If the workbook is connected to another data source, this retrieves the current data (see "Connecting Web Parts to Data" later in this chapter).
Export to Microsoft Office Excel	Exports the workbook to Microsoft Excel.
Commands and Options	Opens the Commands and Options dialog box for formatting, modifying formulas, searching, and setting sheet options.
Help	Opens Microsoft Office 2003 Spreadsheet Component Help.

In addition to entering data directly into an Office Spreadsheet Web Part, you can connect to existing data sources. See "Connecting Web Parts to Data" later in this chapter for information about how to access existing data sources.

Formatting Text, Dates, and Numbers

To make formatting changes to the cells in an Office Spreadsheet Web Part, click the **Commands and Options** button on the toolstrip or on the toolbar to open the Commands and Options dialog box. On the Format tab, you can change text formatting, including bold, italics, underline, horizontal and vertical text alignment in a cell, font color, font, font size, number formats, fill color, merge and unmerge cells, border color, border style, border weight, borders, and text direction (for languages that read left to right or right to left).

You can leave the Commands and Options dialog box as you select and format different cells, so it makes sense to do all your formatting at one time. Select the cell or group of cells you want to format, then choose the appropriate feature on the Format tab.

Entering Formulas

Office Spreadsheet Web Parts can contain formulas as simple as the sum of two cells, and as complex as you want to make them. You can enter formulas directly into cells by entering an = sign and then constructing the formula just as you would in Excel. There's no formula bar in the web part, so to see the formula in a cell, double-click it or open the Commands and Options dialog box and click the Formula tab. This shows the formula and the results of the formula in the active cell.

Except for SUM, which is available by clicking the **AutoSum** button on the toolbar, there is no assistance, such as the Insert Function dialog box in Excel, for constructing formulas with functions. You must enter the formula that includes the function by typing it in the proper syntax. However, there's an extensive help file that lists all the available functions, their proper syntax, and examples. Click the **Help** button on the toolbar, then double-click **Working with Functions** to access the list of available functions by category.

You can use the Formula tab of the Commands and Options dialog box to name cells for easier reference in formulas. To name a cell or range of cells, select the cell or range you want to name, then enter a name in the Name text box on the Formula tab. Use these guidelines to name cells:

- The first character of a name must be a letter or an underscore character.

- Names can contain letters, numbers, periods, and underscore characters.

- Names cannot contain spaces. Use underscores (Net_Sales) or camel case (NetSales) to distinguish words in the name.

- Names are not case sensitive: BUDGET is the same as Budget.

After you name the cells, you can create a formula such as `=Budget-Actual` rather than the more obtuse `=B3-B4`.

Dates and times are treated as numbers in an Office Spreadsheet Web Part. However, to use a date or time in a formula, you must put it in quotation marks to designate it as text. For example, the following formula results in –14:

```
="12/1/2006"-"12/15/2006"
```

However, the following formula results in 0.00558325 because each / is treated as a division symbol:

```
=12/1/2006-12/15/2006
```

If you create a formula that contains cells formatted as dates, be sure the cell that contains the formula is formatted as General.

Searching for Data

As we mentioned earlier, the capacity of an Office Spreadsheet Web Part is much larger than the capacity of an Excel worksheet. You can use the Sheet tab of the Commands and Options dialog box to search for specific cell content. Enter a search term in the Find What text box and click **Find Next** to search for the first occurrence of the term you entered. Click **Find Next** again to continue to the next occurrence.

If you want to limit the search to occurrences that use the same case, check the **Match case** checkbox. To limit to occurrences that match the entire search term, enable **Entire cell only**. For example, if the search term you enter is **Sales**, and you enable the **Entire cell only** checkbox, a cell that contains Net Sales will not be found.

Setting Worksheet and Workbook Options

On the Sheet tab of the Commands and Options dialog box, you can turn off the display of row and column headers and gridlines in a spreadsheet. You can also change the display of the worksheet from left to right, to right to left if you're working in a right-to-left oriented language.

On the Workbook tab of the Commands and Options dialog box, shown in Figure 9-5, you can change the following options that affect the entire workbook.

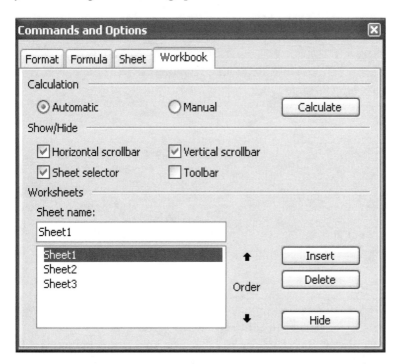

Figure 9-5. *Change workbook options on the Workbook tab.*

- *Calculation*: Just as in Excel, workbooks are set to calculate automatically. However, if you have a large, formula-heavy workbook, you might find that automatic calculation is slowing down data entry. If that's the case, you can switch to manual calculation. To switch to manual, click **Manual**. When you're ready to calculate, click the **Calculate** button and all formulas in the workbook are calculated.

■**Caution** Setting a workbook to calculate manually can be a dangerous practice, especially in a workbook where revisions are made to data that has already been calculated. Users might not realize that formula results haven't been updated, and thereby might use inaccurate results. If you're going to set a workbook to calculate manually, it's best to do it in workbooks where new data is being entered.

- *Show/Hide*: Select the appropriate checkbox to show or hide the vertical scrollbar, the horizontal scrollbar, sheet tabs, and the toolbar.

- *Worksheets*: To rename a worksheet, select the sheet from the Worksheets list, then select the sheet name in the "Sheet name" text box and overwrite it with a new name. You can insert worksheets into an Office Spreadsheet Web Part by clicking the **Insert** button. The sheet is inserted above the sheet you've selected in the Worksheets list.

To delete a sheet, select it from the Worksheets list and click the **Delete** button. Click **Yes** to verify that you want to delete the sheet.

To change the order of worksheets in a workbook, select the sheet you want to move and click the up and down arrow buttons to reposition the sheet.

To hide a worksheet in a workbook, select the sheet and click the **Hide** button. This is especially useful if you have a sheet in a workbook that contains data you're using for lookup lists, or to support formulas that you don't want users to change. The sheet still appears in the list of worksheets, but it's designated as hidden. Select the sheet again and click the **Unhide** button to unhide it.

Printing a Worksheet

It's not easy to say you're out of luck if you want to print a worksheet, but that's the truth. You can print the web page that contains the worksheet, but you cannot print the contents of the web part. If you need to do that, export the workbook to Excel (click the **Export to Excel** button on the toolbar) and print it from there. If a worksheet is too big (too many columns or rows) to fit in Excel, you'll first have to divide it up into multiple worksheets before you export it.

Working with the Office PivotTable Web Parts

As mentioned at the beginning of the chapter, the Office web parts come in several varieties: Office Spreadsheet, Office Datasheet, Office PivotTable, Office PivotChart, and Office PivotView. You've already seen how the Office Spreadsheet Web Part operates. Now we'll take a look at the other four Office web parts. The Office Datasheet, PivotTable and PivotChart Web Parts are fundamentally all the same thing. They each offer a different view of the data but are, in essence, interchangeable with one another. The Office PivotView Web Part combines them all by letting you switch between the other three data views.

If you're experienced with Excel PivotTables, you'll be happy to know that all the functionality that you find in Excel PivotTables and PivotCharts is available in the PivotTable and PivotChart Web Parts, although finding the functionality might be challenging. If you're new to PivotTables, we recommend you learn to use them in Excel before attempting to work with them here in SharePoint. It's important for you to have at least a basic understanding of them to understand their role in SharePoint.

PivotTables make it possible to take large amounts of data and display it, analyze it, and report on it. Rather than presenting a report with 2,000 (or 20,000) individual records, you can use PivotTables to summarize the data, group it together, aggregate it, filter it, count it, and subtotal it so you can identify trends, spot inconsistencies, and analyze the data.

The four SharePoint PivotTable–related web parts are described in more detail later in this chapter, but before we introduce how to connect to data sources, here's a brief overview:

- *Office Datasheet Web Part*: This web part displays data in a tabular format. In other words, it presents it in a detailed view, just like in an Office Spreadsheet Web Part. Use this web part if you want to be able to sort and filter columns of data or enter new data. You can also use it to display specific columns of data from another data source.

- *Office PivotTable Web Part*: This is the primary web part to use when you want to group, aggregate, and subtotal data by rows or by columns.

- *Office PivotChart Web Part*: This web part takes tabular data and presents it in a graphical format. It can be dynamically linked to the data source so it updates as the data is updated.

- *Office PivotView Web Part*: When you want to be able to switch between Datasheet view, PivotTable view, and PivotChart view, this is the web part to use. A simple drop-down menu gives you the best of all worlds.

Connecting Web Parts to Data

Regardless of the type of Office web part you're using, you can connect the web part to existing data sources. In fact, to use any of the Office web parts except for the Office Spreadsheet Web Part, you have to connect them to a data source before you can use them. Additionally, you can connect every sheet in an Office Spreadsheet Web Part to a different data source, while each of the other web parts can typically maintain only one data connection at a time.

You can connect Office web parts to external data sources or to another web part. However, if you connect one web part as the data source for another web part, you cannot use that web part as a data source to connect to another web part. For example, if you have an Office Spreadsheet Web Part filled with transaction data, you can connect that data to an Office PivotTable Web Part to create a pivot table, but you cannot then also connect it to an Office PivotChart Web Part to create a chart. If you need more than one view of the data, use the Office PivotView Web Part so you can switch between Datasheet, PivotTable, and PivotChart views of the same data.

Connecting to External Data Sources

Although SharePoint presents you with a number of options for connecting to data sources, some are clearly better than others. First of all, although this might seem obvious, you have to make sure that the data resides in a shared server location. If it doesn't, everything will look great to you but no one else will be able to see it.

Second, some of the data connection options are old-style 32-bit ODBC (Open DataBase Connectivity) connections. These rely on mapped network drives that aren't reliable. The mapping has to be identical for every user to access the data successfully. If you can avoid using ODBC connections, it's best to do so.

You'll have the most success connecting to SharePoint lists, to Microsoft SQL Server databases, and to Microsoft Business Solutions data (for Great Plains data). You can also connect the data that resides in an Access or other database as long as it's saved in a shared network location, including on the SharePoint site itself.

To connect to an external data source—that is, any data source that isn't on the current web part page—click the **Connect to an External Data Source** link. This opens the Connect Data Source dialog box.

If you have an existing data source connection, specifically an Office Data Connection (ODC) file or a Data Retrieval Service Connection (OXDC) file, you can navigate to the data source and then select it.

If you haven't created an existing data source connection file, you must create one by clicking the **New Source** button to launch the Data Connection Wizard.

Creating a Data Connection to a SharePoint List

To create a new data source connection to a SharePoint list, follow these steps:

1. In the first step of the Data Connection Wizard, select **Data retrieval services**. Click **Next**.

2. Select **Windows SharePoint Services lists**. Click **Next**.

3. Enter the address for the WSS or SPS site. The easiest way to do this is to open the site in a separate browser window, navigate to the site, copy the site address in the address bar (Ctrl+C), then paste it into this text box (Ctrl+V). Delete the specific reference to the home page in the address (for example, `default.aspx`). Click **Next**.

4. In the next step of the wizard, Select a Data Object, select the list you want to connect to. Click **Next**.

5. In the Select Fields step, select the fields you want to include in the connection from the list of available columns. You can select multiple noncontiguous columns by holding the Ctrl key. Click **Add** to add the columns or **Add All** if you want all the columns. Use the **Remove** and **Remove All** buttons to alter your selection. Click the **Move Up** and **Move Down** buttons to set the order of the columns as you want them to appear. Click **Next**.

6. To specify a sort criteria, select the columns you want to sort by. For each column in the Sort Order box, indicate if you want the sort order to be **Ascending** or **Descending**. You can change the sort order of the data in the web part. Click **Next**.

7. If you'd like to retrieve only some of the records, enter filter criteria on the Specify Filter Criteria page, shown in Figure 9-6.

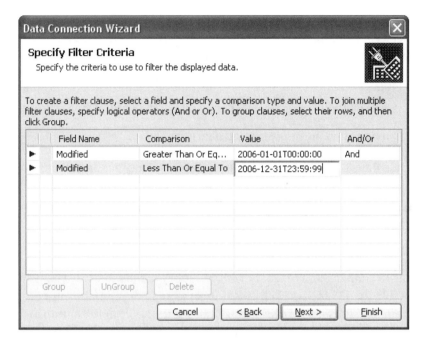

Figure 9-6. *Enter filter criteria on the Specify Filter Criteria page.*

    a. Select the *field name* from the Field Name drop-down list.

    b. Select the *comparison* term. The available comparison terms vary depending on the type of field you've selected. With Yes/No fields, for example, the options are **Equal To**, **Not Equal To**, **Is Null**, and **Is Not Null**.

    c. Select or enter a *value* to compare the contents of the field to. Again, the choices here might be limited based on the comparison. With Yes/No fields, the options are **True** or **False**.

    d. To enter additional filter criteria, select **And** or **Or** and enter a second filter statement. Click **Next**.

8. Indicate if you'd like to limit the number of rows the data connection retrieves. You might want to do this with large databases where a sample of data is sufficient to do the analysis you need. If you choose **Yes**, you must enter a number of rows you want to retrieve. Click **Next**.

9. Enter a name, if you want to change the one provided, and a description of the new data connection. This helps others know what's in this data connection, and is especially useful if you've filtered the data or limited the number of rows.

10. Click **Finish** to create the data connection. This opens the Select Data Source dialog box, similar to the one you used to launch the Data Connection Wizard.

11. Click **Open** to open the newly created data connection.

When you connect to an existing SharePoint list from an Office Spreadsheet Web Part, the data is displayed with Excel list functionality activated. For more information about using Excel list functionality, refer to Appendix A.

Creating a Data Connection to a Database

To create a connection to an Access database, you start out the same way you do for a connection to a SharePoint list: click the **Connect to an External Data Source** link. This opens the Connect Data Source dialog box. Then click the **New Source** button to launch the Data Connection Wizard. From the first step of the Data Connection Wizard, follow these steps:

1. Select **Other/Advanced** from the list of available data sources. Click **Next**.

2. In the Data Link Properties dialog box, on the Provider tab, select the data you want to connect to. For an Access database, follow these steps:

   a. Choose **Microsoft Jet 4.0 OLE DB Provider**. Click **Next**.

   b. Select or enter the database name, or click the ellipsis (**...**) button to open the Select Access Database dialog box. In this case, navigate to the database (in a shared network location) and click **Open**.

   c. Enter appropriate login information to access the database.

   d. Click **Test Connection** to make sure the connection succeeds.

   e. Click **OK**.

3. Back in the Data Connection Wizard, select the table or query that contains the data you want to connect to.

4. Enter a name, if you want to change the one provided, and a description of the new data connection. This helps others know what's in this data connection, and is especially useful if you've filtered the data or limited the number of rows.

5. Click **Finish** to create the data connection. This opens the Select Data Source dialog box, similar to the one you used to launch the Data Connection Wizard.

6. Click **Open** to open the newly created data connection.

If the data you want to connect to resides in a SQL Server, SQL Server OLAP Services, or Oracle database, you follow the same basic steps after selecting the appropriate database from the list of available data sources. However, rather than step 2, you just enter the server name where the database is located and enter the logon credentials. When you click **Next**, you're ready for step 3.

■**Note** If the data source you're trying to connect to lives on another domain, you must enable an Internet Explorer security option that allows IE to access data sources across domains. Go to Tools ➤ Internet Options. On the Security tab, click **Custom Level**. Scroll down the available settings in the Miscellaneous group, and change Access Data Sources across Domains to **Enable** or **Prompt**.

If you decide to disconnect from a database connection, right-click the datasheet and from the shortcut menu, choose External Data ➤ Delete Query.

Connecting to Another Web Part

If you already have data in an Office web part, you can connect another web part to it rather than connecting to an external data source. For example, if you have transaction data in an Office Spreadsheet Web Part, you can use an Office PivotTable Web Part to analyze that data. To connect to another web part, follow these steps:

1. Click the down arrow on the title bar of the web part and choose Modify Shared Web Part.

2. Click the down arrow again and click **Connections**. You have six choices for the type of connection you want to make:

   - *Get Data From*: Use this to connect to another web part that contains tabular data.

- *Filter Data With*: Use this when you have data in another web part that contains a column of data you want to use to filter the data in the PivotView Web Part.

- *Send Data To*: With this you can send all the data in a PivotView Web Part to another web part that displays tabular data.

- *Send Row To*: With this you can send a selected row of data from a PivotView Web Part to another web part for use as a filter or parameter value.

- *Chart Data From*: Connect the PivotView Web Part in PivotChart view to a Spreadsheet Web Part, a PivotView Web Part in PivotTable view, a PivotView Web Part in Datasheet view, or another PivotView Web Part in PivotChart view. The advantage of this connection is that any change in the source data is reflected in the PivotChart.

- *Chart Data To*: Connect the PivotView Web Part in PivotTable view, Datasheet view, or PivotChart view to another PivotView Web Part in PivotChart view. This connection is synchronized with the source data.

After you've selected the type of connection and the screen refreshes, the connection is established.

To disconnect from another web part, reselect the type of connection from the menu. You're prompted to verify that you want to remove the connection.

Using the Office Datasheet Web Part

The Office Datasheet Web Part, shown in Figure 9-7, is designed to offer a tabular or list view of data from another data source. After you've established a data connection (see "Connecting Web Parts to Data" earlier in this chapter), you can view the data, add new data, sort, and filter the data. Click the **Toolbar** button on the toolstrip to access Sort, Filter, and other commands.

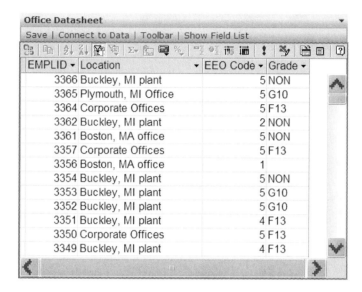

Figure 9-7. *The Office Datasheet Web Part typically displays tabular data.*

If you want to add a quick total to the data, scroll to the bottom of a column and click the **AutoCalc** button. Select the type of total you want from the list that opens. The web part inserts a new totals row at the bottom of the datasheet.

To remove a field from the display, click and drag the field header off the datasheet. When the pointer includes a red X, drop it. To add fields back to the display, click the **Field List** button to add fields to the display. Drag the fields you want to see into the datasheet (the web part places the fields into the Column Area).

Using the Office PivotTable Web Part

A PivotTable, shown in Figure 9-8, differs from a datasheet in that it offers a three-dimensional view of the data.

Employee Ethnicity

Save | Connect to Data | Toolbar | Show Field List

Location ▾			
All			

			Drop Column Fields Here	
Dept ▾	**Ethnic Descr** ▾		Count of Ethnic Descr	
⊟ Accounting	Black	±	1	
	White	±	15	
	Total	±	16	
⊟ Admin, HR & Payroll	Black	±	2	
	White	±	5	
	Total	±	7	
⊟ Administration	White	±	5	
	Total	±	5	
⊟ Analytics	Asian/Pacific Islander	±	2	
	Not Applicable (Non-U.S.)	±	1	
	Not Specified	±	2	
	White	±	2	

Figure 9-8. *You use the Office PivotTable Web Part to summarize, aggregate, and analyze data in columns and rows.*

In a PivotTable, you can put fields in the Column Area, as in a datasheet, but in addition, you can add fields to the Row Area, and summarize them in the Data Area. You can also add fields to the PivotTable in the Filter Area that allow you to filter the data. Figure 9-9 shows an empty PivotTable ready to receive data fields.

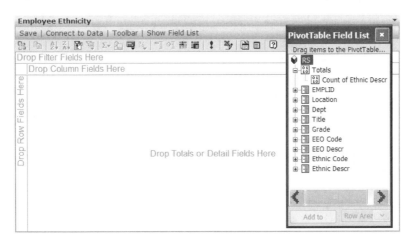

Figure 9-9. *In an Office PivotTable Web Part, you can add fields to the Column, Row, Data, and Filter Areas.*

To begin building a PivotTable, click **Show Field List** on the toolstrip. Drag fields from the field list to the appropriate areas.

■**Note** Just a reminder that if you're unfamiliar with PivotTables, we recommend that you study them in Excel before attempting to work with them in SharePoint. Although they're basically the same, Excel offers extensive help on how to work with PivotTables.

To group items, select the items in the Row Area you want to group. If they're non-contiguous, hold Ctrl to select the items. Right-click the selection and choose **Group**. The PivotTable displays the group to the left of the column. To change the name of the group, follow these steps:

1. Click the **Commands and Options** button on the toolbar.

2. Click the Captions tab.

3. Click the item in the PivotTable you want to rename and then enter a new name in the Caption text box. You can use this method to rename any fields.

Using the Office PivotChart Web Part

The Office PivotChart Web Part, shown in Figure 9-10, converts tabular data to graphical. The available features closely resemble Excel's Chart Wizard, but the PivotChart Web Part isn't nearly as intuitive or easy to use. When you connect the data sources, the web part automatically creates a chart based on the data. However, it might be a long way from the chart you want to see. First of all, the PivotChart Web Part cannot chart noncontiguous data. To chart data that isn't contiguous, you need to rearrange the original data source to make the columns or rows you want to chart contiguous.

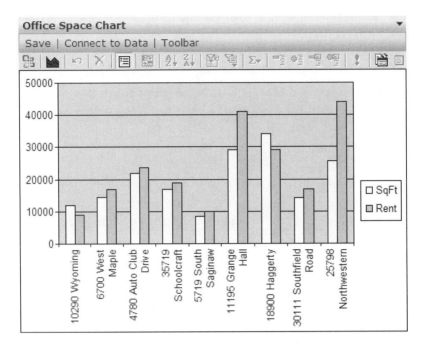

Figure 9-10. *The Office PivotChart Web Part displays data in a graphical format.*

■**Tip** If the data source is a Spreadsheet Web Part, you can easily identify the data you want to chart from the data source itself. To modify the data range displayed in the PivotChart Web Part, select the data you want to chart in the Spreadsheet Web Part, then click the down arrow on the data source's title bar. Choose **Set Chart Range** to establish a new data range for the chart. Using these two web parts together, you can create a nifty reporting interface for your users.

To modify the data ranges within the PivotChart Web Part, follow these steps:

1. Click the **Commands and Options** button on the toolbar.

2. On the General tab of the Commands and Options dialog box, select **Chart Workspace** from the Select drop-down list.

3. Click the Data Range tab, shown in Figure 9-11, to add and remove data series, set a data range for a series, name a series, and set data ranges for category labels.

4. Once you have the correct data ranges set, select the Type tab and choose which chart you want to use.

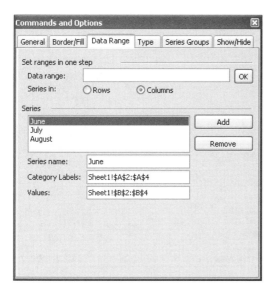

Figure 9-11. *Choose data range options using the Data Range tab.*

Use the other options in the Commands and Options dialog box to change colors, add titles, add data labels, and so on. Remember to select the chart element you want to work with from the Select list on the General tab. The options related to a particular chart element, such as the Legend, are only available if the element is selected.

Using the Office PivotView Web Part

The Office PivotView Web Part, shown in Figure 9-12, offers the ultimate in flexibility. Use this web part if you want to let users switch between Datasheet, PivotTable, and PivotChart views of the same data. Click the View drop-down menu to choose among the three views.

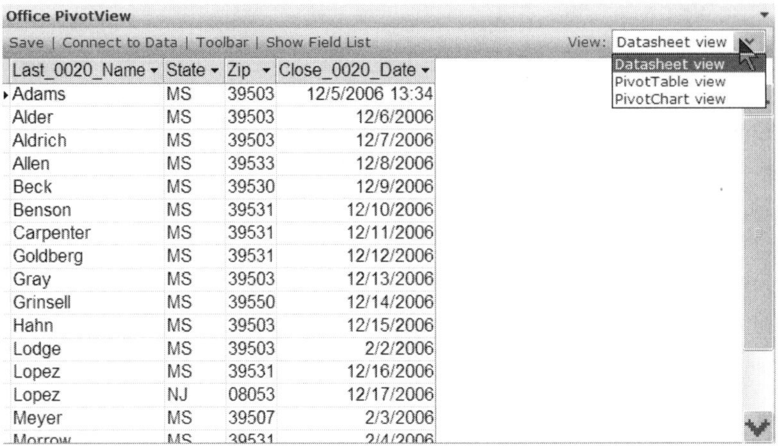

Figure 9-12. *The Office PivotView Web Part lets users choose between the Datasheet, PivotTable, and PivotChart views.*

Modifying Office Web Parts

As you work more with Office web parts, you'll probably get to a place where you want to change some things about them. For example, rather than saying Office Spreadsheet in the title bar, it would be nice if the web part had a descriptive name. You might also want to limit the height or width of the web part as it displays on the web page. These and other options are available from the Office web part task pane (the task pane has the name of the web part in its title bar).

To open the task pane to modify a web part, click **Modify Shared Page** at the top right of the page. Click **Modify Shared Web Parts** and select the web part you want to modify. You can change properties in four categories: Appearance, Layout, Advanced, and Spreadsheet or PivotView. In the following sections, we describe the most important properties that you might want to reset.

Appearance

Appearance properties, shown in Figure 9-13, include the web part Title. We recommend changing the title to something more descriptive. It makes it easier to use in data connections and looks better on the page.

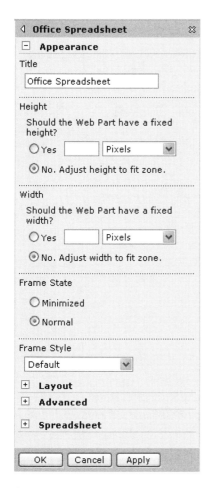

Figure 9-13. *Modify the Appearance properties to set the web part's title, size, and frame style.*

You can also change the Height and Width of the web part from an adjustable size to a fixed size. Use these properties if you want to control how much of the web part is visible on the page.

Depending on how you want the web part to display, you can use the Frame State property to have the web part minimized on opening the page. Users have to know to click the down arrow and choose **Restore** to work with the web part.

In the Frame Style property, you can choose if you want no frame, title bar, and border; title bar only; or the default setting, which includes a frame, title bar, and border.

Layout

Under Layout properties, shown in Figure 9-14, you can hide a web part by clearing the **Visible on Page** checkbox. You might want to do this if its only purpose is to serve as a connector to another web part on the page.

Figure 9-14. *Use the Layout properties to move the part to another zone or hide the part.*

Using the Zone drop-down menu, you can change the position of the web part on the page.

Advanced

In the Advanced properties, shown in Figure 9-15, you can control if you want users to be able to minimize the web part, close it, or change its position (zone change) on a page.

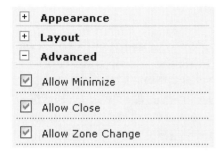

Figure 9-15. *Use the Advanced properties to limit the users' ability to move or close the web part.*

Spreadsheet or PivotView

The Spreadsheet and PivotView options vary depending on whether the web part is a Spreadsheet or a PivotView Web Part. Figure 9-16 shows the PivotView properties.

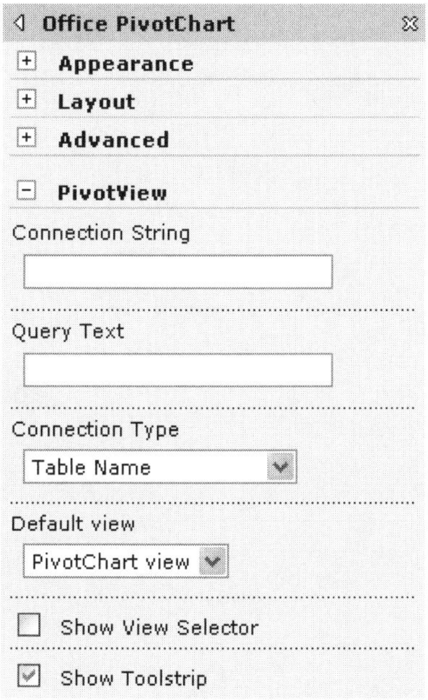

Figure 9-16. *Use PivotChart Web Part's PivotView properties to hide or display the toolstrip.*

When you've finished modifying properties, close the task pane to take you back out of design view.

Summary

In this chapter, we explored the Office web parts, a dynamic way to display and work with data from a variety of sources in a SharePoint site. The Office Spreadsheet Web Part is a useful tool for your online data entry needs, and the Office PivotTable Web Part gives you tremendous power to display, analyze, and aggregate data. Office Datasheets give you flexibility in displaying, sorting, and filtering data, letting you and your users slice and dice data any way you want to see it. Office PivotCharts present a dynamic graphical view of data. Finally, the Office PivotView Web Part lets users decide how they want to see the data.

By adding any or all of these web parts to a SharePoint web part page, you can create exciting dashboards that keep site users up to date with all the current trends by turning raw data into sources of useful information.

In Chapter 10, we take the concept of web parts a step further as we explore how to build custom web parts that are designed to solve your specific business problems.

■■■

CHAPTER 10

Building Excel Spreadsheet Web Parts

You've seen many of the web parts that are included with SharePoint in previous chapters, in which we've used SharePoint web parts to create web part pages. In the last chapter, you learned to create a simple Spreadsheet web part by adding one directly to a web part page from the Web Part Gallery on a Windows SharePoint Services site.

In this chapter, we add another tool for Excel and SharePoint integration: the Windows SharePoint Services Spreadsheet Web Part Add-in for Excel 2003. An Excel add-in is a special type of workbook saved using the XLA extension. Add-ins extend the functionality of Excel, and an add-in usually includes code but can also include worksheets.

When you open an add-in, it isn't displayed like a normal workbook. It's added to the current workbook's Project Explorer, visible only in the Visual Basic Editor. Most add-ins are password protected; you can see them in Project Explorer, but you cannot view or modify the code. Several Excel add-ins are available on the Microsoft site. You can create your own add-ins simply by saving an Excel workbook using the Add-in file type.

With the Windows SharePoint Services Web Part Add-in for Excel 2003, you can create your own web parts in Excel to perform custom calculations or retrieve and display data using an Extensible Markup Language (XML) map. If you haven't worked with XML maps in Excel, you'll find all the information you need to get started in Appendix B.

■**Note** The Spreadsheet Web Part Add-in for Excel 2003 is still being tested (the version used in this chapter is Beta 2). If you download a newer version, the look and feel and the features might be slightly different than is shown in this chapter. Don't let this discourage you; this add-in has been in Beta 2 for almost a year, and many people are using it to create custom web parts.

The simple Payment Calculator web part shown in Figure 10-1 lets the user enter information about the length of the loan, interest rate, and principal, then returns the monthly payment. The user can select other cells, such as the monthly payment, but can't edit them—a key difference between the Office Spreadsheet web part and a custom web part that you create from Excel. The user can select any cell, and use the toolbar commands to copy any cell or export the worksheet to Excel. The exported spreadsheet includes all the same formatting and protection as the web part.

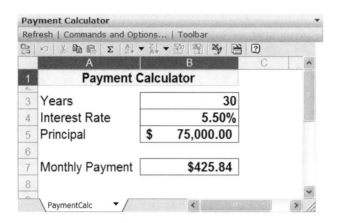

Figure 10-1. *A custom web part created in Excel*

Custom web parts support more Excel features than the Office Spreadsheet web part. You have access to all the formulas that Excel supports—even the financial, statistical, and engineering analysis functions, such as GROWTH, TREND, and NETWORKDAYS, from the Analysis Toolpak. You can use built-in programs such as Goal Seek and other add-ins such as Solver to create your custom web parts. (For more information on installing Solver and the Analysis Toolpak, see Excel Help.)

Note There are both client and server requirements for web parts created with the Spreadsheet Web Part Add-in. Client computers must have the Microsoft Office 2003 Spreadsheet Web Component (owc11.exe) installed. The component is installed by default as part of a Microsoft Office 2003 installation. The Microsoft Office Components for SharePoint Products and Technologies (stspkpl.exe), which include the Office Spreadsheet Web Part must be installed on the server before you can import custom web parts created using the add-in.

Installing the Spreadsheet Web Part Add-In

The Spreadsheet Web Part Add-in is available at no cost from Microsoft. The URL is bulky:
`http://www.microsoft.com/downloads/details.aspx?familyid=dc3d8474-d960-4d14-a9df-9024e39f5463&displaylang=en`.

You can type the link in your browser, but it's easier to simply Google **sharepoint spreadsheet add-in for excel**. (Include SharePoint in the search string—there are a lot of spreadsheet add-ins.) The first item in the search results—Download Details: Windows SharePoint Services Add-in: Spreadsheet—is the link to the download page. Click the link. Follow these steps to install the add-in:

1. On the download page, click the **Download** button.

2. When the File Download - Security Warning dialog box appears, choose **Run** to start the install.

3. Review the Spreadsheet Web Part Add-in license agreement and click **Yes**.

4. In the next dialog box, click **Browse** to choose a location for the add-in. There are two good choices. The default add-ins folder is `C:\Documents and Settings\`*your user name*`\Application Data\Microsoft\AddIns`. The add-ins folder for Office 2003, `C:\Program Files\Microsoft Office\OFFICE11\ADDINS`, is accessible to all users. Choose one of these locations (or another location if you prefer). Click **OK** to save the add-in in the folder.

After the add-in is saved, a message box tells you how to install the add-in in Excel:

1. In Excel, choose Tools ➤ Add-Ins to open the Add-ins dialog box, shown in Figure 10-2.

2. Click the **Browse** button and locate the SpreadsheetWebpart.xla file. Select the file and click **OK** to install the add-in.

Figure 10-2. *Install and enable or disable add-ins for Excel.*

When the add-in is installed, a new command, Create WebPart, appears on the Excel main menu to the right of the Help menu.

■**Note** Add-ins are loaded every time Excel is launched. If you have add-ins that you use infrequently, open the Add-ins dialog box and turn off their checkboxes so they won't be loaded with Excel. This saves memory and shortens the time it takes Excel to launch. To enable an add-in, open the Add-ins dialog box, turn on its checkbox, then close and reopen Excel.

Custom Web Parts

A Spreadsheet Web Part needs five files to run: one preinstalled on the server, one preinstalled on the client, and three that you'll create using the add-in for installation on the server:

- Spreadsheet Web Part Assembly

- XML Spreadsheet

- Solution Specification

- Web Part Definition

- Spreadsheet Component

The Spreadsheet Web Part Assembly is installed on the Windows SharePoint Services site as part of the Office 2003 Web Parts and Components. One Spreadsheet Web Part Assembly can support all the Spreadsheet Web Parts on a site.

The XML Spreadsheet file defines the XML mapping, formatting, validation, and formulas used in your web part. You'll create this file using the Spreadsheet Web Part Add-in.

The Solution Specification file is an XML file that integrates the other components in the web part. You'll create this using the Spreadsheet Web Part Add-in. You can download a separate editor from Microsoft to modify this file.

The Web Part Definition file is an XML file that defines the default property settings for the web part, such as the title and description. It also specifies the location of the Solution Specification file. This file is used when you add a Spreadsheet web part to a web part page or web part catalog. You'll create the Web Part Definition file using the Spreadsheet Web Part Add-in.

The Spreadsheet Component is installed on your users' machines as part of the Office 2003 installation. Users without Office 2003 installed can download and install the Office Web Components (OWCs) separately. However, the OWCs rely on Office 2003 for some features, so users without Office 2003 will have a lesser user experience.

Creating a Simple Custom Web Part

There are three steps to building a custom web part using the Spreadsheet Web Part Add-in:

1. Set up the Excel workbook, which will be used as the XML Spreadsheet file.

2. Use the Spreadsheet Web Part Add-in to specify web part settings.

3. Create the web part.

Setting Up the Excel Workbook

The custom web part can include XML maps, formatting, formulas, and data from an external source. The simple spreadsheet shown in Figure 10-3, which includes formatting and formulas, was used to create the web part shown in Figure 10-1.

	A	B
1	**Payment Calculator**	
2		
3	Years	30
4	Interest Rate	5.50%
5	Principal	$ 75,000.00
6		
7	Monthly Payment	$425.84

Figure 10-3. *The worksheet used to create the custom web part*

The worksheet looks amazingly like the web part. Here are the steps to create a worksheet that you'll use to create a simple custom web part:

1. Enter labels and formulas.

■**Tip** If you want to create the spreadsheet shown in Figure 10-3, there's only one formula, in cell B7:
`=PMT(B4/12,B3*12,-B5)`

---

2. Apply formatting.

3. Select and unlock any cells where the user will enter data. Choose Format ➤ Cells on the menu, or right-click and choose **Format Cells** from the context menu to open the Format Cells dialog box. On the Protection tab, turn off the **Locked** checkbox, then click **OK**.

In your custom web part, users will only be able to modify cells that you just unlocked.

4. Choose Tools ➤ Protection ➤ Protect Sheet to open the Protect Sheet dialog box, shown in Figure 10-4.

Figure 10-4. *Protect the worksheet before creating the web part to protect formulas and labels.*

You don't need to provide a password. Unlike Excel, SharePoint doesn't offer the user an opportunity to enter a password and unprotect the spreadsheet. It just says "No":

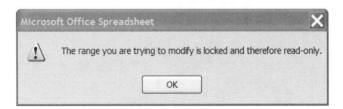

5. Click **OK** to protect the worksheet.

6. Save the workbook. Give it a short descriptive name.

Now you're ready to use the Spreadsheet Add-in to create your custom web part.

Using the Spreadsheet Add-In

Select the worksheet that you want to use to create the web part and click the **Create WebPart** command on the menu bar to open the Spreadsheet Add-in for Microsoft Excel. The add-in is a four-tab dialog box, much like a wizard.

On the General tab, shown in Figure 10-5, you'll identify your SharePoint site, name the web part files, and choose a document library in which to store the web part files.

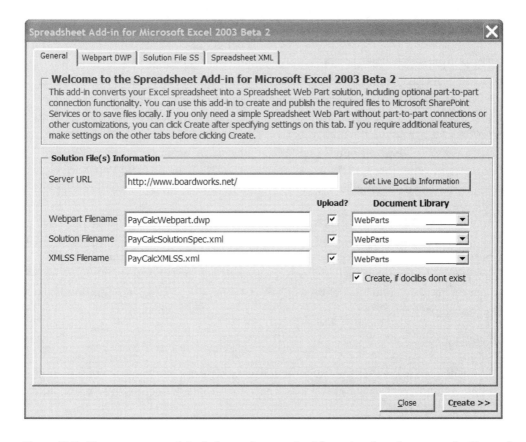

Figure 10-5. *You enter most of the information required for a simple web part on the General tab of the Spreadsheet Add-in.*

Follow these steps to complete the information on the General tab:

1. Enter the URL for your Windows SharePoint Services site in the Server URL text box. If your site is a subsite, use the URL for the subsite.

2. In the Webpart Filename, Solution Filename, and XMLSS Filename text boxes, the suggested file name is the name of the workbook (including the extension), a hyphen, then a description and file extension for the file. Replace the file name and extension with a name that describes the web part. For example, the Webpart Filename for our web part is PayCalcWebPart.dwp.

These three files will be saved in a document library on your SharePoint site. You don't want users to delete or modify the files, so you shouldn't store them in the Shared Documents library. We recommend creating a document library named webparts that isn't listed on the Quick Launch bar. You can create the library in SharePoint, or have the Spreadsheet Add-in create the library for you. The Solution Specification file must be stored on the web site where you want to place the custom web part, and the WebPart Description must be stored on the same site as the Solution Specification file. You might as well store them all together in the same document library. Then, follow these steps:

1. If the library you want to store the web part files in already exists, click the **Get Live DocLib Information** button to populate the three Document Library drop-down lists with the names of the document libraries on the site you specified earlier. Choose the library in each of the drop-down lists. (Don't choose Web Part Gallery— it seems like a good idea, but it won't work.) Clear the **Create, if doclibs dont exist** checkbox.

Or, do the following:

1. If you need to create a new document library, type the name in each of the three Document Library drop-down lists. Leave the **Create, if doclibs dont exist** checkbox turned on.

2. On the Webpart DWP tab, enter a brief name and description for your web part (see Figure 10-6). (If you don't do this, the web part will have the same name as your workbook.)

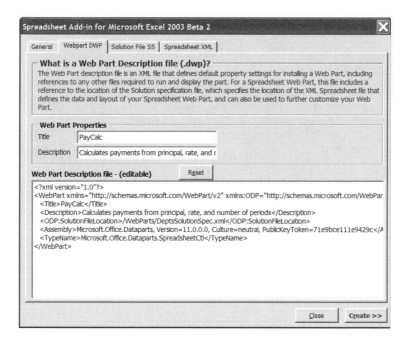

Figure 10-6. *Enter a name and description for your web part.*

Don't click **Create** yet. Continue to the next section to learn how to protect your web part.

Protecting Your Web Part

The default web part settings allow the user to save changes (within the web part, not within the data source), connect to a data source, edit queries, and engage in other random acts of mischief. You can lock down the web part to keep your users from modifying your web part. When you set LockedDown to True, the web part you create will have the following modifications:

- The Connect to Data toolstrip (the menu above the toolbar) command will be hidden

- The Save toolstrip command will be hidden

- The Edit Query and Delete Query commands on the context menu will be disabled

To lock down the web part, follow these steps:

1. Choose the Solution File SS tab, shown in Figure 10-7.

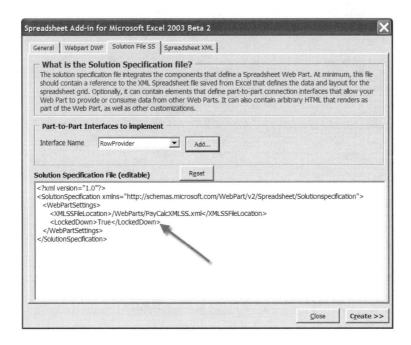

Figure 10-7. *The Solution File SS tab of the Spreadsheet Add-in*

2. Add the following line after the <XMLSSFileLocation> specification between the WebPartSettings start and end tags in the Solution Specification pane, as shown in Figure 10-7:

```
<LockedDown>True</LockedDown>
```

3. You're now ready to create your web part. Click the **Create** button.

The Publishing Files In Progress dialog box opens and shows each file being created (see Figure 10-8).

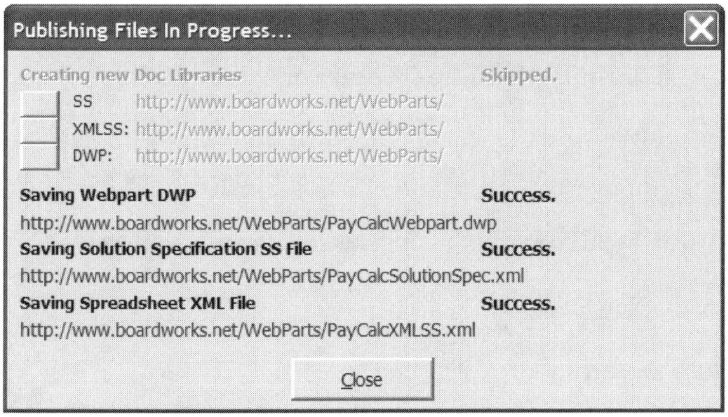

Figure 10-8. *View the web part creation report in the Publishing Files In Progress dialog box.*

When all three files are created, click any of the three gray buttons next to the file names to open the SharePoint document library in Internet Explorer (IE) to view your files.

Adding the Web Part to a Web Part Page

It's relatively easy to add your custom web part to a web part page. There's only one trick: even though you need to publish your web part on a SharePoint site, when you import the web part, the text box control won't allow you to enter a web URL. Before you import the web part, take a minute to make sure your SharePoint site is on the My Network Places list.

Adding Your SharePoint Site to My Network Places

Open My Network Places. (If My Network Places doesn't appear on your Start menu or Desktop, open My Computer, then choose My Network Places in the Other Places list.) Review the list of Network Places. If your SharePoint site is already listed, you're all set. If not, follow these steps to add a Network Place:

1. Open the home page of your SharePoint site in IE.

2. Copy the URL in the address bar.

3. Switch to My Network Places.

4. In the Network Tasks pane, click the **Add a Network Place** link to open the Add Network Place Wizard.

5. In the first step of the wizard, click **Next**.

6. In the second step of the wizard, select **Choose Another Network Location**. Click **Next**.

7. In the third step of the wizard, paste the URL you copied in step 2. Click **Next**.

8. In the fourth step, enter a friendly name for your Network Place. Click **Next**.

9. Click **Finish** to create the Network Place.

You're now ready to add your web part to a page on your SharePoint site.

Importing the Custom Web Part

You can place your custom web part on any web part page on your site. Follow these steps to add the web part:

1. Navigate to the page.

2. Select a view for the web part from the Web Part Page menu:

- If you're in shared view and you want to switch to personal view, click **Modify Shared Page**, then select **Personal View**. When you add your custom web part, only you will see it.

- If you're in personal view and you want to switch to shared view, click **Modify My Page**, then select **Shared View**. When you add your custom web part, it will be available to everyone who views the page.

3. On the Web Part Page menu, choose Add Web Parts ➤ Import to open the Add Web Parts pane, shown in Figure 10-9.

Figure 10-9. *Use the Add Web Parts pane to import your custom web part.*

4. Click the **Browse** button to open the Choose File dialog box.

5. Click the **My Network Places** link.

6. Double-click the Network Place that refers to your SharePoint site.

7. Double-click the document library that contains the files for your custom web part.

8. Select the web part definition file (with a DWP extension) for your web part.

Note If you don't see your web part files, press F5 to refresh the file list in the Choose File dialog box.

---

9. Click **Open**. The Choose File dialog box closes.

10. Click the **Upload** button in the Add Web Parts pane to import the web part.

11. Drag the web part from the Add Web Parts pane and drop it in place on the page (see Figure 10-10).

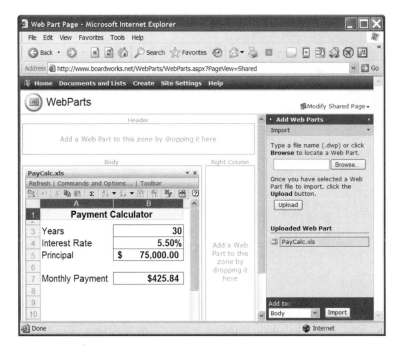

Figure 10-10. *The custom web part installed on the web part page*

12. Click the **Close** button to close the Add Web Parts pane.

13. Test the web part.

Use the drop-down arrow on the web part and choose **Modify Web Part** to change the title bar text or other web part properties.

ADDING YOUR WEB PART TO THE SITE GALLERY

You can use the imported web part anywhere on the page. If you want to use it on another page in the site, you'll need to add the web part definition (DWP) file to the site's Web Part Gallery. Follow these steps:

1. Navigate to the SharePoint page that includes the web part. Click **Site Settings** in the top navigation bar.

2. On the Site Settings page, click the **Go to Top-Level Site Administration** link.

3. On the Top-Level Site Administration page, click the **Manage Web Part Gallery** link.

4. Choose **Upload Web Part**.

5. Click **Browse**. Select the web part definition (DWP) file. You can enter some metadata about the web part: a group name that you can use later in a view to group, sort, or filter. Click **OK**.

If you don't have permissions to add parts to the gallery, you'll be prompted repeatedly for your user-name and password. Just click **Cancel** and consult with your WSS administrator about your permissions.

6. Select the **Type** icon for the new web part to see a preview of the web part.

Remember that the DWP contains references to other files, so the web part is, in effect, site specific. You can import the web part to another site, but when it runs, it will return the following error:

```
Unable to connect to the Solution Specification file
```

If you want to use your web part on another SharePoint site, you'll need to re-create the web part (from Excel) for that site.

Creating a Web Part That Returns a Data Set

That was a good warm up. Now, you'll create a web part that returns a data set with information about documents in a SharePoint library. You'll use the web part on a different SharePoint site. You'll follow similar steps to return data from SQL Server. Your custom web part, shown in Figure 10-11, will retrieve all the documents that have been created or modified on or after January 1, 2006. Users can sort and filter the data set using the commands on the web part toolbar.

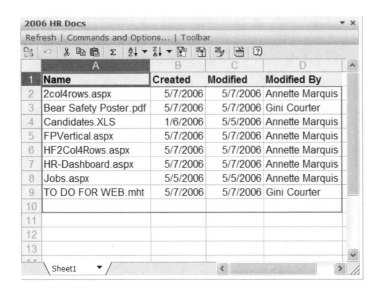

Figure 10-11. *A custom web part, showing only the documents that have been changed since 1/1/2006*

Creating the Data Retrieval Service Connections File

Before you can create a data-bound web part, you need to create a data connection. In this example, you'll use Excel's Data Connection Wizard to create a connection to SharePoint's data retrieval service. The choices that you make in the wizard will be saved in a Data Retrieval Service Connections file. Data Retrieval Service Connections files are saved with the UXDC file extension. Follow these steps to create the worksheet and data-bound web part:

1. Start with a blank Excel worksheet.

2. Choose Data ➤ Import External Data ➤ Import Data from the menu to open the Select Data Source dialog box.

3. Double-click **Connect to New Data Source** to launch the Data Connection Wizard.

4. Select **Data Retrieval Services**, then click **Next**.

5. Choose **Microsoft SharePoints lists** and click **Next**.

6. In the Data Retrieval Service Location, enter the URL for the Windows SharePoint site that contains the list you want to return. Click **Next**.

7. Select the data object (list or library) you want to display in your web part (see Figure 10-12). Click **Next**.

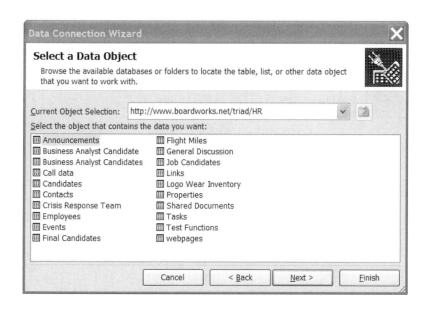

Figure 10-12. *Choose the list you want to display in your web part.*

8. Select the data fields that you want to retrieve (see Figure 10-13). Use the **Add** and **Remove** buttons to move items to the Selected Columns list. Use the **Move Up** and **Move Down** buttons to reorder the list. Click **Next**.

■Note If you want to connect this web part to other web parts, be sure to include the primary key field—the field that contains a unique value that can be used to establish a one-to-many relationship. In SharePoint lists, the ID column is unique.

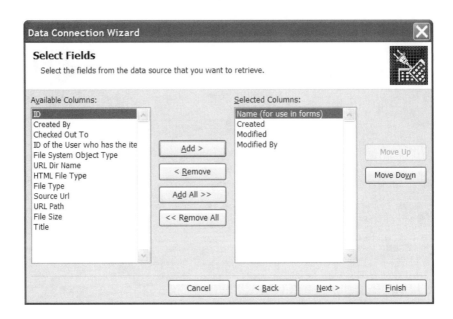

Figure 10-13. *Select the fields you want to display in your web part.*

9. Specify your sort criteria. Use the **Add** and **Remove** buttons to select sort fields. Select each sort field and choose the **Ascending** or **Descending** option. Use the **Move Up** and **Move Down** buttons to order the fields, primary sort on top (see Figure 10-14). Click **Next**.

When you create a filter, the filter criteria must match the data type of the field you're filtering. For example, SharePoint stores Modified and Created dates using this date and time format: YYYY-MM-DD HH:MM:SS. To filter for documents modified after January 1, 2006, the criteria is Modified, greater than or equal to 2006-01-01T00:00:00 (see Figure 10-15).

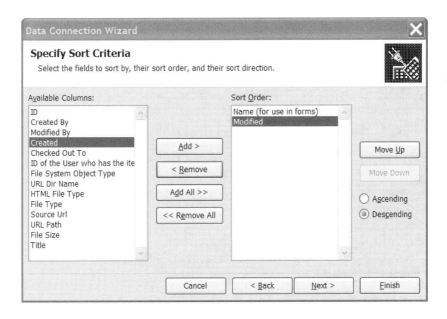

Figure 10-14. *Select the fields you want to use to sort the data.*

10. Specify any filter you wish to apply (see Figure 10-15). Click **Next**.

	Field Name	Comparison	Value	And/Or
►	Modified	Greater Than Or Equa...	2006-01-01T00:00:00	Or
►	Created	Greater Than Or Equa...	2006-01-01T00:00:00	

Figure 10-15. *Set filter criteria to apply to the data set.*

For extremely large data sets, you might wish to limit the number of rows that will be returned.

11. To limit the number of rows, click **Yes**, then use the spin box control to set the maximum number of rows. Click **Next**.

12. Enter a name and description for the Data Retrieval Service Connections file, then click **Finish** to save the file and open the Import Data dialog box.

13. Choose a location for the data, starting at cell A1 of the current worksheet or a new worksheet. Click **OK**.

Excel creates an XML map (see the XML Source task pane in Figure 10-16) and returns the data as an XML list.

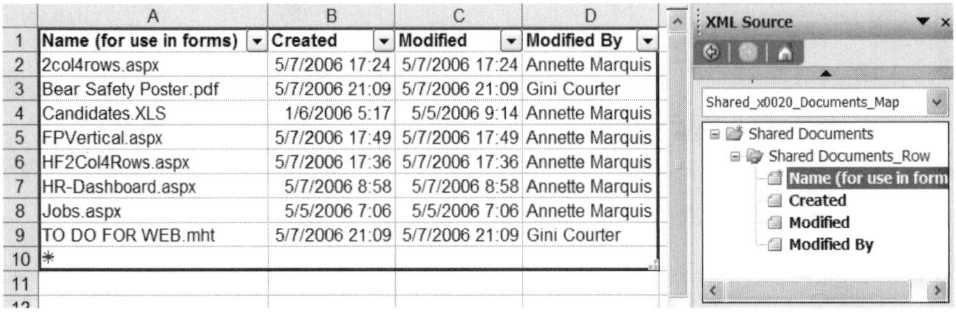

Figure 10-16. *The XML source pane displays the schema for the data.*

Formatting and Saving the XML Spreadsheet

Now, add formulas or apply formatting before creating the custom web part. To add a formula to every row, follow these steps:

1. Insert a column into the XML list.

2. If necessary, drag the handle at the bottom right corner of the list to include the new column in the list.

3. Edit the column heading name.

4. Enter the formula in the first row, then double-click the fill handle to copy the formula down.

Format the column headings and data as you'd like them to appear in your web part. You can edit the column headings; for example, you can change "Name (for use in forms)" to "Name."

When you're finished, save the workbook.

Creating and Importing the Web Part

The instructions for creating a web part and using the web part on a SharePoint web part page appear earlier in this chapter. These steps are the same for every custom web part. Follow the steps in the section "Using the Spreadsheet Add-In" to create the data-bound web part. Follow the steps in the section "Importing the Custom Web Part" to add your web part to a SharePoint web page.

In our example, we used the web part on a completely different web site—a relatively easy way to let a group of users view new additions to a document library on another team's SharePoint site.

Summary

SharePoint's built-in web parts—such as the Office Spreadsheet and Page Viewer Web Parts—are powerful, but if you want advanced Excel functionality, use the SharePoint Spreadsheet Web Part Add-in. The add-in is still in beta, but it's an efficient way to provide your users with all the features of Excel without hours of coding: the ultimate in SharePoint and Excel integration.

APPENDIX A

■■■

Creating and Using Excel Lists

Throughout this book, we've referred to Excel lists, the feature of Excel that makes it possible to synchronize worksheet data with SharePoint (see Chapter 2). Whether or not you want to synchronize a list with SharePoint, using Excel's List command can simplify data entry and put features such as filter, sort, and totals at your fingertips.

Although theoretically any Excel worksheet with columns and rows of data can be called a list, Excel's List command segregates a defined range of cells from the rest of the worksheet, making it possible to combine multiple lists into a single worksheet. Additionally, an Excel list automatically copies formulas and formatting to new rows of data, eliminating the need to do this manually. In this appendix, we'll demonstrate the advantages of using Excel's List command over maintaining lists the traditional way.

Creating a New List

Creating a new list is as simple as entering data into a blank worksheet. A header row isn't required, but comes in handy for other things you might want to do, such as filtering the list. The best way to start is to enter column headings into the worksheet. Follow these steps to create the list:

1. Open a blank worksheet or select an existing worksheet that's large enough to accommodate the list.

2. Enter column headings.

3. Select the column headings.

4. Select Data ➤ List ➤ Create List, or right-click the selected headings and click **Create List** from the context menu.

5. In the Create List dialog box, verify that the correct range is defined in the "Where is the data for your list?" text box. If it isn't, click the **Collapse** button at the right end of the text box and reselect the data.

6. Select the **My list has headers** checkbox.

7. Click **OK** to create the list.

Excel automatically activates the List toolbar and draws a border around the list, separating it from the rest of the worksheet. In addition, it adds a new record row, designated by an asterisk, and turns on AutoFilter, as shown in Figure A-1. When you click outside the list, the List toolbar turns off, the AutoFilter buttons are no longer visible, and the border changes to a thin blue line. Click back inside the list to reactivate the list features.

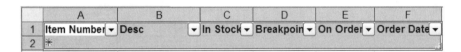

Figure A-1. *The Excel list has the AutoFilter turned on and a new row for data entry.*

Entering Data into a List

To add data to the list, click in the new record row—the row with an asterisk—and start typing. When you reach the end of the row, press Enter to enter the next record.

If you want to add formulas to the list, enter the formula in the first row of data. Excel automatically copies the formula to new rows.

You can also apply text and number formatting to individual cells, and apply conditional formatting to cells or to the entire row. Excel copies the formatting to new rows you enter, and applies conditional formatting as appropriate.

■**Note** If you apply formula-based conditional formatting to the first row, be sure to create the formula to use a relative row reference. For example, in the Conditional Formatting dialog box, change the formula =$B$2="LGA" to =$B2="LGA" to make the column reference B absolute but the row reference 2 relative. This assures that Excel formats the data based on the current row, rather than referring only to the first row of data.

When you've finished entering data, click outside the list to deactivate it.

Redefining the Columns in a List

By default, when you type a header for a column that's adjacent to a defined list, Excel automatically expands the list to include it. List AutoExpansion is one of Excel's AutoCorrect options. If you didn't intend for the column to be added to the list, you can click the **AutoCorrect Options** button that appears next to the column and click **Undo List AutoExpansion**. To turn off this option permanently, click **Stop Automatically Expanding Lists**. You can also insert a column in the middle of a list, and Excel expands the list range to include it.

■**Note** If the AutoCorrect Options button doesn't appear, you might have AutoCorrect turned off. To activate it, select Tools ➤ AutoCorrect Options and click the **Show AutoCorrect Options buttons** checkbox on the AutoCorrect tab of the AutoCorrect dialog box.

If you want to change the range of columns and rows included in a list, click **List** on the List toolbar, then click **Resize List**. You can enter or select a new list range, with a couple caveats: you cannot change the header row of the existing list, and the new list range has to overlap the existing list range. In other words, you can't change a list that was A1:D57 and make the new list E1:G57.

Deleting List Data

You can delete columns and rows in a list without affecting other data in the worksheet. Select the cells in the row you want to delete, rather than selecting the entire row. Then select Edit ➤ Delete Row, or right-click the selected cells and click Delete ➤ Row from the context menu. This deletes a row in the list without impacting data in the worksheet row that's outside the list. For example, say you have a list range of A1:K47. You have another list range of M1:S75. By selecting just the cells you want to delete, you can delete the data in A13:K13 without deleting the data in M13:S13.

Using Database Features and Functions

One of the advantages of using Excel's List command is the ease with which you can sort and filter lists, and toggle totals on and off.

Sorting and Filtering

When you create a list, Excel automatically turns on AutoFilter. The AutoFilter buttons appear on the header row of the list. To sort data in the list, click the down arrow on the column you want to sort. Scroll to the top of the list, then click **Sort Ascending** or **Sort Descending**.

To filter data, select the criteria on which you want to filter from the list of values. If you want to create a custom filter, follow these steps:

1. At the top of the drop-down list, choose **(Custom)** to open the Custom AutoFilter dialog box, shown in Figure A-2. Enter up to two custom filter criteria separated by AND or OR.

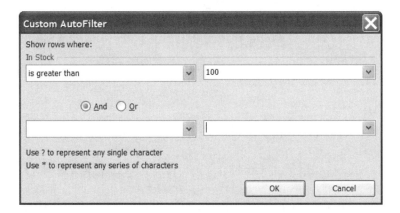

Figure A-2. *Create a custom filter to display records that meet one or two criteria.*

2. Choose from the list of comparison terms such as **equals**, **does not equal**, **is greater than**, and **is less than**, then enter or select the value. This creates the filter statement, such as the following:

    ```
    Show rows where State/Prov equals Alaska or Show rows where
    Revenue is greater than or equal to $50,000.
    ```

3. Click **OK** to apply the filter. Excel hides any rows in the list that don't meet the filter criteria.

You can apply multiple filters to a list by filtering on more than one column. For example, if you want to see all the rows where Revenue is greater than or equal to $50,000 and State/Prov equals Alaska, you'd apply a filter to both the Revenue column and the State column.

■**Tip** To decide whether to use AND or OR in a custom filter, ask yourself this question: in a single row of data, do I want to see the row only if it meets both criteria (AND), or do I want to see the row if it meets either criteria (OR)?

If the AutoFilter buttons distract you, you can turn them off. Select Data ➤ Filter ➤ AutoFilter to toggle off the buttons. Repeat the same steps to turn them back on again.

Adding Totals

The **Toggle Totals Row** button on the List toolbar lets you toggle totals on and off at your discretion. Totals aren't limited to sums—the Totals row includes the choice of eight functions: Average, Count, Count Nums, Max, Min, Sum, StdDev, and Variance. To display totals, follow these steps:

1. Click the **Toggle Totals Row** button on the List toolbar.

2. In the row labeled Totals, click the cell that's in the column you want to total.

3. Select the totals function you want to apply from the drop-down list. Excel displays the applicable total in the cell.

4. Move to the next column you want to total and repeat step 3.

When Excel adds a totals formula in the Totals row to a list, it doesn't just create a standard formula, such as =SUM(D3:D59). Instead, it inserts a subtotals formula, such as =SUBTOTAL(109, D3:D59), where the first argument (in this case, 109) represents the SUM function. The SUBTOTAL function ignores hidden values. The advantage of SUBTOTAL over SUM, AVERAGE, and the other aggregate functions is that it doesn't matter if the data is filtered or not. A correct total is always displayed.

■**Note** The syntax for the SUBTOTAL function is as follows:

```
(SUBTOTAL(function_num, ref1, ref2, ...)
```

Table A-1 shows the function numbers (function_num) for each of the available aggregates used in the SUBTOTAL function.

Table A-1. *Subtotal Function Numbers*

Function	Function_num
AVERAGE	101
COUNT NUMS	102
COUNT	103
MAX	104
MIN	105
STDDEV	107
SUM	109
VARIANCE	110

■**Note** In case you're wondering, the missing function numbers (function_num) are PRODUCT (106), which multiplies all the arguments; STDEVP (108), the standard deviation of a population; and VARP (111), the variance of a population. If you use function numbers 1–11, the SUBTOTAL function includes hidden values; function numbers 101–111 hide hidden values.

When you're adding records to the list, you might find it easier to toggle the Totals row off. To do that, just click the **Toggle Totals Row** button on the List toolbar again.

When Lists Don't Work

Excel's List command is great to use for a lot of your list needs. However, you cannot use Excel lists with the following items:

- *Shared workbooks*: You must unshare the workbook before you can convert a range to a list, or convert the list to a normal range to share a workbook that contains a list.

- *Compare and merge workbooks*: You must convert the list to a normal range before you can compare and merge workbooks.

- *Subtotals*: Excel lists automatically display subtotals using the Totals row (the **Toggle Totals Row** button on the list toolbar). However, you cannot have Excel automatically insert subtotal rows after categories of data. If you need a subtotals report, convert the list to a normal range.

- *Custom views*: You must convert the list to a normal range to create custom views of the worksheet, as covered in the following section.

Converting a List to a Normal Range

If you need to use a feature that Excel's List command doesn't support, you can temporarily or permanently convert the list to a range. To convert a list to a range, right-click the list, then select List ➤ Convert to Range. Alternately, click **List** on the List toolbar and click **Convert to Range**. Confirm your choice by clicking **Yes** when prompted: "Do you want to convert your list to a normal range?" Excel removes the border around the list, deactivates the List toolbar, and turns off the AutoFilter buttons.

To convert the data back to a list, follow the directions in the section "Creating a New List" earlier in this appendix. The only difference is that you want to select the entire range of cells that contain data.

APPENDIX B

◼◼◼

Mapping Excel Spreadsheets for XML

In 1998, the World Wide Web Consortium (W3C) posted goals for a new language that would facilitate data transfer between computers and systems. According to the goals, the new Extensible Markup Language, or XML, would meet specific criteria. The XML draft document describes a standard language with optional features "kept to an absolute minimum," resulting in easy-to-create, human-readable documents. In less than a decade, XML has moved from a set of goals to a language that has undergone frequent and rapid revision. Excel 2003 includes native support for XML (as does Access and InfoPath). In the next version of Office, 2007 Microsoft Office System, every Office application will include native XML support. If you work with SharePoint and Excel, you can't ignore XML.

XML Basics

XML describes data as a hierarchy: a company has departments, departments have employees, employees have first names and last names, and so on. The following simple XML file describes one "record"—an e-mail message:

```
<?xml version = "1.0" ?>
<MESSAGE>
<TO>nwight@triadconsulting.com</TO>
<CC>kmontgomery@boardworks.net</CC>
<FROM>gcourter@triadconsulting.com</FROM>
<DATE>06/01/06</DATE>
<SUBJECT>New Office Location</SUBJECT>
<BODY>Where should this item appear on the meeting agenda?</BODY>
</MESSAGE>
```

■Note If you want to try mapping, importing, and exporting XML, enter the preceding text in Notepad and save it as message.xml. Feel free to make up your own data, but pay particular attention to the tags; for example, <TO> at the start of the To field, and </TO> at the end.

On the surface, XML's form looks much like HTML. Each element (MESSAGE, TO, CC) has a start tag and an end tag, and content is sandwiched between the two. The start tag is enclosed in <> and the end tag in </>. The element name can be in upper case or lower case, but it must be the consistent. Unlike HTML, you can't get sloppy with end tags in XML. They're required.

■Note The XML format isn't designed to handle huge sets of complex data or binary objects such as graphics. Of course, it also isn't designed to work with proprietary data formats.

Every XML document has a root element (also called a document element) that's the highest level of the hierarchy. The last closing tag in the XML document closes the root element (in this example, the MESSAGE element). An XML document that has matching start and end tags for every element and conforms to the hierarchy is called well-formed XML.

■Note A prolog often precedes the start tag for the root element; the prolog can contain an XML declaration stating the XML version the file uses and the schema declaration (more on schemas in a bit).

The preceding XML code is well formed. If you open the document in Internet Explorer, IE knows how to display the document (see Figure B-1).

```
    <?xml version="1.0" ?>
  - <MESSAGE>
      <TO>nwight@triadconsulting.com</TO>
      <CC>kmontgomery@boardworks.net</CC>
      <FROM>gcourter@triadconsulting.com</FROM>
      <DATE>06/01/06</DATE>
      <SUBJECT>New Office Location</SUBJECT>
      <BODY>Where should this item appear on the meeting agenda?</BODY>
    </MESSAGE>
```

Figure B-1. *The message.xml file opened in Internet Explorer*

Even though a browser can display the XML document, there's no way to know if the XML document is correct. It could be missing elements, or have elements included that shouldn't be. The real standard for XML is validity. A valid XML document includes or references a schema: a definition file that describes the structure of the data. The XML is only valid if the data in the XML document complies with the schema, stored as an XML Schema Definition (XSD) file, a type of XML file. Following are the contents of an XSD file that would work for the message.xml file:

```
<?xml version="1.0"?>
<xs:schema xmlns:xs="http://www.w3.org/2001/XMLSchema"
targetNamespace="http://www.triadconsulting.com"
xmlns="http://www.triadconsulting.com"
elementFormDefault="qualified">
<xs:element name="MESSAGE">
    <xs:complexType>
      <xs:sequence>
            <xs:element name="TO" type="xs:string"/>
            <xs:element name="CC" type="xs:string"/>
            <xs:element name="FROM" type="xs:string"/>
            <xs:element name="DATE" type="xs:string"/>
            <xs:element name="SUBJECT" type="xs:string"/>
            <xs:element name="BODY" type="xs:string"/>
      </xs:sequence>
    </xs:complexType>
</xs:element>
</xs:schema>
```

You can also use Document Type Definition (DTD) files to validate XML files, but you can't use DTD files with SharePoint or Excel. Following is a DTD file for message.xml:

```
<!ELEMENT MESSAGE (TO, CC, FROM, DATE, SUBJECT, BODY)>
<!ELEMENT TO (#PCDATA)>
<!ELEMENT CC (#PCDATA)>
<!ELEMENT FROM (#PCDATA)>
<!ELEMENT DATE (#PCDATA)>
<!ELEMENT SUBJECT (#PCDATA)>
<!ELEMENT BODY (#PCDATA)>
```

DTD is an older standard. If someone sends you a DTD file to use with Excel or SharePoint, you'll need to convert it to an XSD file, or create an XSD file from scratch. Neither Excel nor SharePoint support DTD files.

Opening XML Files in Excel

Where does Excel fit in all this? Excel 2003 natively reads and writes XML. To open an XML file in Excel, choose File ➤ Open. XML documents are displayed in the file pane alongside the regular Excel XLS files. When you select an XML document and click Open, you'll be prompted to choose one of three ways to display the XML data in Excel:

- The first choice, as an XML list, inserts the file as an editable list beginning at the active cell. The list is inserted without headers.

- The second choice, XML workbook, opens the file in a new read-only workbook. All elements of the file are inserted, including the prolog.

- The third choice imports the schema (or creates one if the schema doesn't exist or is inaccessible) and loads it in the XML Source task pane so you can place the fields manually in the worksheet.

The XML file described earlier looks like Figure B-2 when it's opened in Excel as an XML list.

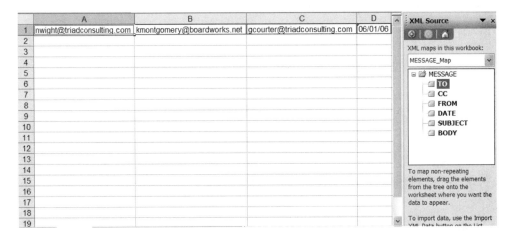

Figure B-2. *The message.xml file opened in Excel*

Excel reads the structure of the file and parses the file appropriately. The message.xml file doesn't include a reference to a schema, so Excel creates an XSD file (see Figure B-3). Fields from the XSD file that Excel created are displayed in the task pane.

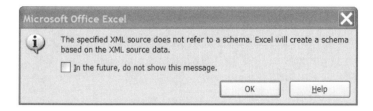

Figure B-3. *The message.xml file doesn't have a schema, so Excel creates one.*

Mapping an XSD in Excel

You can import an XSD file to an Excel workbook, then use the fields in the task pane to create a map in the workbook to indicate where fields from an XML file should be placed in the workbook.

You can create XSD files in Notepad, or use an XML editor such as Altova's XMLSpy (`http://www.altova.com`) or DataDirect Technologies' Stylus Studio (`http://www.stylusstudio.com`). For more information on creating XSD files, see the W3Schools tutorial at `http://www.w3schools.com/schema/default.asp`.

Adding an XSD File to a Workbook

To add an XSD file to a workbook, follow these steps:

1. With Excel open, choose **XML Sources** in the task pane or choose Data ➤ XML ➤ XML Source. The XML Source task pane lets you quickly set up your workbook so it can import and export XML data.

2. Click the **XML Maps** button at the bottom of the task pane to open the XML Maps dialog box (see Figure B-4).

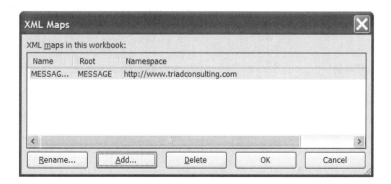

Figure B-4. *Add XSD files to your workbook using the XML Maps dialog box.*

3. Click the **Add** button to open the XML Sources dialog box.

4. Locate the XSD file (all XML files will be displayed, so make sure you're choosing the XSD file), then click **Open** to return to the XML Sources dialog box. You can add more than one XSD file to a workbook.

Tip If you don't have an XSD file, add the XML file in the XML Sources dialog box to have Excel create the XSD file.

---

5. When you've finished adding XSD and/or XML files that Excel will use to create XSD files, click **OK** in the XML Maps dialog box to attach the XSD files to the workbook and display the first XSD file in the task pane.

Adding Fields to the Map

To map the XML fields into the workbook, drag the field from the task pane into a worksheet and drop it on a cell. (To map multiple fields, hold Ctrl while you select the fields in the task pane.) When you drop the field, an option button appears. Click the button to specify whether you're adding your own headers (the default option) or want Excel to add the field name as a header above or to the left of the field (see Figure B-5).

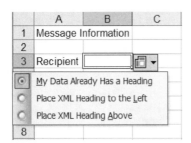

Figure B-5. *Use the option button to have Excel add a field header.*

Figure B-6 shows an XML map created from the message.xsd schema. The map doesn't need to include all the fields in the schema, only the fields you want to display in Excel. You create the labels in Excel, so you don't need to use the XML field names. For example, the TO and FROM fields in the XML file are labeled Recipient and Sender in Figure B-6.

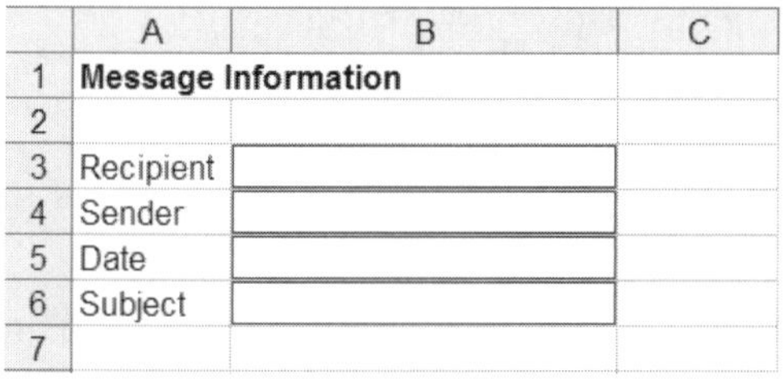

	A	B	C
1	**Message Information**		
2			
3	Recipient		
4	Sender		
5	Date		
6	Subject		
7			

Figure B-6. *An XML map in Excel*

If an XSD field represents a repeating element in the XML file, Excel will create an XML list beginning in the cell where you drop the field.

■**Tip** Although you can add multiple XSD files to a workbook, you can't put elements from more than one XSD into a spreadsheet range. You can map two XSD files next to each other on the same worksheet, but they can't overlap.

Importing XML Data Using the Map

When you import an XML file, the file must include a reference to the XSD file used in the map. The following version of message.xml includes a reference (lines 3, 4, and 5) to two XML namespaces and the XSD file message.xsd. The namespace (xmlns) must be a valid domain. The schema location (line 5) ends with the name of the XSD file:

```
<?xml version="1.0" encoding="utf-8" ?>
<MESSAGE
xmlns="http://www.triadconsulting.com"
xmlns:xsi="http://www.w3.org/2001/XMLSchema-instance"
xsi:schemaLocation="http://triadconsulting.com message.xsd">
    <TO>nwight@triadconsulting.com</TO>
    <CC>kmontgomery@boardworks.net</CC>
    <FROM>gcourter@triadconsulting.com</FROM>
    <DATE>06/01/06</DATE>
    <SUBJECT>New Office Location</SUBJECT>
    <BODY>Where should this item appear on the meeting agenda?</BODY>
</MESSAGE>
```

Follow these steps to import an XML file into the mapped worksheet:

1. Select a cell in the mapped range.

2. Choose Data ➤ XML ➤ Import from the menu.

3. Locate the XML file that you wish to import.

4. Click the **Import** button.

Figure B-7 shows message.xml imported using the Excel map. Only the fields that were mapped are displayed. The headings were added manually.

	A	B
1	Message Information	
2		
3	Recipient	amarquis@uua.org
4	Sender	gcourter@triadconsulting.com
5	Date	06/02/06
6	Subject	Webinar on June 14

Figure B-7. *Importing an XML file using the map*

Even though schemas are used to ensure that an XML file is valid, validation is turned off by default in Excel. If you want to validate the XML against the schema, you need to turn on validation for each map (see Figure B-8).

1. Click in any mapped cell.

2. Choose Data ➤ XML ➤ XML Map Properties to open the XML Map Properties dialog box. If XML Map Properties isn't enabled, you missed step 1.

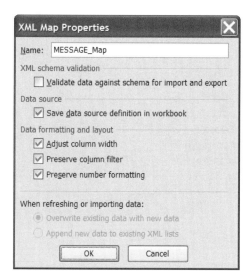

Figure B-8. *Turn on validation for each map you want validated against the schema.*

3. Enable the **Validate data against schema for import and export** checkbox.

4. Click **OK**.

Exporting XML Data Using the Map

Now that you have a mapped workbook, you can enter data into the field elements, then export the data as an XML file. Before exporting, click the **Verify Map for Export** link at the bottom of the task pane. A message box opens to confirm that the map can be used for export (see Figure B-9). The message box also notifies you if any fields in the XSD aren't represented in the map.

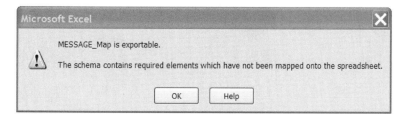

Figure B-9. *Excel determines if the map can be used for export.*

To export data, enter data into the mapped fields. Choose Data ➤ XML ➤ Export. Choose a file name and location, then click the **Export** button. Figure B-10 shows the exported XML file, opened in IE.

```xml
<?xml version="1.0" encoding="UTF-8" standalone="yes" ?>
- <ns1:MESSAGE xmlns:ns1="http://www.triadconsulting.com">
    <ns1:TO>amarquis@uua.org</ns1:TO>
    <ns1:CC>ccowtan@triadconsulting.com</ns1:CC>
    <ns1:FROM>gcourter@triadconsulting.com</ns1:FROM>
    <ns1:DATE>06/02/06</ns1:DATE>
    <ns1:SUBJECT>Webinar on June 14</ns1:SUBJECT>
    <ns1:BODY />
  </ns1:MESSAGE>
```

Figure B-10. *Exported XML file displayed in Internet Explorer*

Every mapped field is included in the XML file. The BODY field was mapped, but empty.

■■■

Resources

Microsoft SharePoint Technologies are relatively new to most business environments. The potential for how SharePoint can improve a team-based organization is enormous. However, for it to be effective, you need access to information from experts in the field—people who are putting SharePoint through its paces and figuring out how to make it work effectively in a wide variety of situations. This appendix provides you with resources that are available in the user and developer community that focus on SharePoint technologies. We've tried to include as many free resources as possible.

■Note Although we've attempted to include only those resources that have stood the test of time, web-based resources are extremely volatile. We apologize in advance if any of these sites are no longer in operation when you try to access them.

General SharePoint Resources

These are resources for "everything SharePoint"—sites with a broad scope and multiple features, including search capabilities.

MSD2D

`http://msd2d.com/default_section.aspx?section=sharepoint`

This developer-to-developer (D2D) site boasts of having thousands of pages of SharePoint information, including tips, news, and discussion forums. The site also contains SharePoint developer blogs, downloadable web parts, and links to other SharePoint resources.

All the content driven off the main SharePoint page is related to SharePoint. In addition, you can access information on Microsoft Exchange, .NET, and Security from the same site.

The Boiler Room—Mark Kruger, SharePoint MVP

http://www.sharepointblogs.com/mkruger/

Mark Kruger is a Microsoft SharePoint MVP (Most Valuable Professional), and his blog contains a number of useful articles and resources. The most valuable resource on the site is "Mark's List of Free SharePoint Web Parts and Tools." Although the list isn't updated as often as we'd like, Mark provides a lengthy list of links to a wide variety of SharePoint resources, including the following:

- Free third-party SharePoint web parts

- SharePoint tools

- SDKs and guides

- SharePoint service packs

- How-tos and tips

- SharePoint resources (Microsoft and non-Microsoft)

For additional free SharePoint web parts, scroll down the home page and check out the list below the Archives on the left side of the page.

SharePoint Portal Server Frequently Asked Questions

http://www.spsfaq.com/

This is the site of Microsoft SharePoint MVP Stephen Cummins. The site has current news and information about SharePoint Portal Server.

SharePoint Hosting

If you're unable to host your own SharePoint server, a number of companies will do that for you. You pay a monthly subscription fee based on the number of users and/or the amount of storage space you need, and they provide all the rest. This is an advantage if you're a small company or if you want to evaluate before you set up your own SharePoint server.

However, be aware that if you set up externally hosted SharePoint sites and then decide to move them inside to your own server, moving them can be a lot of work. In fact, depending on the way the hosting company works, you might end up having to do a lot of manual cutting and pasting to move your content over to avoid paying an expensive hourly rate to have your host migrate your site. If internal hosting is your long range goal, it's a good idea to talk with potential hosting companies beforehand to explore the costs of a future migration.

The following companies offer SharePoint hosting:

- *1&1 Internet*: http://www.1and1.com

- *Apptix*: http://www.sharepointsite.com and http://www.apptix.net

- *SharePoint Experts*: http://www.sharepointexperts.com

SharePoint Training Resources

Whether you're looking for a classroom experience, on-site training for your organization, or resources you can use offline at your own speed, you'll find it on this list.

MindSharp

http://www.sharepointknowledge.com/

This training firm specializes in SharePoint. The owners, Bill English and Todd Bleeker, are Microsoft MVPs, and authors of the *Microsoft SharePoint Products and Technologies Resource Kit* (Microsoft Press, 2004). They offer training, courseware, and professional education. If you register, you can access some white papers and other resources they have available for free.

SharePoint Experts

http://www.sharepointbootcamp.com and http://www.sharepointexperts.com

The SharePoint Experts team offers four intensive SharePoint courses:

- *SharePoint Bootcamp*: "Everything you can do with SharePoint before opening Visual Studio.NET"—and you get your own set of dog tags on the last day!

- *SharePoint Development Bootcamp*: "All .NET, all the time. Code warriors, this is your class."

- *SharePoint Customization Bootcamp*: "ONET and SCHEMA and WEBTEMP—Oh, my!"

- *SharePoint End-user Bootcamp*: "I just work here, can you help me out, too?"

Microsoft SharePoint Portal Server 2003 Training Kit

http://www.microsoft.com/downloads/details.aspx?FamilyId=
BCA45A99-E420-47FD-8AEA-A8743735C710&displaylang=en

This training kit is available as a free download from Microsoft, and contains a self-paced study guide for beginning and advanced users. The download includes demos that can be played in autorun mode or in interactive mode for a hands-on demo.

Excel and SharePoint Add-Ins

Here are the URLs for the add-ins discussed in this book, as well as some other useful add-ins that we use and recommend.

Spreadsheet Web Part Add-In for Microsoft Excel

```
http://www.microsoft.com/downloads/details.aspx?FamilyID=
dc3d8474-d960-4d14-a9df-9024e39f5463&DisplayLang=en
```

Use the Spreadsheet Web Part Add-in for Microsoft Office Excel 2003 to create Spreadsheet Web Parts and save them to a SharePoint site.

Microsoft Excel XML Tools Add-In

```
http://www.microsoft.com/downloads/details.aspx?familyid=
72852247-6AFD-425C-83B1-1F94E4AC2775&displaylang=en
```

Use the Excel 2003 XML Tools Add-in to import, export, and manipulate XML in Excel.

Microsoft SharePoint Sites Worth Noting

SharePoint is a Microsoft technology, so it's not surprising that Microsoft has a lot of valuable SharePoint content on its web sites. Here are some of our frequently used URLs.

Microsoft SharePoint Products and Technologies

```
http://www.microsoft.com/sharepoint/
```

This is Microsoft's official SharePoint site. It has sections specifically geared for IT pros, developers, executives, and end users. On this site, you can get free product trials, technical support, resources, and lots of sales information. Don't let that deter you, however. There's a lot of information here if you dig a bit to find it.

Microsoft Applications for Windows SharePoint Services

```
http://www.microsoft.com/technet/prodtechnol/sppt/wssapps/default.mspx
```

This useful resource has more than 30 predesigned out-of-the-box Windows SharePoint Services templates. You can download and install them on your Windows Server running Windows SharePoint Services for immediate use within your organization. This site includes templates for everything from a board of directors site to a classroom management site. With these sites, you can, among other things, create a recruiting resource center, a public relations worksite, or a site to manage expense reimbursements.

Microsoft SharePoint Products and Technologies Team Blog

`http://blogs.msdn.com/sharepoint/`

This blog is from the Microsoft SharePoint Product Group. If you want to get an idea of what's coming down the road, this blog will help. Focused on Microsoft SharePoint 2007, this blog includes articles about specific new features, beta testing, and the status of the new release.

Index

Import to Windows SharePoint Services
    list dialog box, 21
importing data, using copy and paste,
    131–133
Include content, 25
InfoPath forms, 9
information functions, 86, 99–101
interactive mode, 237
interactive pages, 103
IQY (query) file, 43
ISBLANK function, 99, 101
ISERR function, 101
ISERROR function, 101
ISNA function, 101
ISNONTEXT function, 101
ISNUMBER function, 101
Issue Date column, 133
Issue Tracking site, 139
Issues list template, 20
ISTEXT function, 101
Item-Level Permissions setting, 24

■K

Keep Source Formatting, 152
Kruger, Mark, 236

■L

launching site, 136–137
Layout properties, SharePoint's Office Web
    parts, 192
Layout property, 124
layout template, 170
LEFT function, 95, 97
LEN function, 97
libraries, 8–10
Link to Outlook button, 50
Links list template, 20
Links option, 15
Links web part, 134
list as template option, 25
List button, 38–39, 47
List command, Excel, 217
List Range, 21
List toolbar, 223
lists. *See also* Excel lists
logical functions, 86, 98–99
Lookup function, 86
LOWER function, 97

■M

mailto link, 134
Manage Content option, 20–21, 25
Manage users link, 161
Manage Users page, 130
mapping Spreadsheets for XML
    exporting XML data using map, 233–234
    importing XML data using map,
        231–233
    mapping XSD in Excel, 229–231
    opening XML files in Excel, 228
    overview, 225
    XML basics, 225–227
Match case checkbox, 175
Match Destination Formatting, 152
math functions, 86
    overview, 88
    rounding functions, 89, 91
    standard math functions, 89
MAX function, 92
Maximum function, 32
MEDIAN function, 92
Members option, 15
merge workbooks, 222
metadata, 5
Microsoft Applications for Windows
    SharePoint Services, 238
Microsoft Excel XML Tools Add-in, 238
Microsoft InfoPath forms, 9
Microsoft SharePoint. *See* SharePoint
Microsoft SharePoint Portal Server. *See*
    SharePoint Portal Server
Microsoft Windows Server Active
    Directory (AD), 7
Microsoft Windows SharePoint Services
    (WSS). *See* Windows SharePoint
    Services
MIN function, 92
MindSharp, 237
Minimum function, 32
MINUTE function, 93
MNL Portal, 5
MOD function, 89–90
MODE function, 92
Modify My View button, 122
Modify Settings and Columns option, 23
Modify Shared Page option, 122, 172, 190

Find it faster at http://superindex.apress.com/

Find it faster at http://superindex.apress.com/